NEW YORK TIMES CO. *v.* UNITED STATES

CERTIORA

No. 187

The United
in the Ne
classified
justificatio
No. 1873, 4
U. S. App

Alexand
No. 1873.
Hegarty and *Lawrence J. McKay.*

Solicitor General Griswold argued the cause for the United States in both cases. With him on the brief were *Assistant Attorney General Mardian* and *Daniel M. Friedman.*

William R. Glendon argued the cause for respondents in No. 1885. With him on the brief were *Roger A. Clark,* *Anthony F. Essaye, Leo P. Larkin,* Jr., and *Stanley Godofsky.*

Briefs of *amici curiae* were filed by *Bob Eckhardt* and *Thomas I. Emerson* for Twenty-Seven Members of Congress; by *Norman Dorsen, Melvin L. Wulf, Burt Neu-borne, Bruce J. Ennis, Osmond K. Fraenkel,* and *Marvin M. Karpatkin* for the American Civil Liberties Union; and by *Victor Rabinowitz* for the National Emergency Civil Liberties Committee.

Together with No. 1885, United States v. Washington Post Co. et al., on certiorari to the United States Court of Appeals for the District of Columbia Circuit.

DEFINING DOCUMENTS IN AMERICAN HISTORY

The Free Press

DEFINING DOCUMENTS
IN AMERICAN HISTORY

The Free Press

Editor

Michael Shally-Jensen, PhD

Volume 1

SALEM PRESS
A Division of EBSCO Information Services, Inc.
Ipswich, Massachusetts

GREY HOUSE PUBLISHING

Publisher's Cataloging-In-Publication Data
(Prepared by The Donohue Group, Inc.)

Names: Shally-Jensen, Michael, editor.
Title: The free press / editor, Michael Shally-Jensen, PhD.
Other Titles: Defining documents in American history (Salem Press)
Description: [First edition]. | Ipswich, Massachusetts : Salem Press, a division of EBSCO Information Services; Amenia, NY : Grey House Publishing, [2019] | Includes bibliographical references and index.
Identifiers: ISBN 9781642652857 (set) | ISBN 9781642654172 (v. 1) | ISBN 9781642654189 (v. 2)
Subjects: LCSH: Freedom of the press--United States--History--Sources. | Government and the press--United States--History--Sources.
Classification: LCC KF4774. F74 2019 | DDC 342.730853--dc23

FIRST PRINTING
PRINTED IN THE UNITED STATES OF AMERICA

Table of Contents

Volume 1

LIBERTY, SPEECH, AND THE PRINTED WORD IN EARLY DEBATES

MUCKRAKING, YELLOW JOURNALISM, WAR, SEDITION, AND MORE

Publisher's Note

Defining Documents in American History series, produced by Salem Press, offers a closer look at important historical documents by pairing primary source documents on a broad range of subjects with essays written especially for the series by expert writers, including historians, professors, researchers, and other authorities in the subject under examination. This established series includes thirty-five titles that present documents selected to illuminate specific eras in American history—including *American Revolution, The Civil Rights*, and *World War II*—or to explore significant themes and developments in American society—*Business Ethics, Slavery, Immigration & Immigrant Communities*, and *Native Americans*.

This set, *Defining Documents in American History: The Free Press*, offers in-depth analysis of fifty documents, including letters, newspaper reports, book excerpts, speeches, political debates, testimony, court rulings, legal texts, legislative acts, essays, and excerpts from nonfiction books, and dialogs from dramatic works. These selections explore the intricacies of defining what is meant by freedom of the press and how it is understood and applied in the United States.

The material is organized into four sections, and each section begins with a brief introduction that defines questions and problems related to freedom of the press underlying the subjects addressed in the historical documents.

- **Liberty, Speech, and the Printed Word in Early Debates** including a selection from John Milton's *Areopagitica*, portions of the transcript of John Peter Zenger's trial, and James Madison's 1800 Report, concerning the Sedition Act of 1798;
- **Muckraking, Yellow Journalism, War, Sedition, and More** considers the reporting related to the sinking of the USS Maine, a selection from Lincoln Steffan's article in *McClure Magazine*, "The Shame of Minneapolis," as well as several pivotal Supreme Court decisions: *Schenk v. United States, Abrams v. United States, Gitlow v. New York*, and *Near v. Minnesota*;
- **Radio, Television, Movies, Tapes, and Other Media in Past Decades** includes such significant documents as a discussion of *The War of the Worlds* broadcast, a report concerning Senator Joseph R. McCarthy, Newton Minnow's speech,

"Television and the Public Interest," and the decision in *Hustler Magazine v. Falwell*; and
- **Digital Dilemmas and Other Issues Today,** which begins with the Declaration of the Independence of Cyberspace and includes the Manning-Lamo chat logs, a piece of fake news (Pope Endorses Trump), and the Trump-Putin exchange regarding the media.

These documents provide an overview of the free press and how it affects all of aspects of society. A well-informed citizenry is at the heart of our society. Limits and restrictions can have a negative effect, and equally, so does a press that flouts the conventions of rigorous reporting to engage in cover-ups, obfuscation, or outright misrepresentations of the truth.

Essay Format

Each Historical Document is supported by a critical essay, written by historians and teachers, that includes a Summary Overview, Defining Moment, About the Author, Document Analysis, and Essential Themes. An important feature of each essay is a close reading of the primary source that develops broader themes, such as the author's rhetorical purpose, social or class position, point of view, and other relevant issues. Each essay also includes a Bibliography Additional Reading section for further research.

Appendixes in this book include

- **Chronological List** which arranges all documents by year;
- **Web Resources**, an annotated list of websites that offer valuable supplemental resources;
- **Bibliography**, lists of helpful articles and books for further study; and an
- **Index**

Contributors

Salem Press would like to extend its appreciation to all involved in the development and production of this work. The essays have been written and signed by scholars of history, humanities, and other disciplines related to the essays' topics. Without these expert contributions, a project of this nature would not be possible. A full list of the contributors to this set with their affiliations appears following the Editor's Introduction.

Editor's Introduction

Editor's Introduction

The term "free press" is a commonly used shorthand for "freedom of the press." Both refer to the right to publish without government interference or fear of punishment. In the United States, that right is guaranteed by the First Amendment to the Constitution, which states: "Congress shall make no law respecting an establishment of religion, or prohibiting the free exercise thereof; or *abridging the freedom of speech, or of the press*; or the right of the people peaceably to assemble, and to petition the government for a redress of grievances." [Emphasis added.] It is a right applied to all types of printed material, such as books, newspapers, and pamphlets, as well as other media such as radio, television, film, and the Internet. Freedom of the press has never been an absolute right, however, and it can be curbed or censored, particularly in the following instances: abuse of the rights of others through violation of laws, cases of national security, and matters involving obscenity. In these cases, censorship is generally deemed appropriate. The line between free and illegitimate expression is never clear-cut; rather, it is constantly subject to negotiation by society and often has been established by judicial opinion.

Origins and Early Development

The issue of freedom of the press has stirred controversy since the invention of printing with movable metal type in the mid-fifteenth century. Governments felt threatened by the ready dissemination of information and opinion and responded quickly to restrain the freedom of the press. One method tried early on was licensing of the press, which meant that the printing or sale of any book without prior official approval was forbidden. In 1644 the English poet John Milton criticized licensing of the press in his *Areopagitica*, which called for "the liberty to know, to utter, and to argue freely according to conscience." Licensing laws were abolished in England in 1695, partly as a result of Milton's legacy. Still, the government was able to take action on grounds of "seditious libel" against those who published material—whether true or false—that criticized government policies.

In the American colonies, a significant precedent in the struggle for freedom of the press was the trial of John Peter Zenger in 1735. Zenger, a New York editor, was accused of seditious libel for criticizing the colonial governor. The jury acquitted Zenger on the grounds that his charges were true and could not, therefore, be considered libelous. While this case laid the groundwork for a new standard in cases involving freedom of the press, it did not take hold immediately across the colonies (until after 1804) and was not an accepted defense in England itself until the mid-1800s.

An early attempt by Congress to abridge press freedom, protected in the Constitution of the United States by the adoption (1791) of the First Amendment, was the Sedition Act of 1798, which outlawed false, scandalous, or malicious writings about government and its officials. The act was extremely unpopular and was not renewed when it expired in 1801.

Another attempt at government censorship came in the 1830s, when proslavery southern opponents of abolitionism, or antislavery, sought to prevent the U.S. Post Office from delivering abolitionist tracts to readers in southern states—for fear that the message would spread and incite slaves to revolt. Opponents also felt that these publications misrepresented the reality of slaveholding. Although some success resulted from giving local postmasters discretion, ultimately a blanket ban was not achieved.

The Fourth Estate in War and Peace

By the late nineteenth and early twentieth centuries, the press had developed into a powerful force in American political culture—a true "fourth estate" (or fourth branch of government) that influenced lawmakers and the public alike. Two parallel trends in journalism emerged at this time. One was called "yellow journalism" (after a cartoon character). It used sensational stories and exaggerated claims to drive interest among readers and increase sales, making it an early kind of "fake news." The publisher William Randolph Hearst employed yellow journalism in his efforts to beat out his rival, Joseph Pulitzer. Yellow journalism sometimes had dire consequences. When newspapers falsely blamed Spain for blowing up a U.S. ship in Havana Harbor in 1898, for example, the reporting led to the Spanish-American War. Freedom of expression found itself untethered from the truth and became a negative force.

The second trend, developing around this same time, was "muckraking journalism," so called because it dared to look at the darker side of American life and expose the political corruption and systemic social ills lying beneath the surface. Lincoln Steffens and Upton Sinclair helped define the genre with their book-length examinations of dirty city politics and industrial malfeasance. They were not the only notable writers to contribute to the genre. The exposure of the ills that beset politics, government, business, and other public and private institutes often led to social and political change in the form of new laws and altered attitudes. Muckraking journalism, as a tool of a free press, served the public good, even while it was reviled by those targeted by the investigations and their cronies inside the system.

During World War I, the issues of espionage and sedition arose once again. The Espionage Act of 1917 and its seditious libel amendment of 1918 represented strictures placed on the press to prevent the spread of either criticism of the government or antiwar messages. In a landmark case arising from the use of these restrictions, the U.S. Supreme Court, in *Schenck v. United States* (1919), introduced the standard of a "clear and present danger" in measuring statements or actions that might threaten the government and thus give it legitimate cause to limit press freedom. Chief Justice Oliver Wendell Holmes ruled that "the question in every case is whether the words used are used in such circumstances and are of such a nature as to create a clear and present danger that they will bring about the substantive evils that Congress has a right to prevent." Simply asking Americans to beware of government war propaganda or to follow their conscience in deciding whether or not to fight, did not rise to that level.

A revised Espionage Act was introduced during World War II to protect against disclosure of military secrets. It was not invoked, however, because of the press's own self-discipline in toeing the government line. The same was the case with the Hollywood film industry, which imposed its own codes of conduct to prohibit risqué scenes and unpatriotic themes. In the 1950s, the *Schenck* ruling was employed to restrict communist activities in the United States. Just being affiliated with—or *allegedly* affiliated with—a communist organization could be the death-knell of one's career because communism was committed to the overthrow of capitalist democracies as part of the final solution proposed in the *Communist Manifesto* by Carl Marx and Friedrich Engels. By the 1960s, however, the "clear and present danger" test, and the cultural attitudes it embodied, had given way to the more speech-protective test enunciated in *Brandenburg v. Ohio* (1969); the latter case stipulates that speech cannot be suppressed unless it is "directed to inciting or producing imminent lawless action and is likely to incite or produce such action."

Since then, censorship for national security reasons has been carefully limited. In 1971, the Nixon administration attempted to halt publication of the Pentagon Papers—a set of internal reports about decades of mistakes and misrepresentation regarding the Vietnam War—on the grounds that their publication could endanger national security. The Supreme Court ruled, in *New York Times v. United States* (1971), that prior restraint was unconstitutional in this case. Although the classified documents had been leaked to the press by an inside whistleblower, Daniel Ellsberg, the Court ruled that any government attempt to block news releases prior to publication carried "a heavy burden of presumption against its constitutionality." The injunction against publishing was denied.

Other cases involving national security have concerned attempts to restrict press access to U.S. military operations. During the Persian Gulf War (1991), government control of press access was near total. News outlets objected, but to little effect. In the ensuing Iraq War (from 2003), journalists trained as "embedded" sources, under tight military restrictions, to produce war reporting. Criticism dogged the exercise, however, and questions were raised about the accuracy of some reports. Some prominent members of the press were also blamed for essentially promoting the start of the war, in line with government wishes, without having adequately verified their stories about Iraqi weapons of mass destruction, reporting which proved false.

Similar controversy unfolded in the digital era. When a U.S. Army intelligence analyst, Chelsea (then Bradley) Manning, released massive amounts of information about U.S. actions in the Middle East and elsewhere to WikiLeaks in 2010, she was both vilified as a traitor and honored as a legitimate whistleblower. WikiLeaks, too, won both respect and utter disrepute as a publishing outlet devoted to disseminating confidential materials. Once again, the line between useful truths and dangerous disclosures had to be negotiated in the public square. The process was repeated a few years later in 2013 when a former National Security Agency contractor, Edward Snowden, leaked a cache of secret documents concerning the warrantless surveillance of both foreign nationals and U.S. citizens. Various media outlets published the classified information, although many were careful not to disclose intelligence community methods and sources. Snowden himself was charged with espionage and other crimes, although he soon found asylum in Russia.

Additional Sources of Conflict

Prior restraint of information released by the press has often been an issue outside of national security contexts. In *Near v. Minnesota* (1931), the Supreme Court ruled that no newspaper or magazine could be banned because of its contents regardless of how malicious, scandalous, or libelous they might be. However, the nature of just what is and is not permissible in such publications was refined in subsequent rulings. In the case of school newspapers, the Court more recently stated that administrators may control the content of publications because they are part of the school curriculum (*Hazelwood School District v. Kuhlmeier,* 1988).

Libel, or defamation of character, aimed at public figures is a perennial issue in the court of public opinion—as well as in courts of law. Perhaps the principal ruling in this area is *New York Times Co. v. Sullivan* (1964). The justices of the Supreme Court ruled in that case that public officials claiming they have been libeled must prove "actual malice" or "reckless disregard" for the truth on the part of the source of the allegedly libelous material—as opposed to simply proving damage to one's reputation. Similar requirements were subsequently imposed on "public figures" generally—including movie stars and sports personalities—thus affirming the right of "tabloid" publications to dwell on the lives of the rich and famous. As "entertainment" publications rather than standard news sources, the tabloids, moreover, commonly fabricate stories. The Internet has only compounded the problem, as anonymous writers, hackers, and bots work to contrive material that sways public opinion and turns elections. The "fakery" the experienced by readers of "yellow journalism" over a century ago has been eclipsed by the glut of fake and salacious news of our modern day.

Obscenity, too, remains an issue for those concerned with scribing the line between open expression and offensive words and images. Freedom of the press has frequently been limited in the areas of obscenity and pornography, although the courts have had some difficulty delineating appropriate standards of censorship. In *Roth v. United States* (1957), the Supreme Court ruled that "obscenity is not within the area of constitutionally protected speech or press." It ruled that material that appealed to "prurient interest" and was "utterly without redeeming social value" could be banned. A 1958 case, *One Inc. v. Oleson,* concerned the matter of sending an early LGBT publication in the mails, at a time when homosexual-themed writing was considered indecent. In 1973, in *Miller v. California,* the Court decided that to be obscene, material need merely lack "serious literary, artistic, political, or scientific value." A 1978 case, *FCC v. Pacifica,* tested the application of such definitions to the medium of radio, and resulted in government restrictions being applied. Twenty years later, however, following passage of the Communications Decency Act (1996) regarding regulation of Internet content, the Court ruled that Congress had gone too far and struck down the act.

Other topics examined in the present volume include the rights and responsibilities carried by the press; the value of a free press, generally, in informing the citizenry, and the many challenges it has faced over the decades; the abuses of the press by writers, publishers, and politicians who have sometimes pushed matters to the limit (or beyond it); and, finally, the threat to the dissemination of information posed by monopoly control of news sources and related media.

As long as the First Amendment promise of *freedom of speech, or of the press* remains secure, an American's right to petition the government is guaranteed. So too is the right to openly criticize government laws or policies. Citizens may enjoy these rights as long as they do not harm others or pose a threat to public safety, boundaries that have been, and continue to be, subject to interpretation.

—*Michael Shally-Jensen, PhD*

Bibliography and Additional Reading

Abrams, Floyd. *The Soul of the First Amendment.* New Haven: Yale University Press, 2017.

Bollinger, Lee C. *Uninhibited, Robust, and Wide-Open: A Free Press for a New Century.* New York: Oxford University Press, 2010.

Cook, Timothy E., ed. *Freeing the Presses: The First Amendment in Action.* Baton Rouge: Louisiana State University Press, 2013.

Lebovic, Sam. *Free Speech and Unfree News: The Paradox of Press Freedom in America.* Cambridge: Harvard University Press, 2016.

Lewis, Anthony. *Freedom for the Thought that We Have: A Biography of the First Amendment.* New York: Basic Books, 2007.

Contributors

Anna Accettola, MA
University of California, Los Angeles

Michael P Auerbach, MA
Marblehead, Massachusetts

William E. Burns, PhD
George Washington University

Steven L. Danver, PhD
Walden University

K. P. Dawes, MA
Chicago, Illinois

Amber R. Dickinson, PhD
Oklahoma State University

Tracey DiLascio, JD
Framingham, Massachusetts

Ashleigh Fata, MA
University of California, Los Angeles

Kay Tilden Frost
Washington, D.C.

Aaron George, PhD
Tarleton State University

Aaron Gulyas, MA
Mott Community College

Mark S. Joy, PhD
Jamestown University

Laurence W. Mazzeno, PhD
Norfolk, Virginia

Scott C. Monje, PhD
Tarrytown, New York

Michael J. O'Neal, PhD
Springfield, Missouri

Lisa Paddock, JD
Cape May, New Jersey

Luca Prono, PhD
Bologna, Italy

Jonathan Rees, PhD
Colorado State University—Pueblo

Hannah Rich, MA
Philadelphia, Pennsylvania

Michael Shally-Jensen, PhD
Amherst, Massachusetts

Michele McBride Simonelli, JD
Poland, Ohio

Robert Surbrug, PhD
Bay Path University

Vanessa E. Vaughan, MA
Chicago, Illinois

Anthony Vivian, MA
University of California, Los Angeles

Donald A. Watt, PhD
Middleton, Idaho

Complete List of Contents

Volume 1

LIBERTY, SPEECH, AND THE PRINTED WORD IN EARLY DEBATES

MUCKRAKING, YELLOW JOURNALISM, WAR, SEDITION, AND MORE

Volume 2

RADIO, TELEVISION, MOVIES, TAPES, AND OTHER MEDIA IN PAST DECADES

DIGITAL DILEMMAS AND OTHER ISSUES TODAY

Appendixes

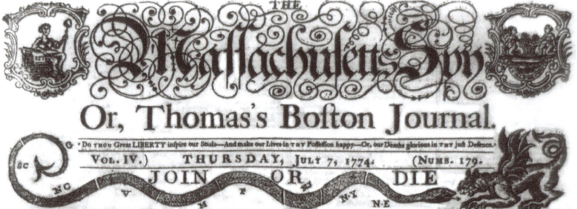

Massachusetts Spy, *July 7, 1774.*

LIBERTY, SPEECH, AND THE PRINTED WORD IN EARLY DEBATES

In this section, we look at five key documents from the mid-1600s to the early 1900s concerning the tension between freedom of expression, particularly in printed form, and government censorship.

John Milton's *Areopagitica* is a statement written in defense of the freedom of speech and of the press. Published in 1644, it was written in opposition to an order by the English Parliament imposing censorship rules and requiring authors to be approved by the government. Although ultimately it did not succeed in its purposes, it stands as a strong early statement for freedom of the press and helped shaped the debate for a time a few decades later when the British government's policy was overturned.

Cato's Letters were a series of essays widely read on both sides of the Atlantic for a period of over three decades in the eighteenth century. The writings of the American Framers often reflected the ideas contained in *Cato's Letters*. The example reproduced here (from 1722) concerns the topic of freedom of speech, a principle incorporated into the First Amendment to the U.S. Constitution.

The trial of John Peter Zenger in 1734 produced a landmark legal decision in the British North American colonies. The verdict given by the jury, as a result of defense arguments by the Scottish lawyer Andrew Hamilton (not to be confused with Alexander Hamilton), was not only broadly applauded but reflected the ideal of a free press, later incorporated into the Bill of Rights.

In 1798, President John Adams signed a law called the Alien and Sedition Acts, a reaction to pending war with France. Among other things, the act prohibited opposition to the government. Those who "write print, utter, or publish … any false, scandalous and malicious writing" against the government could be fined or jailed. James Madison and Thomas Jefferson both strongly opposed the act. Two years after its passage, Madison wrote to the Virginia House of Delegates to explain his objections. His Report of 1800 is examined here.

Finally, in the mid-1830s a debate raged over whether the federal government could order the U.S. Post Office to prevent the dissemination of antislavery tracts in the South, a move supported by slaveholders and their representatives in Congress. President Andrew Jackson took part in the debate, along with Senator John C. Calhoun and, on the other side, opponents of the measure. Local postmasters in southern states were given leave to act as they saw fit, but ultimately the abolitionist publications continued to circulate.

Representative journals of the United States. Copyright 1885. Compiled by A. J. Kane. T. Sinclair & Son, Lith., 506 & 508 North St., Philadelphia. First row: The Union and Advertiser *(William Purcell);* The Omaha Daily Bee *(Edward Rosewater);* The Boston Daily Globe *(Charles H. Taylor);* Boston Morning Journal *(William Warland Clapp);* The Kansas City Times *(Morrison Mumford);* The Pittsburgh Dispatch *(Eugene M. O'Neill). Second row:* Albany Evening Journal *(John A. Sleicher);* The Milwaukee Sentinel *(Horace Rublee);* The Philadelphia Record *(William M. Singerly);* The New York Times *(George Jones);* The Philadelphia Press *(Charles Emory Smith);* The Daily Inter Ocean *(William Penn Nixon);* The News and Courier *(Francis Warrington Dawson). Third row:* Buffalo Express *(James Newson Matthews);* The Daily Pioneer Press *(Joseph A. Wheelock);* The Atlanta Constitution *(Henry Woodfin Grady and Evan Park Howell);* San Francisco Chronicle *(Michael H. de Young);* The Washington Post *(Stilson Hutchins).*

■ From *Areopagitica*

Date: 1644
Author: John Milton
Genre: Published speech

Summary Overview

John Milton's *Areopagitica* is a prose work written in defense of the freedom of speech and of the press. He published it in 1644 in opposition to a new order of the English Parliament that imposed censorship rules and required that authors be approved by the government before publishing.

Milton was a classically educated writer and poet and he makes reference throughout the *Areopagitica* to Greek, Roman, and biblical figures and precedents. The work is named after the Areopagus Hill in Athens, Greece, where politicians and citizens spoke publicly during the Athenian Democracy.

Though the work was well received by Milton's contemporaries, he did not succeed in persuading Parliament to overturn the new censorship rule.

Defining Moment

The English Civil War was a decade-long series of conflicts between the supporters of King Charles I and the English Parliament. At the time, Parliament was a group that could be temporarily assembled or disbanded on the order of the king. However, Parliament had the ability to raise or lower taxes for the government, meaning that it was often the chief fundraiser for the king's projects and lifestyle. In order to ensure his income, the king needed Parliament's support.

Charles quarreled with Parliament in the 1630s over his decision to invade France and he refused to call another parliament for eleven years. Because of this, he had trouble raising money and his attempts at reform eventually caused an armed rebellion in Scotland. To pay for the war, Charles was required to call a parliament in 1640. This parliament, recognizing how much he needed their support, made a long list of demands that would seriously restrict the monarch's power and increase theirs.

Their demands were too much for Charles I and he departed London to raise an army. England was split between the Royalists, led by Charles and his generals, and the Parliamentarians, eventually led by the politician Oliver Cromwell.

As part of its war effort, Parliament abolished several of the king's offices, including the council that had been in charge of censoring publications that were against the monarchy. Writers and publishers took advantage of their new freedom by publishing all kinds of material, including some that criticized the actions of Parliament. In 1643, Parliament passed a Licensing Order that severely limited freedom of the press. The Licensing Order required that all works be approved by Parliament before being given a license to publish and that all publishers register the names of authors with the government. In addition, it gave Parliament power to destroy works they found offensive and to imprison their authors. In issuing the Licensing Order, Parliament essentially replaced the king's censors with their own censors and propagandists.

Milton published *Areopagitica* in the year after the passage of the Licensing Order. He had previously published several pamphlets arguing in favor of legalizing divorce (many attribute these writings to his unhappy home life; his first wife left him shortly after their marriage). The rebukes he received from the censorship officials led him to publish a defense of free speech and criticism of government intervention.

Author Biography

John Milton was born in 1608 in London and received a high-quality education. He read and wrote Greek, Latin, and Italian and travelled extensively in Europe, as was common for young men of the time. His father wanted him to pursue a career in the church, but he was passionate about literature from a young age and hoped to become a professional poet. He studied ancient writings and gained a reputation as a learned scholar, eventually taking private students upon his return to London in 1639. He wrote and published sonnets and other short poems in English, Latin, and Italian, though few of these early works would be published for decades.

Civil war first arose between the supporters of the Parliament and supporters of the King when Milton

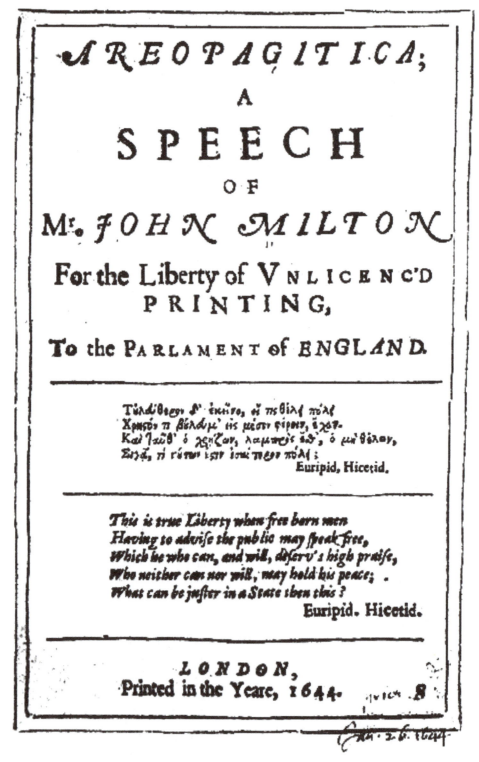

First page of Areopagitica, by John Milton, December 31, 1643.

was in his 30s. He first entered political life when he published what are known as his antiprelatical tracts: he argued that church hierarchy, where a central figure (the pope or archbishop) controlled a network of bishops who each governed their own churches, damaged the connection between the individual and God. He argued that if each individual congregation governed itself, humanity would come closer to divinity and truth. His political and religious beliefs were closely linked. In politics Milton became a famous parliamentary republican, meaning that he supported political systems in which individuals would elect and create their government rather than those in which a central authority figure made the rules.

While Milton taught and published, the English Civil War had turned into open warfare between the armies of the reigning king, Charles I, and Parliament. Charles lost—he was captured, tried, and beheaded in 1649. Milton, who had written several publications in support of the victorious Parliamentarians, was given a government job. His eyesight had been failing for years and by 1652 he was totally blind. He continued to compose works, however, by dictating his writings and poems to scribes.

English politics took another turn in 1660, when Charles II, son of the beheaded king, was restored to the throne. Milton was briefly imprisoned, like many antimonarchy figures, but he was pardoned

Detail from a c. 1629 portrait of John Milton in National Portrait Gallery, London.

and lived the rest of his life in London. He published his ten-book epic poem *Paradise Lost* in 1667, establishing his reputation as the greatest poet of the English language.

HISTORICAL DOCUMENT

I deny not, but that it is of greatest concernment in the Church and Commonwealth, to have a vigilant eye how books demean themselves as well as men; and thereafter to confine, imprison, and do sharpest justice on them as malefactors. For books are not absolutely dead things, but do contain a potency of life in them to be as active as that soul was whose progeny they are; nay, they do preserve as in a vial the purest efficacy and extraction of that living intellect that bred them. I know they are as lively, and as vigorously productive, as those fabulous dragon's teeth; and being sown up and down, may chance to spring up armed men. And yet, on the other hand, unless wariness be used, as good almost kill a man as kill a good book. Who kills a man kills a reasonable creature, God's image; but he who destroys a good book, kills reason itself, kills the image of God, as it were in the eye. Many a man lives a burden to the earth; but a good book is the precious life-blood of a master spirit, embalmed and treasured up on purpose to a life beyond life. 'Tis true, no age can restore a life, whereof perhaps there is no great loss; and revolutions of ages do not oft recover the loss of a rejected truth, for the want of which whole nations fare the worse.

* * * * *

What would ye do then? should ye suppress all this flowery crop of knowledge and new light sprung up and yet springing daily in this city? Should ye set an oligarchy of twenty engrossers over it, to bring a famine upon our minds again, when we shall know nothing but what is measured to us by their bushel? Believe it, Lords and Commons, they who counsel ye to such a suppressing do as good as bid ye suppress yourselves; and I will soon show how. If it be desired to know the immediate cause of all this free writing and free speaking, there cannot be assigned a truer than your own mild and free and humane government. It is the liberty, Lords and Commons, which your own valorous and happy counsels have purchased us, liberty which is the nurse of all great wits; this is that which hath rarefied and enlightened our spirits like the influence of heaven; this is that which hath enfranchised, enlarged and lifted up our apprehensions, degrees above themselves.

Ye cannot make us now less capable, less knowing, less eagerly pursuing of the truth, unless ye first make yourselves, that made us so, less the lovers, less the founders of our true liberty. We can grow ignorant again, brutish, formal and slavish, as ye found us; but you then must first become that which ye cannot be, oppressive, arbitrary and tyrannous, as they were from whom ye have freed us. That our hearts are now more capacious, our thoughts more erected to the search and expectation of greatest and exactest things, is the issue of your own virtue propagated in us; ye cannot suppress that, unless ye reinforce an abrogated and merciless law, that fathers may dispatch at will their own children. And who shall then stick closest to ye, and excite others? not he who takes up arms for coat and conduct, and his four nobles of Danegelt. Although I dispraise not the defence of just immunities, yet love my peace better, if that were all. Give me the liberty to know, to utter, and to argue freely according to conscience, above all liberties.

GLOSSARY

abrogated: repealed, obsolete

And who shall then … Danegelt: those who would join Parliament's war, and who would pay taxes to fund the army (like those in ancient times who paid "Danegelt" to defend the country against the Vikings), will no longer support them

apprehensions: understanding

concernment: concern

demean themselves: act, conduct themselves, behave

dragon's teeth: a reference to an ancient Greek myth in which the hero Cadmus created the city of Thebes by sowing dragon's teeth in a field; the teeth created armed soldiers

engrosser: copier, publisher

for the want of: because of, lacking

Lords and Commons: the two houses of Parliament

malefactors: doers of evil

oft: often

potency: power

progeny: offspring, product

rarefied: refined, made more perfect

Document Themes

In these excerpts from the *Areopagitica,* Milton argues that the virtue of a society is based in its freedom of speech. Books and publications have the spirit of their writers, but can be even more powerful because they can convey knowledge and reason. Those who try to "suppress all this flowery crop of knowledge" are like tyrants who want to suppress and enslave the people by keeping them from the truth.

In the first passage, Milton explains the connection between people and books. He agrees with his opponents that books can act "as malefactors" and that it is unsurprising that Parliament wants to keep "a vigilant eye how books demean themselves." In fact, he argues, the government should take their personification of books one step further and treat them with the respect they give their subjects. Books can be "as active as that soul" who wrote them and can preserve "that living intellect that bred them" for eternity. Because of their power and connection to humanity, destroying a book can be as sinful as killing a man— "he who destroys a good book, kills reason itself." It can be worse, in fact: in the last sentence he states that though the death of a man may sometimes be "no great loss," the destruction of a book is a rejection of truth that can make "whole nations fare the worse."

Milton then appeals to Parliament's political ideals and their identity as the bringers of liberty after the tyranny of the king. In 1644, Parliament was still trying to show England that it would be a better ruler than Charles I. Milton approves of the change in leadership but cautions Parliament not to become "oppressive, arbitrary and tyrannous, as they were from whom ye have freed us." The new government's "mild and free and humane" policies have allowed freedom of speech to flourish. Milton argues that only a free society, founded on "our true liberty," would allow freedom of speech. If Parliament restricts speech, they will be betraying the ideals they claimed to have when they overthrew the king.

—Hannah Rich

Bibliography and Additional Reading

Ackroyd, Peter. *Rebellion: The History of England from James I to the Glorious Revolution.* New York: St. Martin's Griffin, 2015.

Forsyth, Neil. *John Milton: A Biography.* Oxford: Lion Hudson, 2009.

Leonard, John. *The Value of Milton.* New York: Cambridge University Press, 2016.

■ *Cato's Letters*: Of Freedom of Speech

Date: February 4, 1721
Author: Thomas Gordon
Genre: Essay, political tract

Summary Overview

Cato's Letters, a collection of essays written by Thomas Gordon and John Trenchard included this one focusing on the relationship between freedom of speech and political liberty, were widely read essays in the eighteenth century. Ultimately, in addition to the original essays, five editions of the collected essays were published during a period of thirty-five years. However, while they were widely read in Britain, the essays' greatest influence was among the British colonists of North America. The writings of the American founding fathers often reflected the ideas contained in *Cato's Letters*.

Representing the views of the Commonwealthmen, a fringe party in British politics, *Cato's Letters* served to remind the major political parties of their duties as leaders of the country. Written during the ascendancy of the Whig Party (i.e., proconstitutional monarchy, antiestablished religion, and mainly representing middle class/urban wealthy) over the Tories (Conservatives tending to represent landed gentry), Commonwealth supporters saw themselves as the true republicans in their opposition to corruption and governmental restrictions, preferring freedom of thought and expression.

Defining Moment

Although the seventeenth century had more dramatic changes for the British government (House of Tudor to Stuart to Civil War/Interegnum back to Stuart), the 1714 transition from the House of Stuart to the House of Hanover, while permanent, was far from smooth. In addition, when this essay was written in 1721, since the restoration of the monarchy in 1660, the British had been involved in a military conflict more often than not. The costs of these conflicts, in addition to the normal expenses of running a government, created an enormous public debt, with much of the money borrowed when interest rates were high. Needing additional funds, in 1720 the British government gave the South Sea Company a monopoly on British trade with the emerging Spanish and Portuguese colonies in South America. Stock prices for the South Sea Company, and other even less sensible companies, quickly

skyrocketed. However, almost as quickly as it began this so-called South Sea Bubble exploded and prices collapsed. People of all classes who thought they had become wealthy for life, discovered that they were now penniless. Most of the earliest essays in *Cato's Letters* deal with this crash, as the bubble had been caused in part by corrupt government officials.

More than four hundred members of the British House of Commons, and over one hundred members of the House of Lords, were involved with the South Sea Company, although most were just individual investors. The fact that George I was given a position of authority in the company in 1718, added to the perception of government involvement, even though he did not seem to have had any real involvement. The same could not be said, however, of a number of Members of Parliament, since at least three cabinet ministers had accepted bribes from the company. Several other MPs were removed from office for corruption. When Thomas Gordon and John Trenchard met at a coffee house where politics was discussed, they discovered that they agreed on a variety of issues. Trenchard, the older, richer, and more established of the two, invited Gordon to join him in a publishing venture to address the South Sea Bubble and the role of government in general. The result of this relatively brief partnership was the 144 essays known as *Cato's Letters*. The one presented here is the fifteenth in the series.

Author Biography

Thomas Gordon and John Trenchard wrote *Cato's Letters* during the early 1720s. Both are considered part of the Commonwealthmen, a group opposed to excessive government, thus the use of the pseudonym Cato for this series of essays. (Cato was a Roman writer who opposed Julius Caesar's acquisition of power.) Although Gordon is listed as the author of this essay, the two often cowrote essays that are attributed to only one of them.

Thomas Gordon (c. 1691–1750) was co-publisher of *The Independent Whig* from 1720 to 1723, which published the *Cato's Letters* series. He was from Scotland

A COFFEE BROADSIDE OF 1674. The first to be illustrated.

Frontispiece]

The Rules and Orders of the Coffeehouse, similar to coffeehouses where Gordon and Trenchard met.

and was well educated. While teaching in London, just prior to 1720, he wrote political essays that Trenchard admired. This was the basis of their partnership until Trenchard's death in 1723. Gordon continued writing political essays, as well as translating classical works, until his death. He served as first commissioner of wine licenses.

John Trenchard (1662–1723) was educated at Trinity College, Dublin, although his family was English. He was a well-known political essayist from the 1690s until his death. A lawyer by training, he became the commissioner of forfeited estates in Ireland. For just over a year prior to his death, he was a Member of Parliament.

HISTORICAL DOCUMENT

Of Freedom of Speech: That the Same Is Inseparable from Publick Liberty (1721)

Without freedom of thought, there can be no such thing as wisdom; and no such thing as publick liberty, without freedom of speech: Which is the right of every man, as far as by it he does not hurt and control the right of another; and this is the only check which it ought to suffer, the only bounds which it ought to know.

This sacred privilege is so essential to free government, that the security of property; and the freedom of speech, always go together; and in those wretched countries where a man cannot call his tongue his own, he can scarce call any thing else his own. Whoever would overthrow the liberty of the nation, must begin by subduing the freedom of speech; a thing terrible to publick traitors.

...

That men ought to speak well of their governors, is true, while their governors deserve to be well spoken of; but to do publick mischief, without hearing of it, is only the prerogative and felicity of tyranny: A free people will be shewing that they are so, by their freedom of speech.

The administration of government is nothing else, but the attendance of the trustees of the people upon the interest and affairs of the people. And as it is the part and business of the people, for whose sake alone all publick matters are, or ought to be, transacted, to see whether they be well or ill transacted; so it is the interest, and ought to be the ambition, of all honest magistrates, to have their deeds openly examined, and publickly scanned: Only the wicked governors of men dread what is said of them....

Freedom of speech is ever the symptom, as well as the effect, of good government....

Guilt only dreads liberty of speech, which drags it out of its lurking holes, and exposes its deformity and horror to day-light....

The best princes have ever encouraged and promoted freedom of speech; they knew that upright measures would defend themselves, and that all upright men would defend them....

Freedom of speech is the great bulwark of liberty; they prosper and die together: And it is the terror of traitors and oppressors, and a barrier against them. It produces excellent writers, and encourages men of fine genius....

All ministers, therefore, who were oppressors, or intended to be oppressors, have been loud in their complaints against freedom of speech, and the licence of the press; and always restrained, or endeavoured to restrain, both. In consequence of this, they have brow-beaten writers, punished them violently, and against law, and burnt their works. By all which they shewed how much truth alarmed them, and how much they were at enmity with truth....

Freedom of speech, therefore, being of such infinite importance to the preservation of liberty, every one who loves liberty ought to encourage freedom of speech. Hence it is that I, living in a country of liberty, and under the best prince upon earth, shall take this very favourable opportunity of serving mankind, by warning them of the hideous mischiefs that they will suffer, if ever corrupt and wicked men shall hereafter get possession of any state, and the power of betraying their master....

God be thanked, we Englishmen have neither lost our liberties, nor are in danger of losing them.

Let us always cherish this matchless blessing, almost peculiar to ourselves; that our posterity may, many ages hence, ascribe their freedom to our zeal.

The defence of liberty is a noble, a heavenly office; which can only be performed where liberty is....

GLOSSARY

felicity: good fortune

shewing: showing

Document Analysis

This fifteenth essay in the series of *Cato's Letters* followed seven essays written specially about the South Seas Bubble, with most of the others touching on the subject, or inspired by the series of events which created the economic crisis for the nation. However, this essay on the freedom of speech moves beyond the initial focus of the series, dealing more directly with one point of political philosophy. Gordon asserts that true liberty is possible only where there is freedom of speech, including freedom of the press. Suppression of the freedom of expression is the undertaking of tyrants, not responsible leaders who have been elected by the people or true monarchs wishing to sustain the realm. The trust given the government by members of the public includes trusting that the government will keep to a minimum any interference with ordinary human affairs.

Gordon does not differentiate between the freedom of oral speech versus the printed word, because for him they are the same. While he could not have envisioned the forms of communication available to people today, he did understand that it was not possible to limit one form of expression without limiting them all. The "right of every man" was to be able to explore the ideas and concepts that words symbolize, thus allowing for greater understanding. For Gordon, the interchange of discussion, in whatever form, created greater wisdom and liberty for all.

For Gordon, the government's role is to encourage free speech and all that it encompasses. The breadth of what free speech supports includes the security of private property, wisdom, political liberty, and good government. However, from this essay, it seems that the two most important of these are public liberty and good government. In his closing paragraphs, Gordon expresses joy regarding the status of free speech within the British system of government, yet he understands that this is not the global norm, that free speech is something to be zealously guarded.

In his discussion of how governments react to the concept of freedom of speech, Gordon differentiates between good governments and those run by tyrants. He asserts that there is no need to criticize governments in general, as he is not an anarchist. However, he believes that citizens should be able to tell the truth about their government, whether it be praise for good actions or criticism for bad ones. Gordon believes that, in contrast, anyone seeking to be a dictator would "begin by subduing the freedom of speech." He believes that honest leaders support free speech, including speech directed against them, whereas "the wicked" or tyrannical fear anything the people have to say. The liberty to speak freely, for Gordon, creates the liberty to live the type of life all should be able to live.

Essential Themes

While Gordon, or Gordon together with Trenchard, stated in this essay that they believe free speech is not threatened in England, they would not necessarily have published this piece if there were not some concern on their part. The assertion that liberty is only possible with free speech is central to many of the essays comprising *Cato's Letters*. The letters' widespread publication and distribution in Britain's North American colonies during the middle of the eighteenth century had a strong influence on many of those who would come to be known as the founders of the United States. While many of the ideals set forth in the Declaration of Independence, and later the Bill of Rights, reflect the earlier writings of individuals such as John Locke, *Cato's Letters* were one of the central means through which this type of political philosophy was transmitted to a broader audience, especially in the colonies. Gordon and Trenchard added their own touches in essays such as this one, but they were among those advocating a liberal philosophy of life, a philosophy that had at its core the idea of the freedom of speech.

Of central importance to such authors too was the notion that good government was transparent government. People in government who sought to hide their activities were undertaking "publick mischief." The assumption made by Gordon, Trenchard, and others within the liberal school of thought was that the citizens of a nation would rise up against tyrants or "wicked governors." Contrariwise, they believed that those who governed honestly would be supported by the general population. All of this was possible only through the power of free speech, including freedom of inquiry and freedom of the press. These authors, along with the founders of the United States, believed that "freedom of speech is the great bulwark of liberty; they prosper and die together." This philosophy of liberal democracy has become the foundation for virtually all Western governments and for democracies throughout the world.

—*Donald A. Watt*

Bibliography and Additional Reading

Butler, Eamonn. *Classical Liberalism–A Primer*. London: Institute of Economic Affairs, 2015.

McDaniel, Robb A. "Cato's Letters." *The First Amendment Encyclopedia*. Murfreesboro: Middle Tennessee State University, 2019.

McMahon, Marie. *The Radical Whigs: John Trenchard and Thomas Gordon: Libertarian Loyalists to the New House of Hanover*. Lanham, MD: University Press of America, 1989.

Trenchard, John, and Thomas Gordon. "John Trenchard, *Cato's Letters, vol. 1 November 5, 1720 to June 17, 1721* (LF ed.) [1724]." *Online Library of Liberty*. Carmel, IN: Liberty Fund, Inc., 2019.

Zuckert, Michael. "English Radical Whigs: Natural Law and Natural Rights." *Natural Law, Natural Rights, and American Constitutionalism Online Resource*. Princeton, NJ: Witherspoon Institute, 2019.

■ John Peter Zenger Trial Transcript

Date: August 4, 1735
Authors: Andrew Hamilton, James De Lancey, Richard Bradley
Genre: Court Proceedings

Summary Overview

The trial of John Peter Zenger produced a landmark legal decision in the British North American colonies. Although minor in terms of daily life for the colonists, it was a major symbolic victory against the almost absolute power of the colonial governors. The verdict given by the jury, as a result of defense arguments by Andrew Hamilton, was not only broadly applauded, but reflected the ideal of a free press, later incorporated into the Bill of Rights.

Prior to this decision by the jury, the members of which were selected from a pool of individuals seen to favor the governor, the accepted law was that newspapers or magazines could publish articles critical of the government officials only if there was lawful justification. This meant that whether or not what was printed was true, a seditious libel conviction was automatic if governmental permission had not been given for the printing of the criticism. With this decision by a New York jury, the truthfulness of the published statements became relevant when government officials filed a libel charge.

Defining Moment

In the judgment of most historians, the 1732 appointment by the British government of William Cosby as governor of the province of New York and New Jersey was a poor decision for the colonies and colonists. While Cosby was loyal to the crown, he was also self-serving and did little for most colonists. However, friends and allies were richly rewarded, resulting in widespread criticism. Among his critics were the publishers of the *New York Weekly Journal*, one of whom had been the chief judge of the New York Supreme Court, and whom Cosby removed for dissenting against the governor. Desiring to close down the newspaper, Cosby decided to arrest the printer, as few individuals could run a printing press. When two grand juries failed to indict the printer, John Peter Zenger, the governor had him arrested, in November 1734, and held for trial. At an April 1735 hearing, where Zenger's attorneys challenged the legality of his arrest and the seeming conflict of interest of the judges, (since both judges had been appointed by Cosby), Zenger's two attorneys (retained by the *New York Weekly Journal*) were disallowed. Chief Justice De Lancey ruled these attorneys could no longer practice before the Supreme Court.

The two attorneys looked for the most qualified attorney in the region and at the last minute obtained the services of Andrew Hamilton. While Zenger was in jail (his bail had been set at what would have been close to a year's salary for him) he wrote numerous letters that kept the public aware of his plight and rallied support for his cause. When the trial actually started in August 1735, it was much shorter than expected. However, neither was the result an expected one, nor the long-term consequences of the decision.

Author Biographies

Richard Bradley (d. 1752) was identified as Mr. Attorney in the Historical Document. Appointed by the British king to the post, Bradley was the attorney general of New York from 1723 until his death in 1752. While serving in New York he acquired ownership of extensive acreage in Ulster County (New York) and later land in Orange County (New York) for his children.

Andrew Hamilton (1676–1741), aka Andrew Trent, was an immigrant from Scotland, most probably a Jacobite, as he took the name Hamilton after arriving in Virginia, where he studied law. Having passed the Virginia Bar in 1703, he joined a London law firm in 1714. In 1717 he was appointed attorney general of Pennsylvania, and later became provincial agent for that colony. In 1727, he was elected to the Pennsylvania Assembly, becoming Speaker of the Assembly until 1737. By 1735, he was one of the most respected lawyers in the colonies. In 1737 he became a judge in the Vice-Admiralty Court in Philadelphia, serving until his death.

James De Lancey (1703–1760), although educated in England, was a native New Yorker. In 1729, as a member of the New York Assembly, he assisted

The trial, as imagined by an illustrator in the 1883 book Wall Street in History.

in writing a new charter for New York City. After briefly serving as a justice on the court, De Lancey was appointed chief justice of the New York Supreme Court of Judicature in 1733, when he supported the governor's side in a case, while the man who became the previous chief justice did not. (This was the governor who claimed to be libeled by Zenger.) He was appointed lieutenant governor by the king in 1746, but blocked by the new governor. In 1753 he became acting governor upon the death of the governor, and as such presided over the Albany Congress in 1754. For the remainder of his life he alternated between serving as chief justice and colonial governor, depending upon the needs of the colony.

Numb. X.

THE
New - York Weekly JOURNAL,

Containing the freshest Advices, Foreign, and Domestick.

MUNDAY January 7, 1733.

TO THE ENGLISHMAN,

—— With native Freedom brave,
The meanest Briton scorns the highest Slave.
    THE CAMPAIGN.

Since you have taken upon your self the noble Appellation of the Englishman, I am perswaded you will not be displeased if, out of the tender Regard I have to the Honour of my Country, I venture to give you my thoughts upon the Duty of an English Man; and endeavour at the same Time to awaken in you, and all my Country Men, the honest Ambition of Coming up to it in all Respects.

A True English Man in a civil and political Sense, is the greatest Character in Life.

While the Liberties of Rome remained intire, there could be nothing said more to the Honour of a Man, than to say he was a Roman: And for the very same Reason, so long as we continue true to our own Laws and Constitutions, may every freeborn or naturalized Inhabitant of the British Dominions, glory in the Name of English Man? wherein had the Romans the Advantage over us Englishmen? are not our Priviledges, our Rights, our Immunities, as great as ever were theirs? Are we not to all Intents and Purposes as free a People? Are we not as brave? Do we not equal them in all the Arts and Embellishments of Life? Is not even our Wit and Eloquence upon an Equality with theirs? In Navigation, in Trade, in Manufactures, and the several Means of Acquiring Wealth, and furnishing our selves with the Products of distant Countries, they come far short of us. Then as to our Religion, it is as far beyond theirs, as the

Wisdom of God is Superiour to the Inventions of Men.

Considering these inestimable Blessings, which we enjoy in a greater Measure, than any other Nation now in being, what should be the Duty of every English Man, and of you in Particular, but to maintain his happiness and his Birthright to the Utmost? To stand by the free Constitution of his Country with his Discourse, with his Pen and with his Sword? In a Word, with his whole Might and Main? An English Man may speak his Opinion without Doors as well as within Doors: He may, nay he ought to have a jealous Eye, upon the Officers and Servants of his Prince: He may and he ought to allarm his fellow Subjects when he sees any apparent Danger, either from Enemies abroad, or from factions at home. The Prince receives his Information from others and those may be corrupt, and it may be that Nothing less than the Clamours of a Nation can reach the Ears of a Prince, and give him an Opportunity of Detecting the Treachery and Ignorance of those that pretend to serve him. For these Reasons I conjure you, as an English Man, to cry aloud and spare not, when ever you shall see Occasion.

It is the Prerogative of our Prince to choose his Ministers, but it is the Priviledge of the People by their Representatives, to Judge of, and even to arraign the Conduct of those Ministers.

In a Kingdom where an absolute and tyrannical Government prevails, the Prince and his Ministers are in effect the same: But God be praised it is not so with us. Our Laws have fenced the Person of the Prince as it were with a Wall of Brass: He is by them secured from violence, or any

A page from Zenger's New-York Weekly Journal, *January 7, 1733.*

MAZ18847   S.L.C.

115TH CONGRESS
2D SESSION   **S. RES.** _____

Reaffirming the vital and indispensable role the free press serves.

_____

IN THE SENATE OF THE UNITED STATES

Mr. SCHATZ submitted the following resolution; which was referred to the Committee on

_____

RESOLUTION

Reaffirming the vital and indispensable role the free press serves.

Whereas the First Amendment to the Constitution of the United States protects the press from government control and suppression;

Whereas the freedom of the press—

(1) has been recognized as integral to the democratic foundations of the United States since the beginning of the United States; and

(2) has endured and been reaffirmed repeatedly throughout the history of the United States;

Whereas Benjamin Franklin in 1722 wrote, "Whoever would overthrow the Liberty of a Nation, must begin by subduing the Freeness of Speech.";

Senator Bob Menendez (D-N.J.), Ranking Member of the Senate Foreign Relations Committee, submitted this statement for the Senate record in observance of World Press Freedom Day.

MAZ18847   S.L.C.

2

Whereas Thomas Jefferson in 1786 wrote, "Our liberty depends on the freedom of the press, and that cannot be limited without being lost.";

Whereas James Madison in 1789 introduced the freedom of the press in the Bill of Rights to the Constitution of the United States;

Whereas James Madison based the freedom of the press on the Declaration of Rights of the Commonwealth of Virginia, which in 1776 declared, "The freedom of the Press is one of the greatest bulwarks of liberty, and can never be restrained but by despotic Governments.";

Whereas President Ronald Reagan proclaimed August 4, 1985, as Freedom of the Press Day, stating that "Freedom of the press is one of our most important freedoms and also one of our oldest.";

Whereas President Reagan also said, "Today, our tradition of a free press as a vital part of our democracy is as important as ever. The news media are now using modern techniques to bring our citizens information not only on a daily basis but instantaneously as important events occur. This flow of information helps make possible an informed electorate and so contributes to our national system of self-government.";

Whereas Justice Anthony Kennedy wrote in International Soc. for Krishna Consciousness, Inc. v. Lee, 505 U.S. 672 (1992), "The First Amendment is often inconvenient. But that is beside the point. Inconvenience does not absolve the government of its obligation to tolerate speech.";

Whereas the United States Supreme Court also affirmed the history and intent of the freedom of the press in New

Page 2 of the Menendez statement for the Senate record in observance of World Press Freedom Day.

MAZ18847   S.L.C.

3

York Times Co. v. United States, 403 U.S. 713 (1971), stating, "In the First Amendment, the Founding Fathers gave the free press the protection it must have to fulfill its essential role in our democracy. The press was to serve the governed, not the governors. The Government's power to censor the press was abolished so that the press would remain forever free to censure the Government. The press was protected so that it could bare the secrets of government and inform the people. Only a free and unrestrained press can effectively expose deception in government.";

Whereas tyrannical and authoritarian governments and leaders throughout history have sought to undermine, censor, suppress, and control the press to advance their undemocratic goals and actions; and

Whereas the United States, including the long-held commitment to and constitutional protection of the free press in the United States, has stood as a shining example of democracy, self-government, and freedom for the world to emulate: Now, therefore, be it

1   *Resolved,* That—

2   (1) the Senate—

3   (A) affirms that the press is not the enemy

4   of the people;

5   (B) reaffirms the vital and indispensable

6   role that the free press serves to inform the

7   electorate, uncover the truth, act as a check on

8   the inherent power of the government, further

9   national discourse and debate, and otherwise

Page 3 of the Menendez statement for the Senate record in observance of World Press Freedom Day.

MAZ18847   S.L.C.

4

1   advance the most basic and cherished demo-

2   cratic norms and freedoms of the United

3   States; and

4   (C) condemns the attacks on the institu-

5   tion of the free press and views efforts to sys-

6   tematically undermine the credibility of the

7   press as an attack on the democratic institu-

8   tions of the United States; and

9   (2) it is the sense of the Senate that it is the

10   sworn responsibility of all who serve the United

11   States by taking the oath to support and defend the

12   Constitution of the United States to uphold, cherish,

13   and protect the entire Constitution, including the

14   freedom of the press.

Page 4 of the Menendez statement for the Senate record in observance of World Press Freedom Day.

HISTORICAL DOCUMENT

Case for the Prosecution

MR. ATTORNEY. "May it please Your Honors and you, Gentlemen of the Jury. The information now before the Court, and to which the defendant, Zenger, has pleaded 'Not guilty,' is an information for printing and publishing a false, scandalous, and seditious libel in which His Excellency, the Governor of this Province, who is the king's immediate representative here, is greatly and unjustly scandalized as a person that has no regard to law or justice; with much more, as will appear upon reading the information. libeling has always been discouraged as a thing that tends to create differences among men, ill blood among the people, and oftentimes great bloodshed between the party libeling and the party libeled. There can be no doubt but you, Gentlemen of the Jury, will have the same ill opinion of such practices as judges have always shown upon such occasions. But I shall say no more at this time, until you hear the information, which is as follows:

"Be it remembered that Richard Bradley, Attorney General of the king for the Province of New York, who prosecutes for the king in this part, in his own proper person comes here into the Court of the king, and for the king gives the Court here to understand and be informed:

> "That John Peter Zenger, of the City of New York, printer, being a seditious person; and a frequent printer and publisher of false news and seditious libels, both wickedly and maliciously devising the administration of His Excellency William Cosby, Captain Genera] and Governor in Chief, to traduce, scandalize, and vilify both His Excellency the Governor and the ministers and officers of the king, and to bring them into suspicion and the ill opinion of the subjects of the king residing within the Province, on the twenty-eighth day of January, in the seventh year of the reign of George the Second, at the City of New York did falsely, seditiously, and scandalously print and publish, and cause to be printed and published, a certain false, malicious, seditious, scandalous libel entitled *The New York Weekly Journal*."

"In which libel, among other things therein contained, are these words, 'Your appearance in print at last gives a pleasure to many, although most wish you had come fairly into the open field, and not appeared behind entrenchment's made of the supposed laws against libeling, and of what other men had said and done before. These entrenchment's, gentlemen, may soon be shown to you and to all men to be weak, and to have neither law nor reason for their foundation, and so cannot long stand in your stead. Therefore you had much better as yet leave them, and come to what the people of this City and Province (the City and Province of New York meaning) think are the points in question. They (the people of the City and Province of New York meaning) think, as matters now stand, that their liberties and properties are precarious, and that slavery is like to be entailed on them and their posterity if some past things be not amended, and this they collect from many past proceedings." (Meaning many of the past proceedings of His Excellency, the Governor, and of the ministers and officers of the king, of and for the said Province.)

"And the Attorney General likewise gives the Court here to understand and be informed:

> "That the said John Peter Zenger afterwards, to wit on the eighth day of April, did falsely, seditiously and scandalously Print and publish another false, malicious, seditious, and Scandalous libel entitled *The New-York Weekly Journal*.

"In which libel, among other things therein contained, are these words, 'one of our neighbors (one of the inhabitants of New Jersey meaning) being in company and observing the strangers (some of the inhabitants of New York meaning) full of complaints, endeavored to persuade them to remove into Jersey. To which it was replied, c that would be leaping out of the frying pan into the fire; for,' says he, 'we both are under the same Governor (His Excellency the said Governor meaning), and your Assembly have shown with a vengeance what is to be expected from them.' One that was then moving to Pennsylvania (meaning one that was then removing from New York with intent to reside at Pennsylvania), to which place it is reported that several considerable men are removing (from New York meaning), expressed in terms very moving much concern for the circumstances of New York (the bad circumstances of the Province and people of New York meaning), and seemed to think them very much owing to the influence that some men (whom he called tools) had in the administration (meaning the administration of government of the said Province of New York). He said he was now going from them, and was not to be hurt by any measures they should take, but could not help having some concern for the welfare of his countrymen, and should be glad to hear that the Assembly (meaning the General Assembly of the Province of New York) would exert themselves as became them by showing that they have the interest of their country more at heart than the gratification of any private view of any of their members, or being at all affected by the smiles or frowns of a governor (His Excellency the said Governor meaning); both of which ought equally to be despised when the interest of their country is at stake.

"'You,' says he, 'complain of the lawyers, but I think the law itself is at an end. We (the people of the Province of New York meaning) see men's deeds destroyed, judges arbitrarily displaced, new courts erected without consent of the legislature (within the Province of New York

meaning) by which it seems to me trial by jury is taken away when a governor pleases (His Excellency the said Governor meaning), and men of known estates denied their votes contrary to the received practice, the best expositor of any law. Who is there then in that Province (meaning the Province of New York) that can call anything his own, or enjoy any liberty, longer than those in the administration (meaning the administration of government of the said Province of New York) will condescend to let them do it? For which reason I have left it, as I believe more will.)

"These words are to the great disturbance of the peace of the said Province of New York, to the great scandal of the king, of His Excellency the Governor, and of all others concerned in the administration of the government of the Province, and against the peace of the king, his crown, and his dignity.

"Whereupon the said Attorney General of the king prays the advisement of the Court here, in the premises, and the due process of law against the said John Peter Zenger.

"To this information the defendant has pleaded not guilty, but we are ready to prove [Zenger's guilt]."

MR. HAMILTON. "May it please Your Honor, I am concerned in this cause on the part of Mr. Zenger, the defendant. The information against my client was sent me a few days before I left home, with some instructions to let me know how far I might rely upon the truth of those parts of the papers set forth in the information, and which are said to be libelous.

"Although I am perfectly of the opinion with the gentleman who has just now spoken on the same side with me, as to the common course of proceedings meant in putting Mr. Attorney upon proving that my client printed and published those papers mentioned in the information yet I cannot think it proper for me (without doing violence to my own principles) to deny the publication of a complaint, which I think is the right of every freeborn subject to make when the matters so published can be supported with truth.

"Therefore I shall save Mr. Attorney the trouble of examining his witnesses to that point. I do (for my client) confess' that he both printed and published the two newspapers set forth in the information—and I hope that in so doing he has committed no crime."

MR. ATTORNEY. "Then if Your Honor pleases, since Mr. Hamilton has confessed the fact, I think our witnesses maybe discharged. We have no further occasion for them."

MR. HAMILTON. "If you brought them here only to prove the printing and publishing of these newspapers, we have acknowledged that, and shall abide by it."

MR. CHIEF JUSTICE. "Well, Mr. Attorney, will you proceed?"

MR. ATTORNEY. "Indeed, Sir, as Mr. Hamilton has confessed the printing and publishing of these libels, I think the jury must find a verdict for the king. For supposing they were true, the law says that they are not the less libelous for that. Nay, indeed the law says their being true is an aggravation of the crime."

MR. HAMILTON. "Not so neither, Mr. Attorney. There are two words to that bargain. I hope it is not our bare printing and publishing a paper that will make it a libel. You will have something more to do before you make my client a libeler. For the words themselves must be libelous that is, false, scandalous, and seditious or else we are not guilty."

He observed upon the excellency as well as the use of government, and the great regard and reverence which had been constantly paid to it, under both the law and the Gospels. That by government we were protected in our lives, religion, and properties; and for these reasons great care had always been taken to prevent everything that might tend to scandalize magistrates and others concerned in the administration of the government, especially the supreme magistrate. And that there were many instances of very severe judgments, and of punishments, inflicted upon such as had attempted to bring the government into contempt by publishing false and scurrilous libels against it, or by speaking evil and scandalous words of men in authority, to the great disturbance of the public peace. And to support this he cited various legal texts.

From these books he insisted that a libel was a malicious defamation of any person, expressed either in printing or writing, signs or pictures, to asperse the reputation of one that is alive, or the memory of one that is dead. If he is a private man, the libeler deserves a severe punishment, but if it is against a magistrate or other public person, it is a greater offense. For this concerns not only the breach of the peace but the scandal of the government. What greater scandal of government can there be than to have corrupt or wicked magistrates appointed by the king to govern his subjects? A greater imputation to the state there cannot be than to suffer such corrupt men to Sit in the sacred seat of justice, or to have any meddling in or concerning the administration of justice.

From the same books Mr. Attorney insisted that whether the person defamed is a private man or a magistrate, whether living or dead, whether the libel is true or false, or if the party against whom it is made is of good or evil fame, it is nevertheless a libel. For in a settled state of government the party grieved ought to complain, for every injury done him, in the ordinary course of the law. And as to its publication, the law had taken so great care of men's reputations that if one maliciously repeats it, or sings it in the presence of another, or delivers the libel or a copy of it over to scandalize the party, he is to be punished as a publisher of a libel.

He said it was likewise evident that libeling was an offense against the law of God. Acts 23:5: Then said Paul, "I wish not, brethren, that he was the high priest; for it is written Thou shalt not speak evil of the ruler of thy people." 11 Peter 2:10: "Despise government. Presumptuous are they, self-willed, they are not afraid to speak evil of dignities."

He then insisted that it was clear, by the laws of God and man, that it was a very great offense to speak evil of, or to revile, those in authority over us. And that Mr. Zenger had offended in a most notorious and gross manner, in scandalizing His Excellency our governor, who is the king's immediate representative and the supreme magistrate of this Province. For can there be anything more scandalous said of a governor than what is published in those papers? Nay, not only the Governor but both the Council and the Assembly are scandalized. For there it is plainly said that "as matters now stand, their liberties and properties are precarious, and that slavery is like to be entailed on them and their posterity." And then again Mr. Zenger says, "The Assembly ought to despise the smiles or frowns of a governor; that he thinks the law is at an end; that we see men's deeds destroyed, judges arbitrarily displaced, new courts erected without consent of the legislature; that it seems that trials by jury are taken away when a governor pleases; and that none can call anything his own longer than those in the administration will condescend to let him do it."

Mr. Attorney added that he did not know what could be said in defense of a man that had so notoriously scandalized the Governor and the principal magistrates and officers of the government by charging them with depriving the people of their rights and liberties, taking away trial by jury, and, in short, putting an end to the law itself. If this was not a libel, he said, he did not know what was one. Such persons as will take those liberties with governors and magistrates he thought ought to suffer for stirring up sedition and discontent among the people.

He concluded by saying that the government had been very much traduced and exposed by Mr. Zenger before he was taken notice of; that at last it was the opinion of the Governor and the Council that he ought not to be suffered to go on to disturb the peace of the government by publishing such libels against the Governor and the chief persons in the government; and therefore they had directed this prosecution to put a stop to this scandalous and wicked practice of libeling and defaming His Majesty's government and disturbing His Majesty's peace.

Mr. Chambers then summed up to the jury, observing with great strength of reason on Mr. Attorney's defect of proof that the papers in the information were false, malicious, or seditious, which it was incumbent on him to prove to the jury, and without which they could not on their oaths say that they were so as charged.

> It is a commonplace of legal thinking that in a jury trial it is one thing to have the facts on your side, another thing to have the law on your side, a third thing to have the judge on your side, but best of all is to have a respected lawyer. Zenger clearly had the last as well as the first—and his strong points were far weightier than his weaknesses with the jury.

Case for the Defense

MR. HAMILTON. "May it please Your Honor, I agree with Mr. Attorney that government is a sacred thing, but I differ widely from him when he would insinuate that the just complaints of a number of men who suffer under a bad administration is libeling that administration. Had I believed that to be law, I should not have given the Court the trouble of hearing anything that I could say in this cause.

"I own that when I read the information I had not the art to find out, without the help of Mr. Attorney's innuendos, that the Governor was the person meant in every period of that newspaper. I was inclined to believe that they were written by some who, from an extraordinary zeal for liberty, had misconstrued the conduct of some persons in authority into crimes; and that Mr. Attorney, out of his too great zeal for power, had exhibited this information to correct the indiscretion of my client, and at the same time to show his superiors the great concern he had lest they should be treated with any undue freedom.

"But from what Mr. Attorney has just now said, to wit, that this prosecution was directed by the Governor and the Council, and from the extraordinary appearance of people of all conditions, which

I observe in Court upon this occasion, I have reason to think that those in the administration have by this prosecution something more in view, and that the people believe they have a good deal more at stake, than I apprehended. Therefore, as it is become my duty to be both plain and particular in this cause, I beg leave to bespeak the patience of the Court.

"I was in hopes as that terrible Court where those dreadful judgments were given, and that law established, which Mr. Attorney has produced for authorities to support this cause, was long ago laid aside as the most dangerous Court to the liberties of the people of England that ever was known in that kingdom—that Mr. Attorney, knowing this, would not have attempted to set up a star chamber here, nor to make their judgments a precedent to us. For it is well known that what would have been judged treason in those days for a man to speak, has since not only been practiced as lawful, but the contrary doctrine has been held to be law."

"In Brewster's case for printing that subjects might defend their rights and liberties by arms in case the king should go about to destroy them, he was told by the Chief Justice that it was a great mercy he was not proceeded against for his life; for to say the king could be resisted by arms in any case whatsoever was express treason. And yet we see since that time, that Doctor Sacheverell was sentenced in the highest court in Great Britain for saying that such a resistance was not lawful. Besides, as times have made very great changes in the laws of England, so in my opinion there is good reason that [other] places should do so too.

"Is it not surprising to see a subject, upon receiving a commission from the king to be a governor of a Colony in America, immediately imagining himself to be vested with all the prerogatives belonging to the sacred person of his princes? And, which is yet more astonishing, to see that a people can be so wild as to allow of and acknowledge those prerogatives and exemptions, even to their own destruction? Is it so hard a matter to distinguish between the majesty of our sovereign and the power of a governor of The Plantations?' Is not this making very free with our prince, to apply that regard, obedience, and allegiance to a subject, which is due only to our sovereign.

"And yet in all the cases which Mr. Attorney has cited to show the duty and obedience we owe to the supreme magistrate, it is the king that is there meant and understood, although Mr. Attorney is pleased to urge them as authorities to prove the heinousness of Mr. Zenger's offense against the Governor of New York. The several Plantations are compared to so many large corporations, and perhaps not improperly. Can anyone give an instance that the head of a corporation ever put in a claim to the sacred rights of majesty? Let us not, while we are pretending to pay a great regard to our prince and his peace, make bold to transfer that allegiance to a subject which we owe to our king only.

"What strange doctrine is it to press everything for law here which is so in England? I believe we should not think it a favor, at present at least, to establish this practice. In England so great a regard and reverence is had to the judges that if any man strikes another in Westminster Hall while the judges are sitting, he shall lose his right hand and forfeit his land and goods for so doing. Although the judges here claim all the powers and authorities within this government that a Court of King's Bench has in England, yet I believe Mr. Attorney will scarcely say that such a punishment could be legally inflicted on a man for committing such an offense in the presence of the judges sitting in any court within the Province of New York. The reason is obvious. A quarrel or riot in New York can not possibly be attended with those dangerous consequences that it might in Westminster Hall; nor, I hope, will it be alleged that any misbehavior to a governor in The Plantations will, or ought to be, judged of or punished as a like undutifulness would be to our sovereign.

"From all of which, I hope Mr. Attorney will not think it proper to apply his law cases, to support the cause of his governor, which have only been judged where the king's safety or honor was concerned.

"It will not be denied that a freeholder in the Province of New York has as good a right to the sole and separate use of his lands as a freeholder in England, who has a right to bring an action of trespass against his neighbor for suffering his horse or cow to come and feed upon his land or eat his corn, whether enclosed or not. Yet I believe it would be looked upon as a strange attempt for one man here to bring an action against another whose cattle and horses feed upon his grounds that are not enclosed, or indeed for eating and treading down his corn, if that were not enclosed.

"Numberless are the instances of this kind that might be given to show that what is good law at one time and in one place is not so at another time and in another place. So that I think the law seems to expect that in these parts of the world men should take care, by a good fence, to preserve their property from the injury of unruly beasts. And perhaps there may be a good reason why men should take the same care to make an honest and upright conduct a fence and security against the injury of unruly tongues."

MR. ATTORNEY. "I don't know what the gentleman means by comparing cases of freeholders in England with freeholders here. What has this case to do with actions of trespass or men's fencing their ground? The case before the Court is whether Mr. Zenger is guilty of libeling His Excellency the Governor of New York, and indeed the whole administration of the government. Mr. Hamilton has confessed the printing and publishing, and I think nothing is plainer than that the words in the information are 'scandalous, and tend to sedition, and to disquiet the minds of the people of this Province.' If such papers are not libels, I think it may be said that there can be no such thing as a libel."

MR. HAMILTON. "May it please Your Honor, I cannot agree with Mr. Attorney. For although I freely acknowledge that there are such things as libels, yet I must insist at the same time that what my client is charged with is not a libel. And I observed just now that Mr. Attorney, in defining a libel, made use of the words 'scandalous, seditious, and tend to disquiet the people.' But, whether with design or not I will not say, he omitted the word 'false.'"

MR. ATTORNEY. "I think that I did not omit the word 'false.' But it has been said already that it may be a libel notwithstanding that it may be true."

MR. HAMILTON. "In this I must still differ with Mr. Attorney. For I depend upon it that we are to be tried upon this information now before the Court and the jury, and to which we have pleaded 'Not guilty.' By it we are charged with printing and publishing 'a certain false, malicious, seditious, and scandalous libel.' This word 'false' must have some meaning, or else how came it there? I hope Mr. Attorney will not say he put it there by chance, and I am of the opinion that his information would not be good without it. But to show that it is the principal thing which, in my opinion, makes a libel, suppose that the information had been for printing and publishing a certain true libel, would that be the same thing? Or could Mr. Attorney support such an information by any precedent in the English law? No, the falsehood makes the scandal, and both make the libel. And to show the Court that I am in good earnest, and to save the Court's time and Mr. Attorney's trouble, I will agree that if he can prove the facts charged upon us to be false, I shall own them to be scandalous, seditious, and a libel. So the work seems now to be pretty much shortened, and Mr. Attorney has now only to prove the words false in order to make us guilty."

MR. ATTORNEY. "We have nothing to prove. You have confessed the printing and publishing. But if it were necessary, as I insist it is not, how can we prove a negative? I hope some regard will be had to the authorities that have been produced, and that supposing all the words to be true, yet that will not help them. Chief Justice Holt, in his charge to the jury in the case of Tutchin, made no distinction whether Tutchin's papers were true or false; and as Chief Justice Holt has made no distinction in that case, so none ought to be made here; nor can it be shown that, in all that case, there was any question made about their being false or true."

MR. HAMILTON. "I did expect to hear that a negative cannot be proved. But everybody knows there are many exceptions to that general rule. For if a man is charged with killing another, or stealing his neighbor's horse, if he is innocent in the one case he may prove the man said to be killed to be really alive, and the horse said to be stolen never to have been out of his master's stable, etc. And this, I think, is proving a negative.

"But we will save Mr. Attorney the trouble of proving a negative, take the onus probandi [burden of proof] on ourselves, and prove those very papers that are called libels to be true."

MR. CHIEF JUSTICE. "You cannot be admitted, Mr. Hamilton, to give the truth of a libel in evidence. A libel is not to be justified; for it is nevertheless a libel that it is true."

MR. HAMILTON. "I am sorry the Court has so soon resolved upon that piece of law. I expected first to have been heard to that point. I have not, in all my reading, met with an authority that says we cannot be admitted to give the truth in evidence upon an information for libel."

MR. CHIEF JUSTICE. "The law is clear that you cannot justify a libel."

MR. HAMILTON. "I own that, may it please Your Honor, to be so. But, with submission, I understand the word 'justify' there to be a justification by plea, as it is in the case upon an indictment for murder or an assault and battery. There the prisoner cannot justify, but pleads 'Not guilty.' Yet it will not be denied but he may be, and always is, admitted to give the truth of the fact, or any other matter, in evidence, which goes to his acquittal. As in murder he may prove that it was in defense of his life, his house, etc.; and in assault and battery he may give in evidence that the other party struck first: and in both cases he will be acquitted. In this sense I understand the word 'justify' when applied to the case before the Court."

MR. CHIEF JUSTICE. "I pray, show that you can give the truth of a libel in evidence."

MR. HAMILTON. "How shall it be known whether the words are libelous, that is, true or false, but by admitting us to prove them true, since Mr. Attorney will not undertake to prove them false? Besides, is it not against common sense that a man should be punished in the same degree for a true libel, if any such thing could be, as for a false one? I know it is said that truth makes a libel the more provoking, and therefore the offense is greater, and consequently the judgment should be the heavier.

Well, suppose it were so, and let us agree for once that truth is a greater sin than falsehood. Yet, as the offenses are not equal, and as the punishment is arbitrary, that is, according as the judges in their discretion shall direct to be inflicted, is it not absolutely necessary that they should know whether the libel is true or false, that they may by that means be able to proportion the punishment?

"For would it not be a sad case if the judges, for want of a due information, should chance to give as severe a judgment against a man for writing or publishing a lie, as for writing or publishing a truth? And yet this, with submission, as monstrous and ridiculous as it may seem to be, is the natural consequence of Mr. Attorney's doctrine that truth makes a worse libel than falsehood, and must follow from his not proving our papers to be false, or not suffering us to prove them to be true.

"In the case of Tutchin, which seems to be Mr. Attorney's chief authority, that case is against him; for Tutchin was, at his trial, put upon showing the truth of his papers; but he did not. At least the prisoner was asked by the king's counsel whether he would say that they were true. And as he never pretended that they were true, the Chief Justice was not to say so.

"But the point will be clearer on our side from Fuller's case.' Here you see is a scandalous and infamous charge against the late king; here is a charge no less than high treason, against the men in public trust, for receiving money of the French king, then in actual war with the crown of Great Britain; and yet the Court were far from bearing him down with that star chamber doctrine, to wit, that it was no matter whether what he said was true or false. No, on the contrary, Lord Chief Justice Holt asks Fuller, 'Can you make it appear that they are true? Have you any witnesses? You might have had subpoenas for your witnesses against this day. If you take it upon you to write such things as you are charged with, it lies upon you to prove them true, at your peril. If you have any witnesses, I will hear them. How came you to write those books which are not true? If you have any witnesses, produce them. If you can offer any matter to prove what you wrote, let us hear it.' Thus said, and thus did, that great man, Lord Chief Justice Holt, upon a trial of the like kind with ours; and the rule laid down by him in this case is that he who will take upon him to write things, it lies upon him to prove them, at his peril. Now, sir, we have acknowledged the printing and publishing of those papers set forth in the information and, with the leave of the Court, agreeable to the rule laid down by Chief Justice Holt, we are ready to prove them to be true, at our peril."

MR. CHIEF JUSTICE. "Let me see the book."

MR. CHIEF JUSTICE. "Mr. Attorney, you have heard what Mr. Hamilton has said, and the cases he has cited, for having his witnesses examined to prove the truth of the several facts contained in the papers set forth in the information. What do you say to it?"

MR. ATTORNEY. "The law, in my opinion, is very clear. They cannot be admitted to justify a libel, for by the authorities I have already read to the Court it is not the less a libel because it is true. I think I need not trouble the Court over again. The thing seems to be very plain, and I submit it to the Court."

MR. CHIEF JUSTICE. "Mr. Hamilton, the Court is of the opinion that you ought not to be permitted to prove the facts in the papers. these are the words of the book, 'It is far from being a justification of a libel that the contents thereof are true, or that the person upon whom it is made had a bad reputation, since the greater appearance there is of truth in any malicious invective, so much the more provoking it is.'"

MR. HAMILTON. "These are Star Chamber cases, and I was in hopes that practice had been dead with the court."

MR. CHIEF JUSTICE. "Mr. Hamilton, the Court have delivered their opinion, and we expect that you will use us with good manners. You are not to be permitted to argue against the opinion of the Court."

MR. HAMILTON. "With submission, I have seen the practice in very great courts, and never heard it deemed unmannerly to-"

MR. CHIEF JUSTICE. "After the Court have declared their opinion, it is not good manners to insist upon a point in which you are overruled."

MR. HAMILTON. "I will say no more at this time. The Court, I see, is against us in this point - and that I hope I may be allowed to say."

MR. CHIEF JUSTICE. "Use the Court with good manners and you shall be allowed all the liberty you can reasonably desire."

GLOSSARY

Court of King's Bench: a court of common law, merged into the High Court of Justice in 1873

freeholder: owner of property and thus allowed to vote

Star Chambers: secret judicial court held in the Palace of Westminster for trials of the upper class, originally fair but devolving into a political weapon, ending in 1641

traduce: to speak maliciously; to slander

Tutchin's case: John Tutchin, a British, radical Whig who was arrested and convicted of libel three times

Westminster Hall: another name for the Palace of Westminster, where Parliament meets

Document Analysis

Having languished in jail for almost eight months, John Peter Zenger was more than ready to have his trial proceed. For the prosecution, it seemed an open and shut case. Within British case law there were rulings that government officials could not be harshly criticized in print. Doing this was seditious libel, and Zenger's prosecutors were ready to prove that he printed the pieces of paper on which such criticisms of the New York governor appeared. However, for the defense attorney, Andrew Hamilton, this should not be at the heart of the case. Generally a charge of libel was upheld only if the statements made were false, and detrimental to the subject of the statements. Thus, to the surprise of the prosecution, Hamilton, and Zenger, admitted that Zenger had printed the pieces of paper, but claimed it was not libel because the statements were true. Thus, Hamilton argued that this was not just a matter about running a printing press; rather, it was a case that focused on the issue of liberty for British citizens living in New York. Fortunately for Zenger, the jury agreed with Hamilton's position and reached a verdict based on it, rather than on the issue of setting down words on paper.

The first half of the document, which is not a verbatim transcript of the trial but rather includes recollections, focuses on the arguments put forward by the prosecution, although it includes portions of the debate between prosecution and defense. Having outlined a few examples of what the prosecutor believed to be libelous editions of the *New York Weekly Journal*, he went on to assert that what had been printed caused a "great disturbance of the peace" and could even be seen as causing harm to the king. Interrupting the prosecution, Hamilton admitted that these pages had been printed by Zenger. This seemed to have thrown the prosecutor off stride, as what he had focused on proving had just been admitted by the defendant. However, again during the prosecution's statement, Hamilton asserted that what was printed was true. The prosecution argued that in making scandalous statements about the governor, Zenger was libeling the governor, no matter what the actual case might be.

Hamilton, speaking for the defense in the second half of the document, started with the central point of his defense, namely, that it is not libel when "the just complaints of a number of men who suffer under a bad administration" are printed. (Tongue in cheek, Hamilton also welcomed the prosecution's clarification that it was the governor who had done all the scandalous things outlined in the newspaper articles.) Hamilton also noted that some of the legal precedents to which the prosecution referred were from the Star Chamber court, which had been discontinued about a hundred years earlier, and most of its actions had been disavowed. Hamilton claimed that the governor was usurping some of the king's prerogatives by the claims of libel. However, at the end, he returned to his central argument, that libel concerns falsehoods not the printing of truthful statements.

In the closing debate, the prosecution claimed they had nothing to prove, since Zenger had admitted printing the newspaper. Hamilton responded with several examples of how accused people have been acquitted because the full truth was made known in the trial. Inserting himself into the discussion, the judge observed that Hamilton could not introduce "the truth of a libel in evidence." While this was what the judge ruled, Hamilton had presented the idea and "evidence" before the jury, and this was what swayed them to find Zenger not guilty, despite the judge's instructions to find him guilty.

Essential Themes

The outcome of Zenger's trial was more than a not guilty verdict, although that was very important to him. The finding of the jury, after only ten minutes of deliberation, was essentially that truth was a defense against a charge of libel. In the American system of justice, this has been the case ever since, based partially on this verdict and partially on commonsense understandings.

However, there was another, larger concept that came out of this case. This was the fact that a free press was essential for liberty. If a society was to be free, then it had to have virtually unfettered communications. As Hamilton said in court, "The question before the Court and you, Gentlemen of the jury, is not of small or private concern…. No! It may in its consequence affect every free man that lives under a British government on the main of America. It is the best cause. It is the cause of liberty." The jury's validation that the press need not worry when printing the truth about government officials has been a vital part of the heritage of the American political and legal system since that time.

—Donald A. Watt

Bibliography and Additional Reading

Barnett, Lincoln. "The Case of John Peter Zenger." *American Heritage.* Rockville, MD: American Heritage Publishing Co., 1971.

Historical Society of the New York Courts. "Crown v. John Peter Zenger, 1735." *Historical Society of the New York Courts: Legal History Matters.* White Plains, NY: Historical Society of the New York Courts, 2019.

Kluger, Richard. *Indelible Ink: The Trials of John Peter Zenger and the Birth of America's Free Press.* New York: W.W. Norton & Company, 2016.

Linder, Douglas O. "The Trial of John Peter Zenger: An Account." *Famous Trials.* Kansas City: Douglas O. Linder-University of Missouri-Kansas City Law School, 2019.

Miller, Eugene F. "1736: Brief Narrative of the Trial of Peter Zenger." *Online Library of Liberty.* Indianapolis: Liberty Fund, Inc., 2016.

■ James Madison on the Sedition Act of 1798

Date: 1800
Author: James Madison
Genre: Report

Summary Overview

In 1798, on the cusp of war with the French, President John Adams signed a law called the Alien and Sedition Acts. This was a collection of laws designed to protect the new United States from a host of perceived external threats that gave the government the power to deport anyone not considered American, extend the amount of time someone had to live in the United States before being considered an American, and—most relevant to the First Amendment—prohibit opposition to the government. Those who "write print, utter, or publish ... any false, scandalous and malicious writing" against the government could be fined or jailed. Moreover, of course, the government determined what was false, scandalous, or malicious.

James Madison and Thomas Jefferson were both strong opponents of these acts, feeling strongly that the federal government had no right to make these sorts of laws; after all, Adams, Madison, and Jefferson had all lived through the Revolutionary War just a few decades before. Two years after the passage of the Alien and Sedition Acts, Madison wrote to the Virginia House of Delegates to explain his objections to the acts. The excerpt offered below is just one section of what is called the Report of 1800.

Defining Moment

Even though the American colonies had won their freedom from English rule in 1783, the victory was followed by years of fluctuation as the new country tried to hammer out a Constitution that could balance a centralized government that oversaw a nation of semi-independent states. The U.S. Constitution was not drafted until 1787, and was not ratified until 1788. It therefore had been in force for just a decade before the Alien and Sedition Acts were passed; the Bill of Rights and the First Amendment existed, but they had not been well tested.

As the United States faced war with France, there were many French refugees living in the new American states. Using the same sort of logic that later fueled Japanese internment camps during World War II, Congress decided that laws must be put in place

to ensure that those refugees would not try to fight Americans if war were declared. John Adams was part of the Federalist party of government, a party that believed that a strong central government was the only method by which the new country could survive. The formation of the Democratic-Republican party, organized by Madison and Jefferson, was in part a response to this and similar laws, which were perceived to directly violate the new Constitution.

As a result of the 1800 Report and other writings, Virginia and Kentucky both declared that their states were exempt from the Alien and Sedition Acts and that their citizens would not be subject to prosecution under it.

Author Biography

James Madison is frequently considered one of the most influential of America's Founding Fathers. Born in 1751, he wrote the first draft of the Constitution, wrote several of the Federalist Papers, and was a primary sponsor of the Bill of Rights. He served as the fourth president of the United States and died at his Virginia estate in 1836.

Madison was the oldest child of a Virginia planter who owned thousands of acres of land and dozens of slaves. Madison was educated at the College of New Jersey (now Princeton University) and then returned home to join the Virginia militia in 1775.

In 1776, Madison met Thomas Jefferson at the Virginia Convention, and the two became lifelong friends, frequently working together on political projects and supporting each other's careers. In the early years of the United States, Madison supported the Federalists, arguing for a strong central government, the three different branches of government, and worked with John Jay and Alexander Hamilton on the Federalist Papers, which argued for the ratification of the Constitution by each of the young states. While Madison is often called the Author of the Constitution, his arguments in favor of free speech for all was one of his central contributions to American democracy. Madison was a longtime supporter of George Washington and federalism until

The text of the Sedition Act (1798).

FIFTH *CONGRESS* OF THE UNITED STATES:

At the Second Session.

Begun and held at the city of *Philadelphia*, in the state of PENNSYLVANIA, on *Monday*, the thirteenth of *November*, one thousand seven hundred and ninety-seven.

An ACT *concerning aliens.*

BE it enacted by the Senate and House of Representatives of the United States of America, in Congress assembled, *That it shall be lawful for the President of the United States at any time during the continuance of this act, to order all such aliens as he shall judge dangerous to the peace and safety of the United States...*

The text of the Alien Friends Act (1798).

FIFTH CONGRESS OF THE UNITED STATES:

At the Second Session.

Begun and held at the city of *Philadelphia*, in the state of PENNSYLVANIA, on *Monday*, the thirteenth of *November*, one thousand seven hundred and ninety-seven.

An ACT *in addition to the act, entitled "An Act for the punishment of certain crimes against the United States."*

BE it enacted by the Senate and House of Representatives of the United States of America, in Congress assembled. That if any persons shall unlawfully combine or conspire together, with intent to oppose any measure or measures of the government of the United States, which are or shall be directed by proper authority, or to impede the operation of any law of the United States, or to intimidate or prevent any person, holding a place or office in or under the government of the United States, from undertaking, performing or executing his trust or duty; and if any person or persons, with intent as aforesaid, shall counsel, advice or attempt to procure any insurrection, riot, unlawful assembly, or combination, whether such conspiracy, threatening, counsel, advice, or attempt shall have the proposed effect or not, he or they shall be deemed guilty of a high misdemeanor, and on conviction, before any court of the United States having jurisdiction thereof, shall be punished by a fine not exceeding five thousand dollars, and by imprisonment during a term not less than six months nor exceeding five years; and further, at the discretion of the court may be holden to find sureties for his good behaviour in such sum, and for such time, as the said court may direct.

Sect. 2. And be it further enacted, That if any person shall write, print, utter or publish, or shall cause or procure to be written, printed, uttered or published, or shall knowingly and willingly assist or aid in writing, printing, uttering or publishing any false, scandalous and malicious writing or writings against the government of the United States, or either House of the Congress of the United States, or the President of the United States, with intent to defame the said government, or either House of the said Congress, or the said President, or to bring them, or either of them, into contempt or disrepute; or to excite against them, or either or any of them, the hatred of the good people of the United States; or to stir up sedition within the United States; or to excite any unlawful combinations therein, for opposing or resisting any law of the United States, or any act of the President of the United States, done in pursuance of any such law, or of the powers in him vested by the Constitution of the United States; or to resist, oppose, or defeat any such law or act; or to aid, encourage or abet any hostile designs of any foreign nation against the United States, their people or government, then such person, being thereof convicted before any court of the United States, having jurisdiction thereof, shall be punished by a fine not exceeding two thousand dollars, and by imprisonment not exceeding two years.

Sect. 3. And be it further enacted and declared, That if any person shall be prosecuted under this act, for the writing or publishing any libel aforesaid, it shall be lawful for the defendant, upon the trial of the cause, to give in evidence in his defence, the truth of the matter contained in the publication charged as a libel. And the jury who shall try the cause, shall have a right to determine the law and the fact, under the direction of the Court, as in other cases.

Sect. 4. And be it further enacted, That this act shall continue and be in force until the third day of March, one thousand eight hundred and one, and no longer: Provided, that the expiration of the act shall not prevent or defeat a prosecution and punishment of any offence against the law, during the time it shall be in force.

Jonathan Dayton Speaker of the House of Representatives.

Theodore Sedgwick President of the Senate, pro tempore.

Approved July 14, 1798.

John Adams
President of the United States.

I Certify that this Act did originate in the Senate.

Attest,
Sam A. Otis Secretary

The text of An Act for the Punishment of Certain Crimes Against the United States (1798).

Alexander Hamilton's proposal in 1791 for a central bank. At that point, Madison and Jefferson left the party to create the Democratic-Republican party.

Madison campaigned and became president in 1808, where he served two terms. His Congress declared the War of 1812, which led to the British invasion of Maryland and the burning of the White House and other Capital buildings. After the end of his presidency, he worked with Jefferson to create the University of Virginia, but primarily retired from public life. A letter, "Advice to My Country," was published after his death in 1834.

HISTORICAL DOCUMENT

[…]
2. The next point which the resolution requires to be proved is, that the power over the press exercised by the Sedition Act is positively forbidden by one of the amendments to the Constitution.

The amendment stands in these words: "Congress shall make no law respecting an establishment of religion, or prohibiting the free exercise thereof, or abridging the freedom of speech or of the press; or the right of the people peaceably to assemble and to petition the Government for a redress of grievances."

In the attempts to vindicate the Sedition Act it has been contended—

1. That the "freedom of the press" is to be determined by the meaning of these terms in the common law.

2. That the article supposes the power over the press to be in Congress, and prohibits them only from abridging the freedom allowed to it by the common law.

Although it will be shown, on examining the second of these positions, that the amendment is a denial to Congress of all power over the press, it may not be useless to make the following observations on the first of them:

It is deemed to be a sound opinion, that the Sedition Act, in its definition of some of the crimes created, is an abridgment of the freedom of publication, recognised by principles of the common law in England.

The freedom of the press under the common law is, in the defences of the Sedition Act, made to consist in an exemption from all previous restraint on printed publications by persons authorized to inspect and prohibit them. It appears to the committee that this idea of the freedom of the press can never be admitted to be the American idea of it; since a law inflicting penalties on printed publications would have a similar effect with a law authorizing a previous restraint on them. It would seem a mockery to say that no laws should be passed preventing publications from being made, but that laws might be passed for punishing them in case they should be made.

The essential difference between the British Government and the American Constitutions will place this subject in the clearest light.

In the British Government the danger of encroachments on the rights of the people is understood to be confined to the executive magistrate. The representatives of the people in the Legislature are not only exempt themselves from distrust, but are considered as sufficient guardians of the rights of their constituents against the danger from the Executive. Hence it is a principle, that the Parliament is unlimited in its power; or, in their own language, is omnipotent. Hence, too, all the ramparts for protecting the rights of the people—such as their Magna Charta, their Bill of Rights, &c. —are not reared against the Parliament, but against the royal prerogative. They are merely legislative precautions against executive usurpations. Under such a government as this, an exemption of the press from previous restraint, by licensers appointed by the King, is all the freedom that can be secured to it.

In the United States the case is altogether different. The People, not the Government, possess the absolute sovereignty. The Legislature, no less than the Executive, is under limitations of power. Encroachments are regarded as possible from the one as well as from the other. Hence, in the United States the great and essential rights of the people are secured against legislative as well as against executive ambition. They are secured, not by laws paramount to prerogative, but by constitutions paramount to laws. This security of the freedom of the press requires that it should be exempt not only from previous restraint by the Executive, as in Great Britain, but from legislative restraint also; and this exemption, to be effectual, must be an exemption not only from the previous inspection of licensers, but from the subsequent penalty of laws.

The state of the press, therefore, under the common law, cannot, in this point of view, be the standard of its freedom in the United States.

But there is another view under which it may be necessary to consider this subject. It may be alleged that although the security for the freedom of the press be different in Great Britain and in this country, being a legal security only in the former, and a constitutional security in the latter; and although there may be a further difference, in an extension of the freedom of the press, here, beyond an exemption from previous restraint, to an exemption from subsequent penalties also; yet that the actual legal freedom of the press, under the common law, must determine the degree of freedom which is meant by the terms, and which is constitutionally secured against both previous and subsequent restraints.

The committee are not unaware of the difficulty of all general questions which may turn on the proper boundary between the liberty and licentiousness of the press. They will leave it, therefore, for consideration only how far the difference between the nature of the British Government and the nature of the American Governments, and the practice under the latter may show the degree of rigor in the former to be inapplicable to and not obligatory in the latter.

The nature of governments elective, limited, and responsible, in all their branches, may well be supposed to require a greater freedom of animadversion than might be tolerated by the genius of such a government as that of Great Britain. In the latter it is a maxim that the King, an hereditary, not a responsible magistrate, can do no wrong, and that

the Legislature, which in two-thirds of its composition is also hereditary, not responsible, can do what it pleases. In the United States the executive magistrates are not held to be infallible, nor the Legislatures to be omnipotent; and both being elective, are both responsible. Is it not natural and necessary, under such different circumstances, that a different degree of freedom in the use of the press should be contemplated?

Is not such an inference favoured by what is observable in Great Britain itself? Notwithstanding the general doctrine of the common law on the subject of the press, and the occasional punishment of those who use it with a freedom offensive to the Government, it is well known that with respect to the responsible members of the Government, where the reasons operating here become applicable there, the freedom exercised by the press and protected by public opinion far exceeds the limits prescribed by the ordinary rules of law. The ministry, who are responsible to impeachment, are at all times animadverted on by the press with peculiar freedom, and during the elections for the House of Commons, the other responsible part of the Government, the press is employed with as little reserve towards the candidates.

The practice in America must be entitled to much more respect. In every State, probably, in the Union, the press has exerted a freedom in canvassing the merits and measures of public men of every description which has not been confined to the strict limits of the common law. On this footing the freedom of the press has stood; on this footing it yet stands. And it will not be a breach either of truth or of candour to say, that no persons or presses are in the habit of more unrestrained animadversions on the proceedings and functionaries of the State governments than the persons and presses most zealous in vindicating the act of Congress for punishing similar animadversions on the Government of the United States.

The last remark will not be understood as claiming for the State governments an immunity greater than they have heretofore enjoyed. Some degree of abuse is inseparable from the proper use of every thing, and in no instance is this more true than in that of the press. It has accordingly been decided by the practice of the States, that it is better to leave a few of its noxious branches to their luxuriant growth, than, by pruning them away, to injure the vigour of those yielding the proper fruits. And can the wisdom of this policy be doubted by any who reflect that to the press alone, chequered as it is with abuses, the world is indebted for all the triumphs which have been gained by reason and humanity over error and oppression; who reflect that to the same beneficent source the United States owe much of the lights which conducted them to the ranks of a free and independent nation, and which have improved their political system into a shape so auspicious to their happiness? Had "Sedition Acts," forbidding every publication that might bring the constituted agents into contempt or disrepute, or that might excite the hatred of the people against the authors of unjust or pernicious measures, been uniformly enforced against the press, might not the United States have been languishing at this day under the infirmities of a sickly Confederation? Might they not, possibly, be miserable colonies, groaning under a foreign yoke?

To these observations one fact will be added, which demonstrates that the common law cannot be admitted as the universal expositor of American terms, which may be the same with those contained in that law. The freedom of conscience and of religion are found in the same instruments which assert the freedom of the press. It will never be admitted that the meaning of the former, in the common law of England, is to limit their meaning in the United States.

Whatever weight may be allowed to these considerations, the committee do not, however, by any means intend to rest the question on them. They contend that the article of amendment, instead of supposing in Congress a power that might be exercised over the press, provided its freedom was not abridged, was meant as a positive denial to Congress of any power whatever on the subject.

To demonstrate that this was the true object of the article, it will be sufficient to recall the circumstances which led to it, and to refer to the explanation accompanying the article.

When the Constitution was under the discussions which preceded its ratification, it is well known that great apprehensions were expressed by many, lest the omission of some positive exception, from the powers delegated, of certain rights, and of the freedom of the press particularly, might expose them to the danger of being drawn, by construction, within some of the powers vested in Congress, more especially of the power to make all laws necessary and proper for carrying their other powers into execution. In reply to this objection, it was invariably urged to be a fundamental and characteristic principle of the Constitution, that all powers not given by it were reserved; that no powers were given beyond those enumerated in the Constitution, and such as were fairly incident to them: that the power over the rights in question, and particularly over the press, was neither among the enumerated powers, nor incident to any of them; and consequently that an exercise of any such power would be manifest usurpation. It is painful to remark how much the arguments now employed in behalf of the Sedition Act are at variance with the reasoning which then justified the Constitution, and invited its ratification.

From this posture of the subject resulted the interesting question, in so many of the Conventions, whether the doubts and dangers ascribed to the Constitution should be removed by any amendments previous to the ratification, or be postponed in confidence that, as far as they might be proper, they would be introduced in the form provided by the Constitution. The latter course was adopted; and in most of the States, ratifications were followed by propositions and instructions for rendering the Constitution more explicit, and more safe to the rights not meant to be delegated by it. Among those rights, the freedom of the press, in most instances, is particularly and emphatically mentioned. The firm and very pointed manner in which it is asserted in the proceedings of the Convention of this State will be hereafter seen.

In pursuance of the wishes thus expressed, the first Congress that assembled under the Constitution proposed certain amendments, which have since, by the necessary ratifications, been made a part of it; among which amendments is the article containing, among other prohibitions on the Congress, an express declaration that they should make no law abridging the freedom of the press.

Without tracing farther the evidence on this subject, it would seem scarcely possible to doubt that no power whatever over the press was supposed to be delegated by the Constitution, as it originally stood, and that the amendment was intended as a positive and absolute reservation of it.

But the evidence is still stronger. The proposition of amendments made by Congress is introduced in the following terms:

"The Conventions of a number of the States having, at the time of their adopting the Constitution, expressed a desire, in order to prevent misconstructions or abuse of its powers, that further declaratory and restrictive clauses should be added; and as extending the ground of public confidence in the Government will best insure the beneficent ends of its institutions."

Here is the most satisfactory and authentic proof that the several amendments proposed were to be considered as either declaratory or restrictive, and, whether the one or the other as corresponding with the desire expressed by a number of the States, and as extending the ground of public confidence in the Government.

Under any other construction of the amendment relating to the press, than that it declared the press to be wholly exempt from the power of Congress, the amendment could neither be said to correspond with the desire expressed by a number of the States, nor be calculated to extend the ground of public confidence in the Government.

Nay, more; the construction employed to justify the Sedition Act would exhibit a phenomenon without a parallel in the political world. It would exhibit a number of respectable States, as denying, first, that any power over the press was delegated by the Constitution; as proposing, next, that an amendment to it should explicitly declare that no such power was delegated; and, finally, as concurring in an amendment actually recognising or delegating such a power.

Is, then, the Federal Government, it will be asked, destitute of every authority for restraining the licentiousness of the press, and for shielding itself against the libellous attacks which may be made on those who administer it?

The Constitution alone can answer this question. If no such power be expressly delegated, and if it be not both necessary and proper to carry into execution an express power—above all, if it be expressly forbidden, by a declaratory amendment to the Constitution—the answer must be, that the Federal Government is destitute of all such authority.

And might it not be asked, in turn, whether it is not more probable, under all the circumstances which have been reviewed, that the authority should be withheld by the Constitution, than that it should be left to a vague and violent construction, whilst so much pains were bestowed in enumerating other powers, and so many less important powers are included in the enumeration?

Might it not be likewise asked, whether the anxious circumspection which dictated so many peculiar limitations on the general authority would be unlikely to exempt the press altogether from that authority? The peculiar magnitude of some of the powers necessarily committed to the Federal Government; the peculiar duration required for the functions of some of its departments; the peculiar distance of the seat of its proceedings from the great body of its constituents; and the peculiar difficulty of circulating an adequate knowledge of them through any other channel; will not these considerations, some or other of which produced other exceptions from the powers of ordinary governments, all together, account for the policy of binding the hand of the Federal Government from touching the channel which alone can give efficacy to its responsibility to its constituents, and of leaving those who administer it to a remedy, for their injured reputations, under the same laws, and in the same tribunals, which protect their lives, their liberties, and their properties?

But the question does not turn either on the wisdom of the Constitution or on the policy which gave rise to its particular organization. It turns on the actual meaning of the instrument, by which it has appeared that a power over the press is clearly excluded from the number of powers delegated to the Federal Government.

3. And, in the opinion of the committee, well may it be said, as the resolution concludes with saying, that the unconstitutional power exercised over the press by the Sedition Act ought, "more than any other, to produce universal alarm; because it is levelled against that right of freely examining public characters and measures, and of free communication among the people thereon, which has ever been justly deemed the only effectual guardian of every other right."

Without scrutinizing minutely into all the provisions of the Sedition Act, it will be sufficient to cite so much of section 2d as follows: "And be it further enacted, that if any person shall write, print, utter, or publish, or shall cause or procure to be written, printed, uttered, or published, or shall knowingly and willingly assist or aid in writing, printing, uttering, or publishing, any false, scandalous, and malicious writing or writings against the Government of the United States, or either house of the Congress of the United States, or the President of the United States, with an intent to defame the said Government or either house of the said Congress, or the President, or to bring them or either of them into contempt or disrepute, or to excite against them, or either or any of them, the hatred of the good people of the United States, &c. —then such person, being thereof convicted before any court of the United States having jurisdiction thereof, shall be punished by a fine not exceeding two thousand dollars, and by imprisonment not exceeding two years."

On this part of the act, the following observations present themselves:

1. The Constitution supposes that the President, the Congress, and each of its Houses, may not discharge their trusts, either from defect of judgment or other causes. Hence they are all made responsible to their constituents, at the returning periods of election; and the President, who is singly intrusted with very great powers, is, as a further guard, subjected to an intermediate impeachment.

2. Should it happen, as the Constitution supposes it may happen, that either of these branches of the Government may not have duly discharged its trust; it is natural and proper, that, according to the cause and degree of their faults, they should be brought into contempt or disrepute, and incur the hatred of the people.

3. Whether it has, in any case, happened that the proceedings of either or all of those branches evince such a violation of duty as to justify a contempt, a disrepute, or hatred among the people, can only be determined by a free examination thereof, and a free communication among the people thereon.

4. Whenever it may have actually happened that proceedings of this sort are chargeable on all or either of the branches of the Government, it is the duty, as well as right, of intelligent and faithful citizens to discuss and promulge them freely, as well to control them by the censorship of the public opinion, as to promote a remedy according to the rules of the Constitution. And it cannot be avoided that those who are to apply the remedy must feel, in some degree, a contempt or hatred against the transgressing party.

5. As the act was passed on July 14, 1798, and is to be in force until March 3, 1801, it was of course that, during its continuance, two elections of the entire House of Representatives, an election of a part of the Senate, and an election of a President, were to take place.

6. That consequently, during all these elections, intended by the Constitution to preserve the purity or to purge the faults of the Administration, the great remedial rights of the people were to be exercised, and the responsibility of their public agents to be screened, under the penalties of this act.

May it not be asked of every intelligent friend to the liberties of his country, whether the power exercised in such an act as this ought not to produce great and universal alarm? Whether a rigid execution of such an act, in time past, would not have repressed that information and communication among the people which is indispensable to the just exercise of their electoral rights? And whether such an act, if made perpetual, and enforced with rigor, would not, in time to come, either destroy our free system of government, or prepare a convulsion that might prove equally fatal to it?

In answer to such questions, it has been pleaded that the writings and publications forbidden by the act are those only which are false and malicious, and intended to defame; and merit is claimed for the privilege allowed to authors to justify, by proving the truth of their publications, and for the limitations to which the sentence of fine and imprisonment is subjected.

To those who concurred in the act, under the extraordinary belief that the option lay between the passing of such an act and leaving in force the common law of libels, which punishes truth equally with falsehood, and submits the fine and imprisonment to the indefinite discretion of the court, the merit of good intentions ought surely not to be refused. A like merit may perhaps be due for the discontinuance of the corporal punishment, which the common law also leaves to the discretion of the court. This merit of intention, however, would have been greater, if the several mitigations had not been limited to so short a period; and the apparent inconsistency would have been avoided, between justifying the act, at one time, by contrasting it with the rigors of the common law otherwise in force; and at another time, by appealing to the nature of the crisis, as requiring the temporary rigor exerted by the act.

But, whatever may have been the meritorious intentions of all or any who contributed to the Sedition Act, a very few reflections will prove that its baleful tendency is little diminished by the privilege of giving in evidence the truth of the matter contained in political writings.

In the first place, where simple and naked facts alone are in question, there is sufficient difficulty in some cases, and sufficient trouble and vexation in all, of meeting a prosecution from the Government with the full and formal proof necessary in a court of law.

But in the next place, it must be obvious to the plainest minds, that opinions and inferences, and conjectural observations, are not only in many cases inseparable from the facts, but may often be more the objects of the prosecution than the facts themselves; or may even be altogether abstracted from particular facts; and that opinions, and inferences, and conjectural observations, cannot be subjects of that kind of proof which appertains to facts, before a court of law.

Again: it is no less obvious that the intent to defame, or bring into contempt, or disrepute, or hatred—which is made a condition of the offence created by the act—cannot prevent its pernicious influence on the freedom of the press. For, omitting the inquiry, how far the malice of the intent is an inference of the law from the mere publication, it is manifestly impossible to punish the intent to bring those who administer the Government into disrepute or contempt, without striking at the right of freely discussing public characters and measures; because those who engage in such discussions must expect and intend to excite these unfavorable sentiments, so far as they may be thought to be deserved. To prohibit, therefore, the intent to excite those unfavorable sentiments against those who administer the Government, is equivalent to a prohibition of the actual excitement of them; and to prohibit the actual excitement of them is equivalent to a prohibition of discussions having that tendency and effect; which, again, is equivalent to a protection of those who administer the Government, if they should at any time deserve the contempt or hatred of the people, against being exposed to it by free animadversions on their characters and conduct. Nor can there be a doubt, if those in public trust be shielded by penal laws from such strictures of the press as may expose them to contempt, or disrepute, or hatred, where they may deserve it, that, in exact proportion as they may deserve to be exposed, will be the certainty and criminality of the intent to expose them, and the vigilance of prosecuting and punishing it; nor a doubt that a government thus intrenched in penal statutes against the just and natural effects of a culpable administration will easily evade the responsibility which is essential to a faithful discharge of its duty.

Let it be recollected, lastly, that the right of electing the members of the Government constitutes more particularly the essence of a free and responsible government. The value and efficacy of this right depends on the knowledge of the comparative merits and demerits of the candidates for public trust, and on the equal freedom, consequently, of examining and discussing these merits and demerits of the candidates respectively, It has been seen that a number of important elections will take place while the act is in force, although it should not be continued beyond the term to which it is limited. Should there happen, then, as is extremely probable in relation to some or other of the branches of the Government, to be competitions between those who are and those who are not members of the Government, what will be the situations of the competitors? Not equal; because the characters of the former will be covered by the Sedition Act from animadversions exposing them to disrepute among the people, whilst the latter may be exposed to the contempt and hatred of the people without a violation of the act. What will be the situation of the people? Not free; because they will be compelled to make their election between competitors whose pretensions they are not permitted by the act equally to examine, to discuss, and to ascertain. And from both these situations will not those in power derive an undue advantage for continuing themselves in it, which, by impairing the right of election, endangers the blessings of the Government founded on it?

It is with justice, therefore, that the General Assembly have affirmed, in the resolution, as well that the right of freely examining public characters and measures, and of free communication thereon, is the only effectual guardian of every other right, as that this particular right is levelled at by the power exercised in the Sedition Act.

The Resolution next in order is as follows:

> "That this State having, by its Convention, which ratified the Federal Constitution, expressly declared that, among other essential rights, 'the liberty of conscience and of the press cannot be cancelled, abridged, restrained, or modified, by any authority of the United States;' and, from its extreme anxiety to guard these rights from every possible attack of sophistry and ambition, having, with other States, recommended an amendment for that purpose, which amendment was in due time annexed to the Constitution, it would mark a reproachful inconsistency, and criminal degeneracy, if an indifference were now shown to the most palpable violation of one of the rights thus declared and secured, and to the establishment of a precedent which may be fatal to the other."

To place this Resolution in its just light, it will be necessary to recur to the act of ratification by Virginia, which stands in the ensuing form:

> "We, the delegates of the people of Virginia, duly elected in pursuance of a recommendation from the General Assembly and now met in Convention, having fully and freely investigated and discussed the proceedings of the Federal Convention, and being prepared, as well as the most mature deliberation hath enabled us, to decide thereon—DO, in the name and in behalf of the people of Virginia declare and make known that the powers granted under the Constitution, being derived from the people of the United States, may be resumed by them whensoever the same shall be perverted to their injury or oppression; and that every power not granted thereby remains with them, and at their will. That,

therefore, no right of any denomination can be cancelled, abridged, restrained, or modified, by the Congress, by the Senate or House of Representatives, acting in any capacity, by the President, or any department or officer of the United States, except in those instances in which power is given by the Constitution for those purposes; and that, among other essential rights, the liberty of conscience and of the press cannot be cancelled, abridged, restrained, or modified, by any authority of the United States."

Here is an express and solemn declaration by the Convention of the State, that they ratified the Constitution in the sense that no right of any denomination can be cancelled, abridged, restrained, or modified, by the Government of the United States, or any part of it, except in those instances in which power is given by the Constitution; and in the sense, particularly, "that among other essential rights, the liberty of conscience and freedom of the press cannot be cancelled, abridged, restrained, or modified, by any authority of the United States."

Words could not well express in a fuller or more forcible manner the understanding of the Convention, that the liberty of conscience and the freedom of the press were equally and completely exempted from all authority whatever of the United States.

Under an anxiety to guard more effectually these rights against every possible danger, the Convention, after ratifying the Constitution, proceeded to prefix to certain amendments proposed by them a declaration of rights, in which are two articles providing, the one for the liberty of conscience, the other for the freedom of speech and of the press.

Similar recommendations having proceeded from a number of other States, and Congress, as has been seen, having, in consequence thereof, and with a view to extend the ground of public confidence, proposed, among other declaratory and restrictive clauses, a clause expressly securing the liberty of conscience and of the press, and Virginia having concurred in the ratifications which made them a part of the Constitution, it will remain with a candid public to decide whether it would not mark an inconsistency and degeneracy, if an indifference were now shown to a palpable violation of one of those rights—the freedom of the press; and to a precedent, therein, which may be fatal to the other—the free exercise of religion.

That the precedent established by the violation of the former of these rights may, as is affirmed by the resolution, be fatal to the latter, appears to be demonstrable by a comparison of the grounds on which they respectively rest, and from the scope of reasoning by which the power over the former has been vindicated.

First. Both of these rights, the liberty of conscience and of the press, rest equally on the original ground of not being delegated by the Constitution, and, consequently, withheld from the Government. Any construction, therefore, that would attack this original security for the one must have the like effect on the other.

Secondly. They are both equally secured by the supplement to the Constitution, being both included in the same amendment, made at the same time, and by the same authority. Any construction or argument, then, which would turn the amendment into a grant or acknowledgment of power with respect to the press, might be equally applied to the freedom of religion.

Thirdly. If it be admitted that the extent of the freedom of the press secured by the amendment is to be measured by the common law on this subject, the same authority may be resorted to for the standard which is to fix the extent of the "free exercise of religion." It cannot be necessary to say what this standard would be; whether the common law be taken solely as the unwritten, or as varied by the written law of England.

Fourthly. If the words and phrases in the amendment are to be considered as chosen with a studied discrimination, which yields an argument for a power over the press under the limitation that its freedom be not abridged, the same argument results from the same consideration for a power over the exercise of religion, under the limitation that its freedom be not prohibited.

For if Congress may regulate the freedom of the press, provided they do not abridge it, because it is said only "they shall not abridge it," and is not said, "they shall make no law respecting it," the analogy of reasoning is conclusive that Congress may regulate and even abridge the free exercise of religion, provided they do not prohibit it; because it is said only "they shall not prohibit it," and is not said, "they shall make no law respecting, or no law abridging it."

The General Assembly were governed by the clearest reason, then, in considering the Sedition Act, which legislates on the freedom of the press, as establishing a precedent that may be fatal to the liberty of conscience; and it will be the duty of all, in proportion as they value the security of the latter, to take the alarm at every encroachment on the former.

GLOSSARY

animadversion: criticism

encroachments: intrusion on a person's territory or rights

licentiousness: disregarding accepted rules or conventions

noxious: harmful, poisonous, very unpleasant

omnipotent: unlimited power

pernicious: having a harmful effect, often in a gradual way

prerogative: a right or privilege exclusive to a particular individual or class (in England, sovereign right, such as the King)

sovereignty: supreme power or authority

vexation: being annoyed, frustrated, or worried

SUPPLEMENTAL HISTORICAL DOCUMENT

Bill of Rights (1791)

Congress of the United States begun and held at the City of New-York, on Wednesday the fourth of March, one thousand seven hundred and eighty nine.

THE *Conventions* of a number of the States, having at the time of their adopting the Constitution, expressed a desire, in order to prevent misconstruction or abuse of its powers, that further declaratory and restrictive clauses should be added: And as extending the ground of public confidence in the Government, will best ensure the beneficent ends of its institution.

RESOLVED *by the Senate and House of Representatives* of the United States of America, in Congress assembled, two thirds of both Houses concurring, that the following Articles be proposed to the Legislatures of the several States, as amendments to the Constitution of the United States, all, or any of which Articles, when ratified by three fourths of the said Legislatures, to be valid to all intents and purposes, as part of the said Constitution; viz.

ARTICLES in addition to, and Amendment of the Constitution of the United States of America, proposed by Congress, and ratified by the Legislatures of the several States, pursuant to the fifth Article of the original Constitution.

Article the first... After the first enumeration required by the first article of the Constitution, there shall be one Representative for every thirty thousand, until the number shall amount to one hundred, after which the proportion shall be so regulated by Congress, that there shall be not less than one hundred Representatives, nor less than one Representative for every forty thousand persons, until the number of Representatives shall amount to two hundred; after which the proportion shall be so regulated by Congress, that there shall not be less than two hundred Representatives, nor more than one Representative for every fifty thousand persons.

Article the second... No law, varying the compensation for the services of the Senators and Representatives, shall take effect, until an election of Representatives shall have intervened.

Article the third... Congress shall make no law respecting an establishment of religion, or prohibiting the free exercise thereof; or abridging the freedom of speech, or of the press; or the right of the people peaceably to assemble, and to petition the Government for a redress of grievances.

Article the fourth... A well regulated Militia, being necessary to the security of a free State, the right of the people to keep and bear Arms, shall not be infringed.

Article the fifth... No Soldier shall, in time of peace be quartered in any house, without the consent of the Owner, nor in time of war, but in a manner to be prescribed by law.

Article the sixth... The right of the people to be secure in their persons, houses, papers, and effects, against unreasonable searches and seizures, shall not be violated, and no Warrants shall issue, but upon probable cause, supported by Oath or affirmation, and particularly describing the place to be searched, and the persons or things to be seized.

Article the seventh... No person shall be held to answer for a capital, or otherwise infamous crime, unless on a presentment or indictment of a Grand Jury, except in cases arising in the land or naval forces, or in the Militia, when in actual service in time of War or public danger; nor shall any person be subject for the same offence to be twice put in jeopardy of life or limb; nor shall be compelled in any criminal case to be a witness against himself, nor be deprived of life, liberty, or property, without due process of law; nor shall private property be taken for public use, without just compensation.

Article the eighth... In all criminal prosecutions, the accused shall enjoy the right to a speedy and public trial, by an impartial jury of the State and district wherein the crime shall have been committed, which district shall have been previously ascertained by law, and to be informed of the nature and cause of the accusation; to be confronted with the witnesses against him; to have compulsory process for obtaining witnesses in his favor, and to have the Assistance of Counsel for his defence.

Article the ninth... In Suits at common law, where the value in controversy shall exceed twenty dollars, the right of trial by jury shall be preserved, and no fact tried by a jury, shall be otherwise re-examined in any Court of the United States, than according to the rules of the common law.

Article the tenth... Excessive bail shall not be required, nor excessive fines imposed, nor cruel and unusual punishments inflicted.

Article the eleventh... The enumeration in the Constitution, of certain rights, shall not be construed to deny or disparage others retained by the people.

Article the twelfth... The powers not delegated to the United States by the Constitution, nor prohibited by it to the States, are reserved to the States respectively, or to the people.

ATTEST,

Frederick Augustus Muhlenberg, Speaker of the House of Representatives

John Adams, Vice-President of the United States, and President of the Senate

John Beckley, Clerk of the House of Representatives.

Sam. A Otis Secretary of the Senate

SUPPLEMENTAL HISTORICAL DOCUMENT

Transcript of An Act Concerning Aliens, An Act Respecting Alien Enemies, and An Act for the Punishment of Certain Crimes Against the United States

(1798)

FIFTH CONGRESS OF THE UNITED STATES:

At the Second Session,

Begun and help at the city of Philadelphia, in the state of Pennsylvania, on Monday, the thirteenth of November, one thousand seven hundred and ninety-seven.

An Act Concerning Aliens.

SECTION 1. Be it enacted by the Senate and the House of Representatives of the United States of America in Congress assembled, That it shall be lawful for the President of the United States at any time during the continuance of this act, to order all such aliens as he shall judge dangerous to the peace and safety of the United States, or shall have reasonable grounds to suspect are concerned in any treasonable or secret machinations against the government thereof, to depart out of the territory of the United States, within such time as shall be expressed in such order, which order shall be served on such alien by delivering him a copy thereof, or leaving the same at his usual abode, and returned to the office of the Secretary of State, by the marshal or other person to whom the same shall be directed. And in case any alien, so ordered to depart, shall be found at large within the United States after the time limited in such order for his departure, and not having obtained a license from the President to reside therein, or having obtained such license shall not have conformed thereto, every such alien shall, on conviction thereof, be imprisoned for a term not exceeding three years, and shall never after be admitted to become a citizen of the United States. Provided always, and be it further enacted, that if any alien so ordered to depart shall prove to the satisfaction of the President, by evidence to be taken before such person or persons as the President shall direct, who are for that purpose

hereby authorized to administer oaths, that no injury or danger to the United States will arise from suffering such alien to reside therein, the President may grant a license to such alien to remain within the United States for such time as he shall judge proper, and at such place as he may designate. And the President may also require of such alien to enter into a bond to the United States, in such penal sum as he may direct, with one or more sufficient sureties to the satisfaction of the per- son authorized by the President to take the same, conditioned for the good behavior of such alien during his residence in the United States, and not violating his license, which license the President may revoke, whenever he shall think proper.

SEC. 2. And be it further enacted, That it shall be lawful for the President of the United States, whenever he may deem it necessary (for the public safety, to order to be removed out of the territory thereof, any alien who mayor shall be in prison in pursuance of this act; and to cause to be arrested and sent out of the United States such of those aliens as shall have been ordered to depart therefrom and shall not have obtained a license as aforesaid, in all cases where, in the opinion of the President, the public safety requires a speedy removal. And if any alien so removed or sent out of the United States by the President shall voluntarily return thereto, unless by permission of the President of the United States, such alien on conviction thereof, shall be imprisoned so long as, in the opinion of the President, the public safety may require.

SEC. 3. And be it further enacted, That every master or commander of any ship or vessel which shall come into any port of the United States after the first day of July next, shall immediately on his arrival make report in writing to the collector or other chief officer of the customs of such port, of all aliens, if any, on board his vessel, specifying their names, age, the place of nativity, the country from which they shall have come, the nation to which they belong and owe allegiance, their occupation and a description of their persons, as far as he shall be informed thereof, and on failure, every such master and commander shall forfeit and pay three hundred dollars, for the payment whereof on default of such master or commander, such vessel shall also be holden, and may by such collector or other officer of the customs be detained. And it shall be the duty of such collector or other officer of the customs, forthwith to transmit to the office of the department of state true copies of all such returns.

SEC. 4. And be it further enacted, That the circuit and district courts of the United States, shall respectively have cognizance of all crimes and offences against this act. And all marshals and other officers of the United States are required to execute all precepts and orders of the President of the United States issued in pursuance or by virtue of this act.

SEC. 5. And be it further enacted, That it shall be lawful for any alien who may be ordered to be removed from the United States, by virtue of this act, to take with him such part of his goods, chattels, or other property, as he may find convenient; and all property left in the United States by any alien, who may be removed, as aforesaid, shall be, and re- main subject to his order and disposal, in the same manner as if this act had not been passed.

SEC. 6. And be it further enacted, That this act shall continue and be in force for and during the term of two years from the passing thereof.

Jonathan Dayton, Speaker of the House of Representatives.

TH. Jefferson, Vice President of the United States and President of the Senate.

I Certify that this Act did originate in the Senate.

Attest, Sam. A. Otis, Secretary

APPROVED, June 25, 1798.

John Adams

President of the United States.

An Act Respecting Alien Enemies

SECTION 1. Be it enacted by the Senate and House of Representatives of the United States of America in Congress assembled, That whenever there shall be a declared war between the United States and any foreign nation or government, or any invasion or predatory incursion shall be perpetrated, attempted, or threatened against the territory of the United States, by any foreign nation or government, and the President of the United States shall make public proclamation of the event, all natives, citizens, denizens, or subjects of the hostile nation or government, being males of the age of fourteen years and upwards, who shall be within the United States, and not actually naturalized, shall be liable to be apprehended, restrained, secured and removed, as alien enemies. And the President of the United States shall be, and he is hereby authorized, in any event, as aforesaid, by his proclamation thereof, or other public act, to direct the conduct to be observed, on the part of the United States, towards the aliens who shall become liable, as aforesaid; the manner and degree of the restraint to which they shall be subject, and in what cases, and upon what security their residence shall be permitted, and to provide for the removal of those, who, not being permitted to reside within the United States, shall refuse or neglect to depart therefrom; and to establish any other regulations which shall be found necessary in the premises and for the public safety: Provided, that aliens resident within the United States, who shall become liable as enemies, in the manner aforesaid, and who shall not be chargeable with actual hostility, or other crime against the public safety, shall be allowed, for the recovery, disposal, and removal of their goods and effects, and for their departure, the full time which is, or shall be stipulated by any treaty, where any shall have been between the United States, and the hostile nation or government, of which they shall be natives, citizens, denizens or subjects: and where no such treaty shall have existed, the President of the United States may ascertain and declare such reasonable time as may be consistent with the public safety, and according to the dictates of humanity and national hospitality.

SEC. 2. And be it further enacted, That after any proclamation shall be made as aforesaid, it shall be the duty of the several courts of the United States, and of each state, having criminal jurisdiction, and of the several judges and justices of the courts of the United States, and they shall be, and are hereby respectively, authorized upon complaint, against any alien or alien enemies, as aforesaid, who shall be resident and at large within such jurisdiction or district, to the danger of the public peace or safety, and contrary to the tenor or intent of such proclamation, or other regulations which the President of the United States shall and may establish in the premises, to cause such alien or aliens to be duly apprehended and convened before such court, judge or justice; and after a full examination and hearing on such complaint. and sufficient cause therefor appearing, shall and may order such alien or aliens to be removed out of the territory of the United States, or to give sureties of their good behaviour, or to be otherwise restrained, conformably to the proclamation or regulations which shall and may be established as aforesaid, and may imprison, or otherwise secure such alien or aliens, until the order which shall and may be made, as aforesaid, shall be performed.

SEC. 3. And be it further enacted, That it shall be the duty of the marshal of the district in which any alien enemy shall be apprehended, who by the President of the United States, or by order of any court, judge or justice, as aforesaid, shall be required to depart, and to be removed, as aforesaid, to provide therefor, and to execute such order, by himself or his deputy, or other discreet person or persons to be employed by him, by causing a removal of such alien out of the territory of the United States; and for such removal the marshal shall have the warrant of the President of the United States, or of the court, judge or justice ordering the same, as the case may be.

APPROVED, July 6, 1798.

FIFTH CONGRESS OF THE UNITED STATES:

At the Second Session,

Begun and help at the city of Philadelphia, in the state of Pennsylvania, on Monday, the thirteenth of November, one thousand seven hundred and ninety-seven.

An Act in Addition to the Act, Entitled "An Act for the Punishment of Certain Crimes Against the United States."

SECTION 1. Be it enacted by the Senate and House of Representatives of the United States of America, in Congress assembled, That if any persons shall unlawfully combine or conspire together, with intent to oppose any measure or measures of the government of the United States, which are or shall be directed by proper authority, or to impede the operation of any law of the United States, or to intimidate or prevent any person holding a place or office in or under the government of the United States, from undertaking, performing or executing his trust or duty, and if any person or persons, with intent as aforesaid, shall counsel, advise or attempt to procure any insurrection, riot, unlawful assembly, or combination, whether such conspiracy, threatening, counsel, advice, or attempt shall have the proposed effect or not, he or they shall be deemed guilty of a high misdemeanor, and on conviction, before any court of the United States having jurisdiction thereof, shall be punished by a fine not exceeding five thousand dollars, and by imprisonment during a term not less than six months nor exceeding five years; and further, at the discretion of the court may be holden to find sureties for his good behaviour in such sum, and for such time, as the said court may direct.

SEC. 2. And be it farther enacted, That if any person shall write, print, utter or publish, or shall cause or procure to be written, printed, uttered or published, or shall knowingly and willingly assist or aid in writing, printing, uttering or publishing any false, scandalous and malicious writing or writings against the government of the United States, or either house of the Congress of the United States, or the President of the United States, with intent to defame the said government, or either house of the said Congress, or the said President, or to bring them, or either of them, into contempt or disrepute; or to excite against them, or either or any of them, the hatred of the good people of the United States, or to stir up sedition within the United States, or to excite any unlawful combinations therein, for opposing or resisting any law of the United States, or any act of the President of the United States, done in pursuance of any such law, or of the powers in him vested by the constitution of the United States, or to resist, oppose, or defeat any such law or act, or to aid, encourage or abet any hostile designs of any foreign nation against United States, their people or government, then such person, being thereof convicted before any court of the United States having jurisdiction thereof, shall be punished by a fine not exceeding two thousand dollars, and by imprisonment not exceeding two years.

SEC. 3. And be it further enacted and declared, That if any person shall be prosecuted under this act, for the writing or publishing any libel aforesaid, it shall be lawful for the defendant, upon the trial of the cause, to give in evidence in his defence, the truth of the matter contained in publication charged as a libel. And the jury who shall try the cause, shall have a right to determine the law and the fact, under the direction of the court, as in other cases.

of March, one thousand eight hundred and one, and no longer: Provided, that the expiration of the act shall not prevent or defeat a prosecution and punishment of any offence against the law, during the time it shall be in force.

Jonathan Dayton, Speaker of the House of Representatives.

Theodore Sedgwick, President of the Senate *pro tempore*.

I Certify that this Act did originate in the Senate.

Attest, Sam. A. Otis, Secretary

APPROVED, July 14, 1798

John Adams

President of the United States.

Transcriptions courtesy of the Avalon Project at Yale Law School.

Document Analysis

Given that freedom of speech was one of the most important issues to Madison during his political career, it is not surprising that he would offer a passionate opposition to the Alien and Sedition Acts. This excerpt focuses on his belief that the acts are clearly unconstitutional. He focuses on the words "abridging the freedom of speech." The acts had declared that the amendment focused solely on declaring the press free from prior restraints on publication, essentially saying that they were governed by the common law as developed in England. This essentially meant that, once accused, authors could defend their writing by trying to prove that it was not libelous or offensive to the government but true and valid. Madison felt that this was far too difficult a test, and unfair. While Madison admits here that the freedom of the press can be abused, he expresses the idea that it would be better to see a few salacious items published than to remove the possibility of a free press entirely.

Essential Themes

In writing to his friend Thomas Jefferson regarding the Alien and Sedition Acts, Madison did not mince words; he wrote "The Alien bill proposed in the Senate is a monster that must forever disgrace its parents." To Madison, freedom of speech was directly tied to the ability of citizens to criticize their government, to impeach their representatives, and to demand accountability from those they had elected. It is generally agreed that the Constitution begins with the words "We, the People," in order to emphasize that the government is made up of the duly elected representatives of the citizens of the United States. Without the freedom of the press, Madison suggests, states might be held together only by the weak Articles of Confederation, which did nothing to support any unity between the states—or, worse still, by laws under the control of the English monarchy.

Madison stated that the phrasing of the amendment went farther than just keeping Congress from making laws or rulings about the press, so long as its freedom was not abridged; he argued that the amendment was designed to keep the government from interfering with free publication in any way whatsoever.

At another point, Madison takes up the issue of government punishment for inappropriate speech or writing. He first points out that the average person is extremely unlikely to be able to prove every fact to be true to the full satisfaction of a court of law. But second, and perhaps more important, he points out that beliefs and opinions are drawn from facts, but cannot inherently be proven. The most a person could hope to do is to show his or her logical train of thought and how one drew one's opinion from the facts.

In some ways, this may be an even more important protection for critical journalism. After all, it is one thing to report facts; high-quality journalists then and now check their sources, document their research, and verify their discoveries. However, the best journalists do not simply report facts. They draw conclusions from those facts and present those conclusions. The job of journalism is not just to report that something happened, but also to explain why it matters. Different journalists may have different opinions on why something matters, but it is clear that Madison believed it was better to let every opinion be spoken than to restrict what could and could not be said.

In this way, Madison's 1800 Report may be the most full-throated support for the First Amendment and a free press that exists. He argues for absolutely no limitations on the press at any time. Ultimately, he also states that Virginia does not agree with the acts, and will not persecute its citizens for any supposed crime according to the acts.

Thomas Jefferson went a step further than Madison's declaration, arguing that states had the right to nullify federal laws. Madison strongly opposed state nullification, even though his 1800 Report was later used to support it.

—*Kay Tilden Frost*

Bibliography and Additional Reading

Hoffer, Peter Charles. *The Free Press Crisis of 1800: Thomas Cooper's Trial for Seditious Libel.* Lawrence: University Press of Kansas, 2011.

Jefferson, Thomas, and James Madison. *James Madison to Thomas Jefferson, With Notes.* 1798. Manuscript/Mixed Material. https://www.loc.gov/item/mjm013485/.

"Virginia and Kentucky Resolutions." *Bill of Rights Institute.* https://billofrightsinstitute.org/founding-documents/primary-source-documents/virginia-and-kentucky-resolutions/.

Vile, John R., William D. Pederson, and Frank J. Williams, eds. *James Madison: Philosopher, Founder, and Statesman.* Athens: Ohio University Press, 2008.

■ Debates over the Circulation of "Incendiary Publications"

Dates: December 7, 1835, February 4, 1836, March 25, 1836
Authors: Andrew Jackson, John Calhoun, Hiland Hall
Genre: Presidential address; congressional committee reports

Summary Overview

These three documents comprise the key portions of the mid-1830s debate over whether or not the federal government should order the U.S. Post Office to prevent the spread of "incendiary publications." "Incendiary publications," in this context, refers to antislavery, abolitionist newspapers, magazines, and pamphlets that were increasing in number in the northern states and which had begun appearing in southern states where slavery was permitted. Slave owners and southern politicians feared that these abolitionist writings would fuel slave uprisings and disrupt the "domestic tranquility" of the southern states.

In the first, President Andrew Jackson, as part of his constitutionally required annual message to Congress, calls for federal legislation to prevent the Post Office from delivering antislavery publications to southern states. In the second, South Carolina Senator John Calhoun echoes Jackson's concerns about this material, but argues that that the federal government does not have the power to prohibit such materials. The solution, as Calhoun saw it, was for the federal government to throw its weight behind the state government's efforts to prevent to circulation of abolitionist writings. Finally, Representative Hiland Hall of Vermont presents an argument that the federal government is expressly prohibited by the First Amendment to the Constitution from making judgments about what political opinions may or may not be communicated by mail.

Defining Moment

By the 1830s, the abolition movement—a social reform movement focused on ending slavery in the United States—had begun to grow in numbers and influence. Many of their ideas spread through the numerous newspapers, magazines, and pamphlets published by various antislavery organizations. In 1835, one of these organizations—the American Anti-Slavery Society—engaged in a broad campaign to convey their arguments not to their supporters in the northern states but rather to slaveholders, politicians, and prominent citizens of the southern states. Led by William Jay, Lewis Tappan, and Arthur Tappan, the organization attempted to use the U.S. Post Office to mail materials from New York City, where they were headquartered, to states where slavery was legal.

Their efforts first ran into trouble not in the South, but in the North, where many local postmasters pledged to prevent the publications from being sent South. When materials did make their way to the intended destinations, there was often trouble. One example occurred in Charleston, South Carolina, where a mob seized the offending materials from the local post office and burned them.

The threat of further abolitionist mail campaigns spurred President Andrew Jackson, in late 1835, to call for legislation that would empower postal officials to keep such materials from being delivered to their targets in slaveholding states. The proposal became part of a wider debate over the new Post Office being debated by Congress. As we see in these documents, there was division over this proposal on a number of fronts. South Carolinian John C. Calhoun shared Jackson's concerns about abolitionist literature and the havoc it might cause but had serious concerns over whether it was the federal government's place to intervene. Vermont Congressman Hiland Hall was concerned that such legislation was prohibited by the First Amendment and would open the door to further abuses by the federal government and diminish the press freedom guaranteed by the Bill of Rights.

Hall's concerns were not heard in Congress; when he tried to present his report, he was silenced and had to release the report in a newspaper, the *National Intelligencer*. While Jackson's supporters attempted to suppress Hall's report, ultimately they failed to achieve their goal of officially sanctioned antiabolition censorship; the 1836 Post Office Bill not only failed to give postmasters the authority to confiscate antislavery materials, it threatened with fines and prison time postmasters who attempted to prevent material from being delivered.

Authors' Biographies

In 1835, Andrew Jackson (1767–1845) was in the midst of his second term as seventh president of the United States. Before reaching the White House, Jackson had

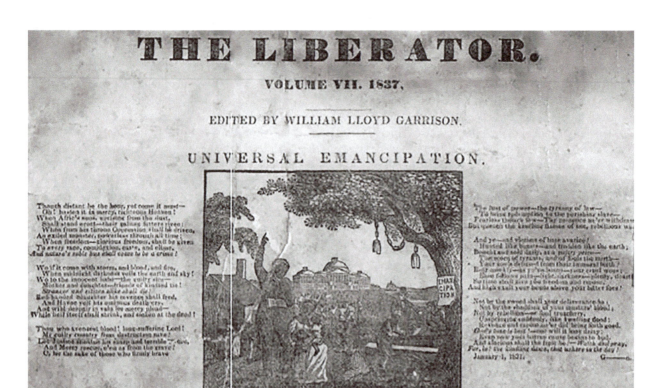

Abolitionist publications like The Liberator *were caught up in debates related to the mailing of incendiary publications. (An issue of* The Liberator *depicting African Americans next to a lynching tree. From Volume VII. 1837. Edited by William Lloyd Garrison. Published by Isaac Knapp, Cornhill, Boston, Massachusetts.)*

a storied career as a military officer in the U.S. Army, was a lawyer, and had served in both the House of Representatives and the Senate. Jackson's presidency had already weathered a number of crises that stoked the fires of political division. One of them—the "Nullification Crisis"—had pit Jackson and his broad view of how the president could wield the power of the federal government against John C. Calhoun, at the time his vice president. This was a showdown over a tariff law, but also over the power of the federal government as opposed to that of the states. Their rivalry would surface in this debate over the powers of the postal service.

John Calhoun (1782–1850), after being Jackson's vice president until 1832, served as a senator from South Carolina. Throughout his career he advocated for the rights of political minorities against the majority; usually this manifested in the form of favoring the

supremacy of the individual states over the federal government. It was his position that states had the authority to "nullify" federal laws that brought him into conflict with Jackson as vice president. His arguments about the question of prohibiting antislavery materials in the mail reflects his view that the states were sovereign over their own affairs.

The third author, and the one most concerned about the press freedom issues at the heart of this debate, was Hiland Hall (1795–1885). Hall served as one of Vermont's congressional representatives from 1833 to 1843, elected first as an Anti-Jackson candidate, then becoming a member of the new Whig Party. Hall also served governor of Vermont for two years (1858–1860) and was a delegate to the unsuccessful Peace Conference of 1861 that attempted to avert civil war following the secession of southern states.

HISTORICAL DOCUMENT

Andrew Jackson, Seventh Annual Address to Congress, 7 December 1835

I must also invite your attention to the painful excitement produced in the South by attempts to circulate through the mails inflammatory appeals addressed to the passions of the slaves, in prints and in various sorts of publications, calculated to stimulate them to insurrection and to produce all the horrors of a servile war. There is doubtless no respectable portion of our countrymen who can be so far misled as to feel any other sentiment than that of indignant regret at conduct so destructive of the harmony and peace of the country, and so repugnant to the principles of our national compact and to the dictates of humanity and religion. Our happiness and prosperity essentially depend upon peace without our borders, and peace depends upon the maintenance in good faith of those compromises of the Constitution upon which the Union is founded. It is fortunate for the country that the good sense, the generous feeling, and the deep-rooted attachment of the people of the nonslaveholding States of the Union and to their fellow-citizens of the same blood in the South have given so strong and impressive a tone

to the sentiments entertained against the proceedings of the misguided persons who have engaged in these unconstitutional and wicked attempts … as to authorize the hope that those attempts will no longer be persisted in. But if these expressions of the public will shall not be sufficient to effect so desirable a result, not a doubt can be entertained that the nonslaveholding States, so far from countenancing the slightest interference with the constitutional rights of the South, will be prompt to exercise their authority in suppressing so far as in them lies whatever is calculated to produce this evil.

In leaving the care of other branches of this interesting subject to the State authorities, to whom they properly belong, it is nevertheless proper for Congress to take such measures as will prevent the Post-Office Department, which was designed to foster an amicable intercourse and correspondence between all the members of the Confederacy, from being used as an instrument of an opposite character. The General Government, to which the great trust is confided of preserving inviolate the relations created among the States by the Constitution, is especially bound to avoid in its own action anything that may disturb them. I would therefore call the special attention of Congress to the subject, and respectfully suggest the propriety of passing such a law as will prohibit, under severe penalties, the circulation in the Southern States, through the mail, of incendiary publications intended to instigate the slaves to insurrection....

Report from the Select Committee on the Circulation of Incendiary Publications, 4 February 1836

The Select Committee fully concur with the President ... as to the character and tendency of the papers, which have been attempted to be circulated in the South, through the mail, and participate with him in the indignant regret, which he expresses at conduct so destructive of the peace and harmony of the country, and repugnant to the Constitution, and the dictates of humanity and religion. They also concur in the hope that, if the strong tone of disapprobation which these unconstitutional and wicked attempts have called forth, does not arrest them, the non-slaveholding States will be prompt to exercise their power to suppress them, as far as their authority extends. But while they agree with the President as to the evil and its highly dangerous tendency, and the necessity of arresting it, they have not been able to assent to the measure of redress which he recommends; that Congress should pass a law prohibiting under severe penalty the transmission of incendiary publications, though the mail, intended to instigate the slaves to insurrection.

After the most careful and deliberate investigation, they have been constrained to adopt the conclusion that Congress has not the power to pass such a law: that it would be a violation of one of the most sacred provisions of the Constitution, and subversive of reserved powers essential to the preservation of the domestic institutions of the slaveholding states....

[The Committee] refer to the amended Article of the Constitution which ... provides that Congress shall pass no law, which shall abridge the liberty of the press, a provision, which interposes ... an insuperable objection to the measure recommended by the President....

Madison, in his celebrated report to the Virginia Legislature in 1799, against the Alien and Sedition Law, ... conclusively settled the principle that Congress has no right, in any form, or in any manner, to interfere with the freedom of the press...

Assuming [the Sedition Act] to be unconstitutional ... which no one now doubts, it will not be difficult to show that if, instead of inflicting punishment for publishing, the act had inflicted punishment for circulating through the mail, for the same offense, it would have been equally unconstitutional. The one would have abridged the freedom of the press as effectually as the other. The object of publishing is circulation, and to prohibit circulation is, in effect, to prohibit publication. They have both a common object. The communication of sentiments and opinions to the public, and the prohibition of one may as effectually suppress such communication, as the prohibition of the other, and, of course, would as effectually interfere with the freedom of the press, and be equally unconstitutional....

[I]f it be admitted, that Congress has the right to discriminate in reference to their character, what papers shall, or what shall not be transmitted by the mail, [that] would subject the freedom of the press, on all subjects, political, moral, and religious, completely to its will and pleasure....

The principle on which the Sedition Act was condemned, as unconstitutional, was a general one, and not limited to its application, to that act. It withdraws from Congress all right of interference with the press, in any form, or shape whatever; and the Sedition Law was put down, as unconstitutional, not because it prohibited publications against the Government, but because it interfered, at all, with the press. The prohibition of any publication on the ground of its being immoral, irreligious, or intended to excite rebellion, or insurrection, would have been equally unconstitutional; and from parity of reason, the suppression of their circulation, through the mail, would be no less so....

Nothing is more clear, than that the admission of the right on the part of Congress to determine what papers are incendiary, and as such to prohibit their circulation through the mail, necessarily involves the right to determine, what are not incendiary and to enforce their circulation. Nor is it less certain, that to admit such a right would be virtually to clothe Congress with the power to abolish slavery, by giving it the means of breaking down all the barriers which the slave holding States have erected for the protection of their lives and property. It would give Congress without regard to the prohibitory laws of the States the authority to open the gates to the flood of incendiary publications, which are ready to break into those States, and to punish all, who dare resist, as criminals. Fortunately, Congress has no such right. The internal peace and security of the States are under the protection of the States themselves, to the entire exclusion of all authority and control on the part of Congress. It belongs to them, and not to Congress, to determine what is, or is not, calculated to disturb their peace and security, and of course in the case under consideration, it belongs to the Slave holding States to determine, what is incendiary and intended to incite to insurrection, and to adopt such defensive measures, as may be necessary for their security, with unlimited means of carrying them into effect, except such as may be expressly inhibited to the States by the Constitution....

If, consequently, the right to protect her internal peace and security belongs to a State, the general Government is bound to respect the measures adopted by her for that purpose, and to cooperate in their execution, as far as its delegated powers may admit, or the measure may require. Thus, in the present case, the slave-holding States having the unquestionable right to pass all such laws as may be necessary to maintain the existing relation between master and slave, in those States, their right, of course, to prohibit the circulation of any publication, or any intercourse, calculated to disturb or destroy that relation is incontrovertible. In the execution of the measures, which may be adopted by the States for this purpose, the powers of Congress over the mail, and of regulating commerce with foreign nations and between the States, may require cooperation on the part of the general Government; and it is bound, in conformity with the principle established, to respect the laws of the State in their exercise, and so to modify its acts, as not only not to violate those of the States, but, as far as practicable, to cooperate in their execution....

Regarding [the above principle] as established ... the Committee ... have prepared a Bill ...

prohibiting under penalty of fine and dismissal from other, any Deputy Postmaster, in any State, Territory or District, from knowingly receiving and putting into the mail, any letter, packet, pamphlet, paper, or pictorial representation, directed to any Post office or person in a State, Territory or District, by the laws of which the circulation is forbidden....

Report of the Minority of Committee on Post Offices and Post Roads on the President's Message, 25 March 1836

[T]he establishment of a censorship over all publications ... must necessarily operate with extreme harshness.... In order to make the law effectual, a censor must be appointed in the vicinity of every printing press, whose duty it would be to examine every number of every periodical, and every edition of all other publications, for which a mail circulation was sought, and certify their fitness for such circulation to the postmasters.... One of the obvious legal effects of this mode of legislation would be to transfer the power of determining a publisher's right to circulate, and also his right of property in the publications, from a jury of his peers to the summary discretion of any one of many thousand individuals. The medium of mail circulation has become so useful and important to the press of the country, and would be so trammeled and obstructed by the previous submission of all matters to be transmitted to the tribunal of a licenser, that this species of censorship could be scarcely less exceptionable and oppressive than a censorship that should extend to the restraint of the actual printing of publications. On the whole, a law of this description would be in such direct opposition to all the preconceived opinions of the People of this country, so abhorrent to their notions of the principles of civil liberty, and so utterly destructive of the freedom of the press, that the undersigned will not permit themselves seriously to apprehend that, under any possible circumstances, such a law can ever find a place on our statute book....

The second mode of legislation [is] prohibiting the circulation by mail of such publications as the States shall prohibit.... If one State has a right to call on

Congress to enact laws to prevent the effect of a mail circulation of publications within its limits, any other State has the same right; and if the judgment of one State is to be received as evidence of the evil tendency of particular publications, the judgment of every other State must have the same force, and impose the same obligation on Congress. A statute, therefore, founded on this principle, would provide that it should be an offense against the United States for any person to send through the mail into any State any publication the circulation of which might be prohibited by the laws of such State. A statute of this description would not only punish the citizen of Massachusetts before the federal court in his State for sending publications by mail on the subject of slavery into Georgia, but would also punish the citizen of Georgia, before the federal court in his State, for sending a publication on any subject into Massachusetts, that subject, whatever it might be, having previously come under the interdict of the law of Massachusetts…. One State might prohibit the dissemination of the Catholic doctrine; another, that of the Protestant; one that of one political sentiment, and another that of its opposite….

We are then thrown back on the question of what authority Congress possesses over "incendiary publications," by the grants of power contained in the Constitution, under the restrictions on the exercise of those powers found in that instrument? … The mode which this species of legislation provides, for executing the judgment which the Government forms of the character of publications, is most exceptionable and alarming. It does not, like other statutes, provide for the trial and punishment of the actual offender, but for the manual seizure and destruction of the article which it judges to be offensive. It deprives the citizen of his right of trial by jury to determine the fact of the unlawfulness of the publication, and takes from him his property without any "process of law" whatever. In this respect it is a direct violation of the fifth article of the amendment to the constitution. It is a censorship of the Press, committed to this summary discretion of any single Post Master—a censorship exercised in secret and upon evidence which can only be reached by an inquisitorial scrutiny into the contents of the mails, which must at once destroy all confidence in this security for any purpose. It is believed that a law with such odious features could not long be tolerated by any free people….

The minority have not been able to come to the conclusion that Congress possesses the constitutional power to restrain the mail circulation of the publications specified in the message. On the contrary, they believe that any legislation for that purpose would come in direct conflict with that clause in the Constitution which prohibits Congress from making any law "abridging the freedom of speech or of the press." … The meaning of the term abridge is not qualified in the Constitution by the specification of any particular degree beyond which the liberty of the press is not permitted to be diminished. The slightest contraction or lessening of that liberty is forbidden. Nor does the Constitution point out any particular mode by which the freedom of the press may not be abridged. All modes of abridgment whatever are excluded, whether by the establishment of a censorship, the imposition of punishments, a tax on the promulgation of obnoxious opinions, or by any other means which can be devised to give a legislative preference, either in publication or circulation, to one sentiment emanating from the press, over that of another. Otherwise, the clause, by being susceptible of evasion, would be nugatory and useless. It was not against particular forms of legislation but to secure the substance of the freedom of the press, that the clause was made a part of the Constitution. The object of publication is circulation. The mere power to print, without the liberty to circulate, would be utterly valueless. The Post Office power, which belongs to the General Government, is an exclusive power. Under that power Congress has the entire control of the whole regular circulation of the country. Neither a State nor individuals, in opposition to the will of Congress, can establish or carry on the business of such circulation. A power, therefore, in Congress to judge of the moral, religious, political, or physical tendency of publications, and to deny the medium of mail circulation to those it deemed of an obnoxious character, would not only enable Congress to abridge the freedom of the press, but absolutely and completely to destroy it….

Those who denied the constitutionality of the sedition act, and among them Mr. Madison, in his elaborate and able report, made to the Virginia House of Delegates in 1799, contended that the clause of the Constitution which provides that Congress shall make no law "abridging the freedom of speech, or of the press," was to be understood as a clear prohibition of all power in Congress over the subject of the press, and that consequently Congress could make no law in any manner affecting it, or in other words, could express no legislative opinion of the character and tendency of its productions. This doctrine is believed to have obtained the almost universal assent of the People of the United States, and especially of that portion of the People of the Union for whose peculiar benefit the proposed legislation is intended. In this doctrine the undersigned concur; and if it be admitted as the true doctrine, if it be admitted that Congress can make no law in any manner affecting the press, they cannot conceive what possible ground remains for argument, in favor of the constitutionality of the legislation now in contemplation.... It will be readily conceded that Congress, under the post office power, may make any law which is necessary and proper to secure the safe, convenient, and expeditious transportation of the mail.... Nor will the undersigned undertake to say that Congress could not, under its post office power, prohibit the use of the mail for transportation of articles calculated to produce mischief or crime, in cases where its legislation would not come in conflict with any of the prohibitory clauses of the Constitution. The sending through the mail of forged papers, as checks, drafts, or bank bills, might present a strong case to the consideration of Congress.... [Nevertheless], They hold that the prohibitory clauses of the Constitution are coextensive with the whole instrument; that they restrain, absolutely and completely, the conferred powers, and that they cannot, under any presence, be violated without a violation of the Constitution.... The prohibition of "incendiary publications" from mail circulation is not within the legitimate scope of the post office power; the power of proscribing them not being at all necessary to the safe, convenient, or expeditious transportation of the mail.... A law to prevent their circulation would be founded in erroneous and unconstitutional principles. Under color of providing for the convenient transportation of the mail, and of preventing its use for evil purposes, it would assume a power in Congress to judge of the tendency of opinions emanating from the press; a power to discriminate between packages, not in reference to their bulk or form, but in relation to the sentiments they might be designed to inculcate. One class of opinions, meeting the approbation of Congress, is permitted a free circulation; another class of opinions, which Congress denominate "dangerous, seditious, and incendiary," is prohibited.... The People of the United States never intended that the Government of the Union should exercise over the press the power of discriminating between true and erroneous opinions, of determining that this sentiment was patriotic, that seditious and incendiary, and therefore wisely prohibited Congress all power over the subject. The minority of the committee respectfully submit to the House that Congress does not possess the constitutional power to distinguish from other publications, of like size and form, the "incendiary publications" specified in the Message of the President, or in any way to restrain their mail circulation.

GLOSSARY

abridge: to limit or reduce

"all the members of the Confederacy": a reference to the individual states of the United States

disapprobation: strong disapproval

incendiary: something likely to cause outrage and, potentially, violence

Document Analysis

Jackson begins by discussing the "painful excitement" caused by the transmission of abolitionist material to the South. Here, he characterizes the materials as being "appeals addressed to the passions of slaves" and argues that the intent of the publications as being to ignite a violent slave uprising. He argues that such materials are "destructive to the peace and harmony of the country." As such, these attempts violate the notion of a "good faith" acceptance of both slave and free states of the union. Since some of the compromises between free and slave states exist in the Constitution, Jackson makes a legal (and rhetorical) jump to declaring the abolitionist efforts to be "unconstitutional." He calls for legislation that would prevent the transmission of such incendiary materials through the mail. In doing so, he characterizes the postal service as a tool "to foster an amicable intercourse" between all states; thus, he positions abolitionist efforts as a perversion and misuse of the postal service.

John Calhoun, in the February 1836 report, concurs with Jackson's characterization of these antislavery materials but does not feel that Congress has the authority to pass the type of sweeping law for which the president called. Calhoun cites the First Amendment and arguments against the eighteenth-century Sedition Act. All is not lost, however; Calhoun argues that state laws against incendiary publications are lawful and that the federal government has a responsibility to help enforce those laws. Calhoun's committee has prepared legislation that orders postmasters to enforce bans on material under state law.

Hall's March report raises the same points as Calhoun with regard to the First Amendment and the precedent of the Sedition Act. However, Hall's goal is to assert the absolute prohibition on federal action to "abridge" the free press. Where Calhoun uses these arguments in the service of his wider concerns about state and federal power, Hall argues that Calhoun's proposal would put the federal government in the position of determining which state laws to help enforce and which to ignore. Hall's reading of the First Amendment prohibits *any* federal interference in the freedom of the press.

Essential Themes

These three statements encapsulate some of the major arguments consuming the United States in the decades leading up to the Civil War. The driving force behind these arguments was slavery, but in this case, as in other cases, the institution of slavery was the impetus for debates without being the subject of the debates. In the case of the Jackson and Calhoun arguments, the point of contention is the continual tension between the power of the federal government and that of the states' governments. With regard to question of banning abolitionist publications from delivery by the postal service, Jackson's support for broad federal power is in keeping with his sweeping use of federal and executive power in instances such as the removal of the Cherokee and other tribes from the southeastern United States and his willingness to use the army to enforce tariff collection in South Carolina. Calhoun's insistence that state-level legislation should be adequate to ban abolitionist materials—that the federal government has the responsibility to compel compliance with state law but not the authority to ban materials from the post itself—is an extreme position in support of state power, an echo of his support for the "nullification" of the tariff laws by South Carolina (the position which led to Jackson's deployment of the military). This tension between state and federal power would increase in coming decades.

Hiland Hall's argument against censorship of the mail is based on the kind of strict interpretation of the Bill of Rights that would typify press freedom debates in the later nineteenth century until the present. Here, Hall takes a position that the Constitution provides no authority for Congress to order the Post Office to discriminate against particular political ideas. The First Amendment prohibits Congress from "abridging" freedom of speech or press: Hall argues—as did James Madison before him and many free press advocates after him—that this prohibition is total.

—Aaron Gulyas

Bibliography and Additional Reading

Harrold, Stanley. *American Abolitionism: Its Direct Political Impact from Colonial Times into Reconstruction.* Charlottesville: University of Virginia Press, 2019.

John, Richard R. "Hiland Hall's "Report on Incendiary Publications": A Forgotten Nineteenth Century Defense of the Constitutional Guarantee of the Freedom of the Press." *The American Journal of Legal History* 41, no. 1 (1997): 94–125.

Meacham, Jon. *American Lion: Andrew Jackson in the White House.* New York: Random House, 2009.

Wyatt-Brown, Bertram. *Lewis Tappan and the Evangelical War against Slavery.* Baton Rouge: Louisiana State University Press, 1997.

Muckraking, Yellow Journalism, War, Sedition, and More

In this section we present documents representing a range of converging historical themes extending from the end of the nineteenth century to the middle of the twentieth.

Near the turn of the century, a brand of journalism that came to be known as "muckraking" journalism emerged. Theodore Roosevelt is credited with coining the term *muckraking* when he referred in a speech to the "Muck-Rake" in John Bunyan's classic novel *Pilgrim's Progress*. Muckraking was investigative journalism that sought to expose political corruption and scandalous conditions in society. In doing so it illustrated the value of a free press—for in other, less democratic nations it was impossible to publish criticism of the government (local or national) or to describe social problems accurately. (Jail or other threats could result.) In the United States, as in other growing democracies, such published accounts were welcome by reformers and agents of change.

In this section, we include a few examples of turn-of-the-century reform-era writing to show the free press at work. The first document is a famous 1890 account by Jacob Riis called *How the Other Half Lives*. It concerns life in the slums of the Lower East Side of Manhattan, particularly the dismal life experienced by children. Another example is presented in "The Shame of Minneapolis" by Lincoln Steffens. The article describes the corruption, bribery, cronyism, graft, and other political ills affecting the city of Minneapolis, Minnesota, under its crooked mayor at the time. This document is followed by an excerpt from the 1906 novel *The Jungle*. In it, the writer Upton Sinclair describes the unsanitary conditions in Chicago's meat-packing district, as well as the dangers of working in processing facilities there. Finally, in "The Passing of the War Virtues" (1907), the social reformer Jane Addams suggests that a fairer society can be achieved

only if the older military values that are considered founding virtues of the American social order are replaced by a newer understanding that focuses on beneficial social growth.

We also look briefly at another trend in journalism occurring in the same period, namely, "yellow journalism," or news reporting that seeks to sensationalize in order to win a following and advance a point of view—bending the truth in the course of doing so. In 1898, New York newspapers intent on both starting a war and selling more papers blamed Spain for the sinking of the U.S.S. *Maine* in Havana Harbor. The result was the start of the Spanish-American War, even though Spain was not at fault in the ship's sinking. In this case, the free press did more harm than good.

Several documents concerning World War I–era definitions of "sedition," or "seditious libel," are also included in the present section. This material serves to illustrate the limitation placed on freedom of speech and the press during times of war. We hear from two persons accused of crimes under the 1918 Sedition Act, Eugene Debs and Scott Nearing; and we review a variety of landmark U.S. Supreme Court decisions—*Schenk v. United States* (1919), *Abrams v. United States* (1919), and *Gitlow v. New York* (1925)—that lay out the legal standards involved or otherwise consider what sedition amounts to in spoken or written statements. One other court case included here looks at a somewhat related issue, namely, "prior restraint" of the press, or the prohibiting of a publication prior to its release to the public (*Near v. Minnesota*, 1931).

A few general statements of principles concerning the idea of a free press are also provided here. We reproduce a 1928 speech by President Calvin Coolidge on the relationship between a free press and a "free government." Nearly twenty years later, the issue again arose in the context of World War II (and its aftermath)

"The Evil Spirits of the Modern Daily Press." Nasty little printer's devils such as "Paid Puffery" and "Suggestiveness" spew forth from the modern daily press. (Sydney B. Griffin (1854-1923)–Puck cartoon of November 21, 1888)

SPANIARDS SEARCH WOMEN ON AMERICAN STEAMERS

DRAWN BY FREDERIC REMINGTON

Male Spanish officials strip search an American woman tourist in Cuba looking for messages from rebels; front page "yellow journalism" from Hearst (artist: Remington)

and was addressed by a special commission of experts who produced a report, "A Free and Responsible Press" (1947). The following year, Congress decided that it was okay for the United States to broadcast propaganda to foreign countries but not inside the United States (see the "Smith-Mundt Act"). In that same year, too, the United Nations (UN) General Assembly issued a "Universal Declaration of Human Rights" that included among its provisions a statement on the rights of free speech and a free press.

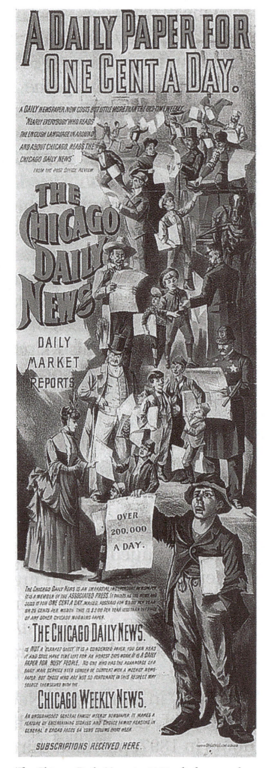

The Chicago Daily News *in 1901 relied on newsboys hawking the headlines.*

From *How the Other Half Lives*

Date: 1890
Author: Jacob Riis
Genre: Nonfiction (excerpt)

Summary Overview

In 1890, *New York Evening Sun* reporter Jacob Riis published an extensive book on life in the slums of the East Side of Manhattan. Riis's book, which served as the inspiration for social reformers in New York, graphically depicted the life of squalor in which the residents—particularly the children—of this area lived. This excerpt describes how a number of children lived in these conditions, avoiding school, the reformatory, and the dangers of life on the street. Riis calls upon readers to combat poverty in New York by focusing on improving the lives of children, such as the ones he describes in the book.

Defining Moment

The American Industrial Revolution represented a great set of opportunities for those seeking employment, not only for Americans but also for countless immigrants. German Jews fleeing the 1848 revolution, Irish men and women escaping the 1846–51 potato famine, and many other groups of laborers unable to find work in their homelands all braved harsh travel conditions and long delays in New York Harbor to arrive in what they thought would be a better way of life. According to the census data, New York's population just prior to the Civil War was 805,658; by 1890, the population had exceeded 1.5 million.

The tremendous influx of immigrants in New York City occurred without corresponding development. To be sure, New York City had been constructing tenement houses, but immigrants simply packed into them in numbers far too great to make any space hospitable. Apartments were tiny, overpriced, poorly ventilated and lit, and dilapidated. Many tenements were not fit properly for sewage and water, resulting in widespread public health dangers and the spilling of waste into alleys and roads. In the streets, the situation was no better: according to an 1866 report, tons of garbage and other waste littered the streets and blocked sewers, and cattle marched through crowded streets, endangering anyone in their paths.

The issue was not lost on the government, but it could do little to address the problems. In 1867, the New York City Council of Hygiene, for example, passed regulations that required tenements to be built with such features as proper ventilation, fire escapes, bathrooms, and sewer linkage. While such laws were largely ineffective (enforcement was extremely difficult), they did at least generate awareness about this issue. In fact, these laws laid the groundwork for later local, state, and federal laws.

In 1890, Riis, who at the time was a police reporter whose work occasionally appeared in the New York media, launched a personal investigation into the conditions in New York City's slums. Riis had the benefit of using a new piece of technology: a flash camera, capable of illuminating dark tenement apartments, alleys, basements, and other places where immigrants lived and took shelter. A social reformer, Riis was himself an immigrant who had arrived in 1870. He used this experience and motivation to pen an in-depth book on life in the slums of New York's East Side, complete with stark photos of the most vulnerable of the slums' residents: the children.

Author Biography

Jacob Riis was born on May 3, 1849, in Ribe, Denmark. In 1870, at the age of twenty-one, he immigrated to the United States in search of work. However, he found little success and resorted to begging and taking shelter in police barracks. Riis performed a wide range of odd jobs before he found employment as a police reporter. Committed to correcting the social ills that he had experienced, he continued to take tours of the slums and tenements in New York after the success of *How the Other Half Lives*. He was befriended by New York City police commissioner Theodore Roosevelt and was later offered a chance to serve in Roosevelt's presidential administration but declined. Riis continued to advocate for open space and parks in New York until his death on March 26, 1914.

Bandit roost (59 Mulberry Street in New York City) by Jacob Riis, 1888.

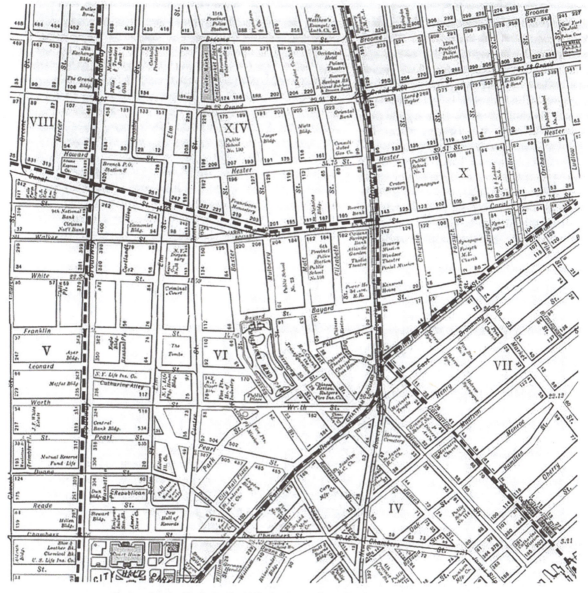

Section of lower Manhattan in 1899, showing Mulberry Bend Park (created on the site of Mulberry Bend in 1895 after Riis's disclosures), Chinatown, Five Points, Jewish neighborhoods on Bayard and Baxter Streets, and adjacent wards.

A map of the area Jacob Riis surveyed while collecting material for How the Other Half Lives.

Portrait of S. S. McClure. (Published in The World's Work, *1914)*

Jacob Riis, journalist, c. 1905. (Photographed by Pirie MacDonald)

HISTORICAL DOCUMENT

The problem of the children becomes, in these swarms, to the last degree perplexing. Their very number makes one stand aghast. I have already given instances of the packing of the child population in East Side tenements. They might be continued indefinitely until the array would be enough to startle any community. For, be it remembered, these children with the training they receive—or do not receive—with the instincts they inherit and absorb in their growing up, are to be our future rulers, if our theory of government is worth anything. More than a working majority of our voters now register from the tenements. I counted the other day the little ones, up to ten years or so, in a Bayard Street tenement that for a yard has a triangular space in the centre with sides fourteen or fifteen feet long, just room enough for a row of ill-smelling closets at the base of the triangle and a hydrant at the apex. There was about as much light in this "yard" as in the average cellar. I gave up my self-imposed task in despair when I had counted one hundred and twenty-eight in forty families. Thirteen I had missed, or not found in. Applying the average for the forty to the whole fifty-three, the house contained one hundred and seventy children. It is not the only time I have had to give up such census work. I have in mind an alley—an inlet rather to a row of rear tenements—that is either two or four feet wide according as the wall of the crazy old building that gives on it bulges out or in. I tried to count the children that swarmed there, but could not. Sometimes I have doubted that anybody knows just how many there are about. Bodies of drowned children turn up in the rivers right along in summer whom no one seems to know anything about. When last spring some workmen, while moving a pile of lumber on a North River pier, found under the last plank the body of a little lad crushed to death, no one had missed a boy, though his parents afterward turned up. The truant officer assuredly does not know, though he spends his life trying to find out, somewhat illogically, perhaps, since the department that employs him admits that thousands of poor children are crowded out of the schools year by year for want of room. There was a big tenement in the Sixth Ward, now happily appropriated by the beneficent spirit of business that blots out so many foul spots in New York—it figured not long ago in the official reports as "an out-and-out hogpen"—that had a record of one hundred and two arrests in four years among its four hundred and seventy-eight tenants, fifty-seven of them for drunken and disorderly conduct. I do not know how many children there were in it, but the inspector reported that he found only seven in the whole house who owned that they went to school. The rest gathered all the instruction they received running for beer for their elders. Some of them claimed the "flat" as their home as a mere matter of form. They slept in the streets at night. The official came upon a little party of four drinking beer out of the cover of a milk-can in the hallway. They were of the seven good boys and proved their claim to the title by offering him some.

The old question, what to do with the boy, assumes a new and serious phase in the tenements. Under the best conditions found there, it is not easily answered. In nine cases out of ten he would make an excellent mechanic, if trained early to work at a trade, for he is neither dull nor slow, but the short-sighted despotism of the trades unions has practically closed that avenue to him. Trade-schools, however excellent, cannot supply the opportunity thus denied him, and at the outset the boy stands condemned by his own to low and ill-paid drudgery, held down by the hand that of all should labor to raise him. Home, the greatest factor of all in the training of the young, means nothing to him but a pigeon-hole in a coop along with so many other human animals. Its influence is scarcely of the elevating kind, if it have any. The very games at which he takes a band in the street become polluting in its atmosphere. With no steady hand to guide him, the boy takes naturally to idle ways. Caught in the street by the truant officer, or by the agents of the Children's Societies, peddling, perhaps, or begging, to help out

the family resources, he runs the risk of being sent to a reformatory, where contact with vicious boys older than himself soon develop the latent possibilities for evil that lie hidden in him. The city has no Truant Home in which to keep him, and all efforts of the children's friends to enforce school attendance are paralyzed by this want. The risk of the reformatory is too great. What is done in the end is to let him take chances—with the chances all against him. The result is the rough young savage, familiar from the street. Rough as he is, if anyone doubt that this child of common clay have in him the instinct of beauty, of love for the ideal of which his life has no embodiment, let him put the matter to the test. Let him take into a tenement block a handful of flowers from the fields and watch the brightened faces, the sudden abandonment of play and fight that go ever hand in hand where there is no elbow-room, the wild entreaty for "posies," the eager love with which the little messengers of peace are shielded, once possessed; then let him change his mind. I have seen an armful of daisies keep the peace of a block better than a policeman and his club, seen instincts awaken under their gentle appeal, whose very existence the soil in which they grew made seem a mockery. I have not forgotten the deputation of ragamuffins from a Mulberry Street alley that knocked at my office door one morning on a mysterious expedition for flowers, not for themselves, but for "a lady," and having obtained what they wanted, trooped off to bestow them, a ragged and dirty little band, with a solemnity that was quite unusual. It was not until an old man called the next day to thank me for the flowers that I found out they had decked the bier of a pauper, in the dark rear room where she lay waiting in her pine-board coffin for the city's hearse. Yet, as I knew, that dismal alley with its bare brick walls, between which no sun ever rose or set, was the world of those children. It filled their young lives. Probably not one of them had ever been out of the sight of it. They were too dirty, too ragged, and too generally disreputable, too well hidden in their slum besides, to come into line with the Fresh Air summer boarders. With such human instincts and cravings, forever unsatisfied, turned into a haunting curse; with appetite ground to keenest edge by a hunger that is never fed, the children of the poor grow up in joyless homes to lives of wearisome toil that claims them at an age when the play of their happier fellows has but just begun. Has a yard of turf been laid and a vine been coaxed to grow within their reach, they are banished and barred out from it as from a heaven that is not for such as they. I came upon a couple of youngsters in a Mulberry Street yard a while ago that were chalking on the fence their first lesson in "writin'." And this is what they wrote: "Keeb of te Grass." They had it by heart, for there was not, I verily believe, a green sod within a quarter of a mile. Home to them is an empty name. Pleasure? A gentleman once catechized a ragged class in a down-town public school on this point, and recorded the result: Out of forty-eight boys twenty had never seen the Brooklyn Bridge that was scarcely five minutes' walk away, three only had been in Central Park, fifteen had known the joy of a ride in a horse-car. The street, with its ash-barrels and its dirt, the river that runs foul with mud, are their domain. What training they receive is picked up there. And they are apt pupils. If the mud and the dirt are easily reflected in their lives, what wonder? Scarce half-grown, such lads as these confront the world with the challenge to give them their due, too long withheld, or—. Our jails supply the answer to the alternative.

A little fellow who seemed clad in but a single rag was among the flotsam and jetsam stranded at Police Headquarters one day last summer. No one knew where he came from or where he belonged. The boy himself knew as little about it as anybody, and was the least anxious to have light shed on the subject after he had spent a night in the matron's nursery. The discovery that beds were provided for boys to sleep in there, and that he could have "a whole egg" and three slices of bread for breakfast put him on the best of terms with the world in general, and he decided that Headquarters was "a bully place." He sang "McGinty" all through, with Tenth Avenue variations, for the police, and then settled down to the serious business of giving an account of himself. The examination went on after this fashion:

"Where do you go to church, my boy?"

"We don't have no clothes to go to church." And indeed his appearance, as he was, in the door of any New York church would have caused a sensation.

"Well, where do you go to school, then?"

"I don't go to school," with a snort of contempt.

"Where do you buy your bread?"

"We don't buy no bread; we buy beer," said the boy, and it was eventually the saloon that led the police as a landmark to his "home." It was worthy of the boy. As he had said, his only bed was a heap of dirty straw on the floor, his daily diet a crust in the morning, nothing else.

Into the rooms of the Children's Aid Society were led two little girls whose father had "busted up the house" and put them on the street after their mother died. Another, who was turned out by her step-mother "because she had five of her own and could not afford to keep her," could not remember ever having been in church or Sunday-school, and only knew the name of Jesus through hearing people swear by it. She had no idea what they meant. These were specimens of the overflow from the tenements of our home-heathen that are growing up in New York's streets to-day, while tender-hearted men and women are busying themselves with the socks and the hereafter of well-fed little Hottentots thousands of miles away. According to Canon Taylor, of York, one hundred and nine missionaries in the four fields of Persia, Palestine, Arabia, and Egypt spent one year and sixty thousand dollars in converting one little heathen girl. If there is nothing the matter with those missionaries, they might come to New York with a good deal better prospect of success.

By those who lay flattering unction to their souls in the knowledge that to-day New York has, at all events, no brood of the gutters of tender years that can be homeless long unheeded, let it be remembered well through what effort this judgment has been averted. In thirty-seven years the Children's Aid Society, that came into existence as an emphatic protest against the tenement corruption of the young, has sheltered quite three hundred thousand outcast, homeless, and orphaned children in its lodging-houses, and has found homes in the West for seventy thousand that had none. Doubtless, as a mere stroke of finance, the five millions and a half thus spent were a wiser investment than to have let them grow up thieves and thugs. In the last fifteen years of this tireless battle for the safety of the State the intervention of the Society for the Prevention of Cruelty to Children has been invoked for 138,891 little ones; it has thrown its protection around more than twenty-five thousand helpless children, and has convicted nearly sixteen thousand wretches of child-beating and abuse. Add to this the standing army of fifteen thousand dependent children in New York's asylums and institutions, and some idea is gained of the crop that is garnered day by day in the tenements, of the enormous force employed to check their inroads on our social life, and of the cause for apprehension that would exist did their efforts flag for ever so brief a time.

Nothing is now better understood than that the rescue of the children is the key to the problem of city poverty, as presented for our solution to-day; that character may be formed where to reform it would be a hopeless task. The concurrent testimony of all who have to undertake it at a later stage: that the young are naturally neither vicious nor hardened, simply weak and undeveloped, except by the bad influences of the street, makes this duty all the more urgent as well as hopeful. Helping hands are held out on every side. To private charity the municipality leaves the entire care of its proletariat of tender years, lulling its conscience to sleep with liberal appropriations of money to foot the bills. Indeed, it is held by those whose opinions are entitled to weight that it is far too liberal a paymaster for its own best interests and those of its wards. It deals with the evil in the seed to a limited extent in gathering in the outcast babies from the streets. To the ripe fruit the gates of its prisons, its reformatories, and its workhouses are opened wide the year round. What the showing would be at this end of the line were it not for the barriers wise charity has thrown across the broad highway to ruin—is building day by day—may be measured by such results as those quoted above in the span of a single life.

GLOSSARY

bier: a coffin on its stand

catechize: to instruct or teach

deputation: a delegation representing or acting on another's behalf

proletariat: working class; wage earners

ragamuffin: a ragged, unkempt child

tenement: an apartment building or similar living unit—typically a rundown one

Document Analysis

Although considered one of the nation's first "investigative reporters," Riis, in *How the Other Half Lives*, does not shy away from showing his own emotion when he reports the sights and stories encountered in the tenements, alleys, and streets of the East Side. In this excerpt, Riis puts particular focus on the children living in this environment, reminding readers of the fact that the "future rulers" of the nation are living in abject squalor and in near-constant danger.

Riis takes the reader on a tour of a tenement in which so many people reside that it is nearly impossible to count them all. In one house, Riis takes an informal census but, acknowledging that there were more than a dozen children missing, instead makes a rough estimate of exactly how many children were living in the small, dark enclosures in each apartment. Riis is hardly alone in his inability to count all of the children living in these houses; he says that truant officers are similarly handicapped, knowing that there could be thousands of children who should be in school but go missing. Bodies wash up in the river, he reports, with no one coming forth to identify them.

Without formal schooling and even a stable home in which to rest and eat, the children of the East Side slums were largely left to their own devices, Riis reports. Many may actually have serviceable skills worthy of gaining them good-paying jobs, but strict restrictions imposed by labor unions have kept these children from honing their skills in trade schools. A large number of these children would, therefore, find unskilled positions at meager wages with long hours.

Those children who do not find employment, Riis says, fall victim to their idleness. They spend their days hiding from truant officers and other officials because if they are caught, they could be sent to a reformatory. There, life does not necessarily improve, as they encounter other delinquent children, who could force and/or influence them into a life of crime. A child in such conditions becomes a "rough young savage," Riis says.

These young savages, however, are still children, Riis states. They still have a willingness to make the world a better place, citing an example of children gathering flowers for a deceased woman, whose coffin was in the street. These children need school, he argues, as well as clothes and attention. Riis provides a number of case studies as evidence: a young boy who does not attend church because he fears he has no decent clothes; a young girl who only knows of Jesus Christ because she has heard people using his name when swearing; and still another girl whose stepmother has turned her out on the streets because the woman "could not afford to keep her."

Riis states that the protection and nurturing of New York's children is central to successfully combating urban decay and poverty. Adults should change their views of the children on the streets, looking past their "savagery" and at their innocence and potential, Riis writes. In doing so, society can relieve children of the burdens of poverty and crime and help them reach their full potential.

Essential Themes

Riis was himself an immigrant, living much in the same conditions as those he documented and photographed when developing *How the Other Half Lives*. As a result, his book both enlightens the reader and serves as an imperative for the social reform Riis advocated throughout his career. New Yorkers were likely aware of

the city's slums as well as the plight of the immigrants who crowded into the city's tenements and streets. However, his book painted an in-depth portrait of the dangers and horrors of life in the slums of New York.

Riis had the benefit of using a camera and flash powder during his investigation. Flash technology, newly developed in the 1880s, enabled him to photograph the faces of the children and others living in the alleys and basements as well as the overcrowded and dark apartments in the tenement houses. He also documented the countless images he saw in the streets: the children who spent their days either working in low-skilled, low-wage jobs or evading truant officers in order to keep away from the even worse criminal behavior found in the reformatories and social service centers. This use of photographic equipment made Riis a pioneer in the field of photojournalism.

As shown in this excerpt, Riis uses the images and experiences of the children he encountered to create a social and moral imperative for others to follow. Riis unflinchingly details the extent to which slum dwellers suffered—the sewage in the streets, the bodies in the river, and the people packed in small, dark quarters. Riis challenges his readers to use this information to influence the future of New York. According to Riis, the rest of the population had an obligation to ensure that these children had every opportunity to become educated and upstanding members of society.

—*Michael P. Auerbach*

Bibliography and Additional Reading

"About Jacob Riis." *Victorian Richmond Hill*. New York: Richmond Hill Chapter, Queens Historical Society, 1980.

Anbinder, Tyler. *Five Points: The Nineteenth Century New York City Neighborhood that Invented Tap Dance, Stole Elections, and Became the World's Most Notorious Slum*. New York: Simon, 2001.

Baba, Mary. "Irish Immigrant Families in Mid-Late Nineteenth Century America." *Yale-New Haven Teachers Institute*. Yale-New Haven Teachers Institute, 1990.

Lubove, Roy. *The Progressives and the Slums: Tenement House Reform in New York City, 1890–1917*. Pittsburgh: university of Pittsburgh Press, 1963.

Markel, Howard. *Quarantine! East European Jewish Immigrants and the New York City Epidemics of 1892*. Baltimore: Johns Hopkins University Press, 1999.

■ The Sinking of the USS *Maine*

Date: 1898
Author: *New York Journal*
Genre: Newspaper editorial

Summary Overview

The USS *Maine* sank in Havana Harbor on February 15, 1898, just a few weeks after President William McKinley sent the battleship there in order to protect American interests on the island during the Cuban Revolution against Spain. Two hundred sixty-six sailors died in the blast. While nobody knew for sure what exactly caused the explosion, modern investigations strongly suggest that it was an accident. Nonetheless, New York newspapers intent on both starting a war and selling more papers blamed Spain for the tragedy. By turning the explosion into a major scandal, their coverage goaded the McKinley administration to start the Spanish-American War two months later.

Defining Moment

The Cuban War for Independence against Spain had begun in 1895. Civil unrest on the island threatened American assets, but this alone was not enough for most Americans to support entering the conflict on the side of the Cubans. America had always been an isolationist country, yet the idea of being an empire on par with those in Europe was becoming increasingly appealing in some circles.

There was already substantial public pressure to rescue Cuba before President William McKinley sent the USS *Maine* to Havana in January 1898. While McKinley claimed it was a friendly visit, many observers suspected that it was a first step toward war.

Later that month, a letter by a Spanish minister criticizing McKinley had leaked to the *New York Journal*, but this alone did not cause the conflict. The *Journal's* owner, William Randolph Hearst, kept seven correspondents in Cuba to dig up more dirt in order to both sell papers and provoke an international conflict. The Spanish government tried very hard to avoid war with the United States because it knew that it could not protect its still far-flung empire, but Hearst did his best to thwart peace and rouse antagonisms.

The *Maine* exploded the night of February 15, 1898, surprising Americans everywhere. The captain, Charles Sigsbee, was one of a hundred survivors out of 350 onboard. The slogan "Remember the Maine!" was not the product of either the *New York Journal* or its competitor in the yellow press, the *New York World*. It was a kind of spontaneous result of the public connecting the sinking of the *Maine* to Spain as a result of both papers' coverage leading up to the explosion. In other words, the sinking of the *Maine* caused the Spanish American War because newspapers like William Randolph Hearst's *New York Journal* did not wait for the Navy to investigate what caused the explosion; they blamed Spain for it first.

William McKinley remained reluctant to start a war even after the *Maine* had sunk. After the tragedy, McKinley demanded that Spain end its conflict with Cuban rebels and recognize their independence immediately. When the Spanish response was complicated and noncommittal, the U.S. president asked Congress for a declaration of war and got one.

There were many underlying reasons for the war besides the sinking of the *Maine*. American desire for control of Cuba dated back to the 1850s. In the 1890s, Cuba was the source of most of America's sugarcane. Cuba contained lots of valuable coffee plantations. It could serve as a base for coaling stations for American ships.

The Spanish-American War was the country's only serious foreign entanglement between the end of the Civil War and the start of World War I. The war itself did not last the summer. American casualties proved minimal. Success in that conflict played a major role in getting America to step out of its isolationist past and play a major role in world affairs. The creation of a U.S. empire during that conflict, however small, played a major role in preparing the nation for its role in World War I less than twenty years later.

A Navy board of inquiry investigated the explosion and determined, one month later, that it had been caused by a mine. It did not specifically blame Spain for the explosion. Nor did it acknowledge that U.S. Navy ships had had some trouble with spontaneous explosions. The *New York Journal* specifically blamed the explosion on Spain before President McKinley released the board's report; the paper reported, on February 17—the

Pulitzer's treatment in The World *emphasizes horrible explosion.*

Hearst's treatment in the New York Journal *was more effective and focused on the enemy who set the bomb—and offered a huge reward to readers.*

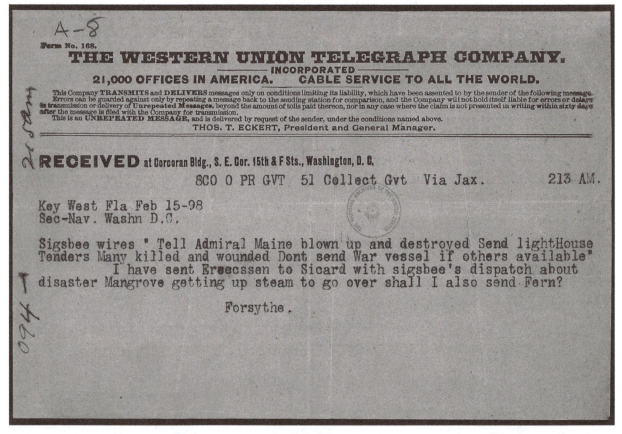

Telegram sent by Captain James Forsythe, commanding, Naval Station Key West, forwarding word from Charles Sigsbee, Captain, USS Maine of the sinking of his ship.

same day as the editorial reproduced here—that "The Warship Maine was Split in Two by an Enemy's Infernal Machine." The *Journal* included a drawing depicting a scene with wires running into the *Maine* from a nearby Spanish fort. Modern research commissioned by Admiral Hyman Rickover in 1974 strongly suggests that the sinking of the *Maine* was caused by an accidental coal fire in the engine room, and explicitly rules out the possibility of an external explosion.

Author Biography

While the exact author of the accompanying editorial is impossible to identify, we do know that the *Journal's* owner, William Randolph Hearst, had great control over the paper's editorial content and supported war with Spain as an attempt to increase newspaper sales. William's father George had earned his fortune as a miner, and bestowed it on William at the time of his death in 1890. He bought the once-stately *New York Journal* in 1895. He promptly hired staff who were willing and experienced at creating stories and graphics that emphasized sex, violence, and scandal to sell newspapers. This tactic was known as "Yellow Journalism." Hearst would use his fame as a populist editor to try several runs for office but found his efforts derailed by stories of his moral failings and hard left-wing politics. Before he died in 1951, Hearst was immortalized as the model of the media tycoon in Orson Welles' 1941 movie classic, *Citizen Kane*.

HISTORICAL DOCUMENT

Spain's Victory of Peace

To five hundred thousand Cubans starved or otherwise murdered have been added an American battleship and three hundred American sailors lost as the direct result of the dilatory policy of our government toward Spain. If we had stopped the war in Cuba when duty and policy alike urged us to do the *Maine* would have been afloat today, and three hundred homes, now desolate, would have been unscathed.

It was an accident, they say. Perhaps it was, but accident or not, it would never have happened if there had been peace in Cuba, as there would have been if we had done our duty. And it was an accident of a remarkably convenient kind for Spain. Two days ago we had five battleships in the Atlantic. Today we have four. A few more such accidents will leave us at the mercy of a Spanish fleet.

Two years ago our naval superiority over Spain was overwhelming. Two successive administrations have waited patiently for Spain to overcome that disadvantage by buying and building ships enough to bring her navy up to an equality with ours. That process proving too slow, it is now being hastened by the accidental destruction of the American fleet. At this rate it ought not to take long for Spain's naval strength to surpass our own.

As to the immediate cause of the disaster that has bereaved so many American households and robbed the American navy of one of the most valued elements of its fighting strength, we heed Captain Sigsbee's appeal to sound judgment. The Government has set an investigation on foot, and the *Journal* has independently undertaken another. Between them the truth will soon be known. If it be found that the Spanish authorities have fought about this calamity, so profitable to themselves, no power from the White House to Wall Street will be able to restrain the American people from exacting a terrible retribution. And Spain's innocence must be clearly proven. All the circumstances of the case fix the burden of proof upon her. The *Maine* was lying in one of her harbors, under the guns of her fortresses, with the warships at hand. The removal of the *Maine* meant a tremendous reduction in the odds against her in the event of the conflict that all Spanish Havana desired. The chances against such a removal by accident were millions to one, and yet the removal occurred. In such circumstances polite expressions of regret count for nothing. The investigations must clearly disclose Spain's innocence or her guilt will be assumed.

But while we must wait for definite evidence before formally charging Spain with the shameful treachery, which all the world is ready to suspect her, we need wait for nothing before instituting such a change of policy it will relieve us of the fear of future troubles. The anarchy in Cuba, which for three years has reached the sympathies of all Americans but the dehumanized stock-jobbers of Wall-Street, has become an intolerable evil to American interests. It has destroyed three hundred seamen. We have endured it long enough. Whether a Spanish torpedo sank the *Maine* or not, peace must be restored in Cuba at once. We cannot have peace without fighting for it, let us fight and have it over with. It is not likely that the entire Spanish navy would be able to do us as much harm in open battle as we suffered in Havana Harbor in one second for a state of things that was neither peace or war.

The investigation into the injuries if the *Maine* may take a week, but the independence of Cuba can be recognized today. The Spanish Government can receive today such a notice as freed Mexico when it was addressed to Louis Napoleon. The Vesuvius can be recalled today from her odious work of doing police service for Spain against the Cuban patriots and sent to join the defenders of America. The American fleet can move on Havana today and plant the flag of the Cuban Republic on Morro and Cabana. It is still strong enough for that in the absence of further "accidents." And if we take such action as that, it is extremely unlikely that any other accident will happen.

[*New York Journal*, February 17, 1898.]

GLOSSARY

Louis Napoleon: nephew of Napoleon Bonaparte; emperor of France between 1852 and 1870

Morro and Cabana: a castle and a fortress in Havana Harbor

stock-jobbers: Wall Street traders

SUPPLEMENTAL HISTORICAL DOCUMENT

The *Maine* Blown Up

Terrible Explosion on Board the United States Battleship in Havana Harbor

MANY PERSONS KILLED AND WOUNDED

All the Boats of the Spanish Cruiser Alfonso XII, Assisting in the Work of Relief

None of the Wounded Men Able to Give Any Explanation of the Cause of the Disaster

Havana, Feb. 15 – At 9:45 o'clock this evening a terrible explosion took place on board the United States battleship *Maine* in Havana Harbor.

Many persons were killed or wounded. All the boats of the Spanish cruiser Alfonso XII. are assisting.

As yet the cause of the explosion is not apparent. The wounded sailors of the *Maine* are unable to explain it. It is believed that the battleship is totally destroyed.

The explosion shook the whole city. The windows were broken in nearly all the houses.

The correspondent of the Associated Press says he has conversed with several of the wounded sailors and understands from them that the explosion took place while they were asleep, so that they can give no particulars as to the cause.

WHAT SENOR DE LOME SAYS

He Declares That No Spaniard Would Be Guilty of Causing Such a Disaster

Senor de Lome, the departing ex-Minister of Spain to this country, who arrived in this city last night, and went to the Hotel St. Marc, at Fifth Avenue and

Thirty-ninth Street, was awakened on the receipt of the news from Havana.

He refused to believe the report at first. When he had been assured of the truth of the story he said that there was no possibility that the Spaniards had anything to do with the destruction of the *Maine*.

No Spaniard, he said, would be guilty of such an act. If the report was true, he said, the explosion must have been caused by some accident on board the warship.

THE MAINE'S VISIT TO HAVANA

First American Warship to Visit Cuba Since the Struggle Began

The *Maine* was ordered to Havana on Jan. 24 last, and was the first American warship to visit that port since the outbreak of the Cuban rebellion. In explanation of the visit of the American battleship to Cuba Secretary Long issued the following statement:

"So far from there being any foundation for the rumors yesterday of trouble at Havana, matters are now in such condition that our vessels are going to resume their friendly calls at Cuban ports and go in and out just as the vessels of other nations do. The *Maine* will go in a day or two on just such a visit. The department has issued orders for vessels to attend the public celebrations in Mobile and the Mardi Gras at New Orleans."

The *Maine* was commanded by Capt. Charles D. Sigsbee. Her other officers were Lieut. Commander Richard Wainwright, Lieuts. G. F. Holman, John Hood, and C. W. Yungen, Lieuts. (junior grade) G. W. Blow, J. T. Blandin, F. W. Jenkins, Cadets J. H. Holden, W. T. Cluverius, Amos Bronson, and D. F. Boyd, Jr.; Surgeon L. G. Heneberger, Paymaster C. W. Littlefield, Chief Engineer L. G. Nowell, Passed Assistant Engineer E. C. Bowers, Assistant Engineers J. R. Morris and D. R. Merritt, Cadet Engineers Pope, Washington, and Arthur Grenshaw, Chaplain J. P. Chidwick, and Lieutenant of Marines A. W. Catlin.

The commander of the *Maine*, Capt. Sigsbee, is a favorite in the Navy Department. For four years he was Chief of the Hydrographic Office, and by his energy brought the office up to a high standard.

He justified the department's judgment in the selection by running his ship straight into a dock in New York harbor to avoid sinking a packed excursion boat. This was a display of quick judgment, nerve, and pluck that pleased the department so highly that the Captain was sent a complimentary letter.

ARMAMENT OF THE MAINE

A Second-Class Battleship Built at the Brooklyn Navy Yard

The *Maine* was placed in commission Aug. 17, 1895. She is a twin-screw, armored turret ship, of the belted type, and is known as a second-class battleship. Like the Texas, the *Maine* was built at a Government navy yard. The Texas was built at Norfolk; the *Maine* at the New York Navy Yard. Both ships were authorized when Secretary Whitney began the work of rehabilitating a then degenerate navy.

The *Maine* is of Navy Department designs throughout. The hull was built by navy yard workmen, and the engines were constructed by the Quintard Iron Works. That firm obtained the contract on its bid of $735,000. There were no other bidders.

The vitals of the ship are protected from gunfire by an armor belt 180 feet in length. This belt has a maximum thickness of 11 1/2 inches. Below the water line the armor tapers to a thickness of 6 inches. To deflect an end-on or a fore-and-aft fire, heavy armored and sharply inclined V-shaped bulkheads are placed forward and aft, the ends joining the armor belt. The bulkheads are 6 inches thick, and well backed.

In her main battery the ship mounts four 10 inch and six 6-inch rifles. A number of guns of smaller caliber are distributed in advantageous places. The 10-inch rifles are mounted in pairs in two steel turrets. One of these is situated aft, the other forward. The turret armor is 10 1/2 inches thick. The protective power of these massive shields is increased by their circular shape, which tends to deflect a missile unless the impact is directly given.

The guns are breech-loading rifles, with bores 10 inches in diameter. The length of each gun is 329 inches. The weight is a little more than 24 tons. From them a full-service charge of 250 pounds of powder throws a 500-pound shell a distance of nine miles, with an initial velocity of 2,000 feet per second.

The 6-inch rifles are of the breech-loading pattern. These weapons measure 196 inches in length and weigh five tons each. The powder charge is fifty pounds. The weight of the shell is 100 pounds.

The secondary battery consists of six 6-pounders, eight 1-pounders, two revolving cannon, and two Gatlings. The heaviest of the rapid-fire guns throws a six-pound projectile at a velocity of 1,870 feet per second. The *Maine* has twin screw, vertical triple-expansion engines of an aggregate indicated horse power, including air and circulating pumps, of 9,000. The cylinders are 35 1/2, 57, and 88 inches in diameter by 36 inches stroke, and make 132 revolutions per minute at full power. The principle of interchangeability of parts, so characteristic of American machinery, has in these engines been carried out to the fullest extent.

All the cylinders have piston valves of the same size- 22 inches in diameter- there being one for the h. p., two for the i. p., and three for the l. p. cylinders. The valves are worked by Stephenson double-bar links. The cylinders are jacketed and fitted with liners of hard cast iron. The condensers are of composition and are cylindrical, 6 feet 5 1/2 inches at internal diameter. There are 5,140 brass tubes in each condenser, 5/8-inch internal diameter, and 8 feet 4 inches long between tube sheets, giving a cooling surface in each condenser of 7,010 square feet. Each condenser has a Blake combined air and circulating pump. There are two vertical air pumps worked by a beam, one horizontal circulating pump, and a single steam cylinder which works all the pumps.

There are eight single-ended boilers of the usual cylindrical or "Scotch" type, each 14 feet 8 inches in diameter and 10 feet long, designed for a working pressure of 135 pounds. Each boiler has three corrugated steel furnaces, made, like all others in this country, by the Continental Iron Works of Brooklyn, 42 inches in internal diameter. Each boiler has 118 stay tubes and 401 plain tubes, all of mild steel, 2 1/4 inches external diameter and 6 feet 7 inches long. The total grate surface is 553 square feet, and the total heating surface about 18,800 square feet. The boilers are in two separate water-tight firerooms.

The forced draught is on the closed ash-pit system, the air being led to the ash pits by ducts under the fireroom floors. The blowers are driven by inclosed three-cylinder engines, and are arranged to draw the air from engine and firerooms so as to give thorough ventilation. This system of forced draught has been stated by Commodore Melville to be, in his opinion, preferable to that by closed firerooms, as it is under much more complete control, and when a fire is cleaned or coaled, the draught is shut off, thus preventing the chilling effect of the cold air on the hot tube sheets.

The *Maine* is the only one of the vessels of above 5,000 tons which is so fitted, and it will be noted that her firerooms are fore and aft. In large ships with athwartship firerooms, it is very difficult to locate the blowers and air ducts so that they will not interfere with overhauling and repairs and will also ventilate the firerooms, and for this reason the closed fireroom system is used on them. The screw propellers are of manganese bronze and are four-bladed. The diameter is 14 feet 6 1/2 inches; mean pitch, 16 feet 1 inch; developed area of each, 65.5 square feet.

The vessel is designed to carry a crew of 800 men. She has accommodations for a flag officer and staff.

SENOR DE LOME ARRIVES

He Reaches the City with His Family From Washington En Route for Spain

Senor Dupuy de Lome, the ex-Minister from Spain to the United States, arrived in New York last night en route for his home. He reached Jersey City by the Congressional Limited over the Pennsylvania

Railroad tracks at 8:55 P. M. His wife and their two sons and a valet completed the party.

They were met at the station by J. V. Jordan, proprietor of the Hotel St. Marc at Thirty-ninth Street and Fifth Avenue, and an old friend of Senor de Lome. The arrival attracted little or no attention. Half a dozen newspaper reporters were the only persons present except Mr. Jordan and the train hands at the station. As he alighted from the Pullman car, Senor de Lome was accosted by the reporters. He raised his hat in reply to their salutation, and replied to all inquiries that he had nothing to say. Then he hurried across the platform after Senora de Lome and her boys to the elevator, which took him to the street level.

There Mr. Jordan's private carriage, with two dark-brown horses, was awaiting them. Senor de Lome, with his elder son, occupied the front set, the valet sat on the box with the coachman, and Mr. Jordan remained afoot. The carriage boarded a Desbrosses Street ferryboat, and then learning that time would be saved by going by the Twenty-third Street line, the carriage turned and drove aboard the New Brunswick, which was lying in the slip. The New Brunswick is the ferryboat that was placed at the disposal of President McKinley when he visited the city to attend the banquet of the National Manufacturers' Association.

At the New York ferry house two detectives from the Central Office, Campbell and Barrett, were on hand in case of necessity. There was no necessity. No one else was in waiting, Spaniard or Cuban. As the carriage dashed out of the ferry house the detectives jumped into a cab and drove after it. Three cabs full of reporters followed the detectives. They drove down Twenty-fourth Street to Fifth Avenue to Thirty-ninth Street, where the ex-Minister and his party alighted at the private door of the Hotel St. Marc.

They did not register, but went immediately to the rooms on the second floor which had been prepared for them, and ten minutes later Senora de Lome, in reply to a note, sent down word that Senor de Lome was very tired and had gone to bed. Mr. Jordan said he did not know what Senor de Lome's immediate plans were, but his valet had told him that the party intended sailing for Europe by some steamer that started at 10 o'clock in the morning. The valet could not or would not remember the name of the steamer.

Thirty large trunks which the party brought with them from Washington were checked to the White Star pier, where the Britannic is moored, ready to sail at noon to-day.

[Source: https://archive.nytimes.com/www.nytimes.com]

Document Themes and Analysis

Dishonest newspaper coverage of the USS *Maine* was both remarkable and to be expected. People found it scandalous that the United States could not protect its own sailors. Although most events are clearer in hindsight, the tragedy of the *Maine*'s sinking is turned by this editorial from Hearst's *Journal* into a scandal for popular consumption. The piece's raising the prospect that Spain had committed "shameful treachery" in connection with the disaster by itself illustrates the newspaper's intent to provoke a war over the matter.

Besides wanting to sell newspapers, Hearst believed in the cause of Cuban liberation and wanted to advance it. He had even tried to smuggle small arms into Cuba on the *Maine*—until the Spanish discovered them. He read the American public's mood as being for war against Spain, and therefore stoked the fires of conflict even before the *Maine* faced its fate. Coverage like the *Journal*'s helps explain why Americans of all social classes rallied behind the cause of war. Hearst's coverage of Cuba made the cause of Cuban liberation seem noble. The war did the impossible in that it let America free people from tyranny and become an empire at the same time. What was different is that America would become a new kind of empire, one that would control far flung colonies economically if not politically. While the United States did gain a few actual colonies including Puerto Rico and the Philippines, the thinking at the time was that these would not cause the Americans to become corrupt like the European imperial powers had.

After the sinking of the *Maine*, the *New York Journal* did all it could to incite a U.S. attack against the Spanish on the island. In particular, the paper blamed the McKinley administration for waiting too long, thus giving the Spanish the opportunity to blow up the ship. While the *Journal* announces its own investigation of the sinking separate from the one that the government had begun, it also promises vengeance against Spain if that country is implicated. The use of the term "accidents," in quotation marks, strongly suggests that the paper's investigation had already arrived at its conclusion. So does the assertion that the chance that the explosion had been the result of an accident is "millions to one."

With no cause for the explosion having been definitively identified, implicating Spain became the easiest course of action for newspapers and the credulous public. The sinking of the *Maine* was the straw that broke the camel's back, for yellow journalism, for readers, and, ultimately, for the McKinley administration. After further news stories and editorials continued to come out, beating the drum for war, McKinley dropped his reluctance and embarked on war.

Hearst could not have waited any longer. At the end of the editorial, the paper recommends that the United States move into Cuba before the wreck of the *Maine* had even been examined on account of the "anarchy" that existed on the island. The *Journal* argued for immediate recognition of Cuban independence. And, indeed, Cuba would get its independence at the start of the conflict and would keep it afterward, aligning itself with the United States until the advent of Fidel Castro's peasant revolution in 1959.

—*Michele McBride Simonelli*

Bibliography and Additional Reading

Fisher, Lewis. "Destruction of the Maine (1898)." *Law Library of Congress*, August 4, 2009. https://www.loc.gov/law/help/usconlaw/pdf/Maine.1898.pdf.

History Matters, "Shameful Treachery": Hearst's Journal Blames Spain." http://historymatters.gmu.edu/d/5471.

Lears, Jackson. *Rebirth of a Nation: The Making of Modern America, 1877–1920*. New York: Harper, 2009.

Thomas, Evan. *The War Lovers: Roosevelt, Lodge, Hearst, and the Rush to Empire, 1898*. New York: Back Bay Books, 2010.

■ Lincoln Steffens: "The Shame of Minneapolis"

Date: 1903
Author: Lincoln Steffens
Genre: Magazine article

Summary Overview

Lincoln Steffens (1866–1936) was a New York City journalist whose name is often associated with early twentieth-century "muckraking"—investigative journalism, often sensational, that exposed scandal and corruption. "The Shame of Minneapolis" was an exposé published in *McClure's Magazine* in January 1903, but the title does not give the full story of the article, for its subtitle reads "The Rescue and Redemption of a City That Was Sold Out." Essentially, the article tells the story of corruption, bribery, cronyism, graft, and a host of other political ills that beset the city of Minneapolis, Minnesota, under its mayor, Albert Alonzo "Doc" Ames, who served four terms (not always consecutively) beginning in 1876. Steffens also details the work of a grand jury leader, Hovey C. Clarke, who brought to light evidence that led to Ames resigning from office and actually fleeing the city, and the work of city council president D. Percy Jones, who became acting mayor, to clean up city government in Minneapolis. This article appeared in an issue of *McClure's* that also had articles by the muckrakers Ida Tarbell (on Standard Oil) and Ray Baker (on corruption among union leaders); this issue sold out in three days and helped establish *McClure's* as one of the leading organs of the muckraking movement. The article was later published in a 1904 collection of similar pieces, *The Shame of the Cities*, but by that time Ames had been driven from office.

Defining Moment

In an attempt to expose political corruption and prompt reforms, Steffens no doubt hoped for as broad an audience as possible. In reality, however, the readership of magazines like *McClure's* was mostly a body of white, middle-class Americans—virtually the same demographic that formed the heart of the Progressive movement. Progressivism and "muckrakers" like Steffens went hand in hand—Progressive politicians and activists used the writings of the muckrakers as evidence of the problems that existed and needed reform. The muckrakers, in turn, were often closely associated with the leaders of the Progressive movement. Steffens, for

example had been a friend and confidant of Theodore Roosevelt since the days when Steffens was a New York police reporter and Roosevelt chaired the city's Board of Police Commissioners.

The working poor, whose votes and tax dollars were manipulated by political machines like those Steffens attacked, were not a major part of the audience he reached. Many were recent immigrants who read English with difficulty, or not at all. But one of the ironies of Progressive attempts to reform city government is that the urban poor often thought the machine "worked" for them, since it bought their votes patronage and favors—therefore, they often resented the Progressive's reform agenda.

Author Biography

Joseph Lincoln Steffens was born in San Francisco, California, on April 6, 1866. His father, Joseph Steffens, was a prosperous businessman. In 1870, the family moved to Sacramento, California.

Steffens attended the University of California at Berkeley, graduating in 1889. His father financed some travel and further study in Europe. Steffens studied a variety of subjects at the universities in Berlin, Heidelberg, and Leipzig in Germany, and at the Sorbonne in Paris. In 1891, he married Josephine Bontecou, an American student he met in Leipzig. They moved to New York City in 1892. Steffens became a reporter for the *New York Evening Post*. He covered a number of different news beats, but eventually became the first police reporter for the *Post*.

In 1897, Steffens became the city editor of the *New York Commercial Advertiser* and gathered round him a staff of talented writers. In 1901, S. S. McClure offered the Steffens the job of managing editor of *McClure's* magazine. Many of the writers that Steffens recruited became prominent examples of the "muckraker" genre. Steffens left *McClure's* in 1906, when he and several other writers bought the *American Magazine*. In 1909, however, he sold his share in the magazine as a result of disagreements with some of the other owners over editorial policy. He spent the rest of his life as a

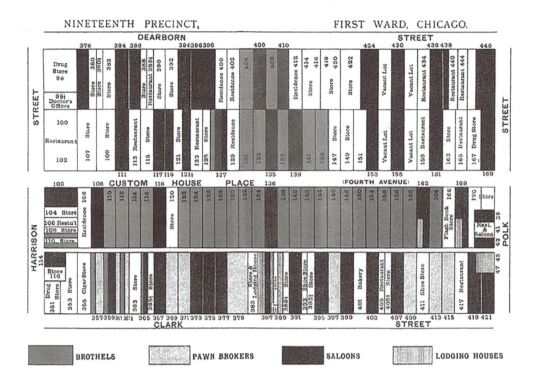

This map of the 19th Precinct and 1st Ward at Chicago by W. T. Stead in his book If Christ came to Chicago! A Plea for the Union of All Who Love in the Service of All Who Suffer, *records 46 saloons, 37 "houses of ill-fame," and 11 pawnbrokers in 1894. Stead is considered a pioneer journalist of the "new journalism," which paved the way for the modern tabloid.*

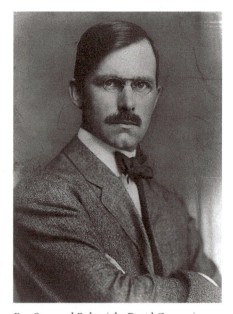

Ray Stannard Baker (aka David Grayson) c. 1900.

Lincoln Steffens, American muckraking journalist, c. 1894.

Steffans wrote for McClure's Magazine, *was an American illustrated monthly periodical popular at the turn of the 20th century, credited with having started the tradition of muckraking journalism and helped direct the moral compass of the day.*

freelance writer, and also travelled widely, speaking in support of liberal political causes and the labor movement. In 1931, he published his autobiography, which was a financial success, and revived interest in some of his earlier work. Steffens's first wife, Josephine, died in 1911. In 1924, he married Ella Winter. They settled in Carmel, California, and had one son, Steffens's only offspring. While on a speaking tour in Chicago in 1933, Steffens had a heart attack. It did not totally disable him, but ended his public touring and speaking. He worked from his home in Carmel for the rest of his life, and died there on August 9, 1936.

HISTORICAL DOCUMENT

Whenever anything extraordinary is done in American municipal politics, whether for good or for evil, you can trace it almost invariably to one man. The people do not do it. Neither do the "gangs" "combines" or political parties. These are but instruments by which bosses (not leaders; we Americans are not led, but driven) rule the people, and commonly sell them out. But there are at least two forms of the autocracy which has supplanted the democracy here as it has everywhere it has been tried. One is that of the organized majority by which, as in Tammany Hall in New York and the Republican machine in Philadelphia, the boss has normal control of more than half the voters. The other is that of the adroitly managed minority. The "good people" are herded into parties and stupefied with convictions and a name, Republican or Democrat; while the "bad people" are so organized or interested by the boss that he can wield their votes to enforce terms with party managers and decide elections. St. Louis is a conspicuous example of this form. Minneapolis is another. Colonel Ed. Butler is the unscrupulous opportunist who handled the non-partisan minority which turned St. Louis into a "boodle town." In Minneapolis "Doc" Ames was the man.

Minneapolis is a New England town on the upper Mississippi. The metropolis of the Northwest, it is the metropolis also of Norway and Sweden in America. Indeed, it is the second largest Scandinavian city in the world. But Yankees, straight from Down East, settled the town, and their New England spirit predominates. They had Bayard Taylor lecture there in the early days of the settlement; they made it the seat of the University of Minnesota. Yet even now, when the town has grown to a population of more than 200,000, you feel that there is something Western about it too—a Yankee with a small Puritan head, an open prairie heart, and a great, big Scandinavian body. The Roundhead takes the Swede and Norwegian bone out into the woods, and they cut lumber by forests, or they go out on the prairies and raise wheat and mill it into fleet-cargoes of flour. They work hard, they make money,

they are sober, satisfied, busy with their own affairs. There isn't much time for public business. Taken together, Miles, Hans, and Ole are very American. Miles insists upon strict laws, Ole and Hans want one or two Scandinavians on their ticket. These things granted, they go off on raft or reaper, leaving whoso will to enforce the laws and run the city.

The people who were left to govern the city hated above all things strict laws. They were the loafers, saloon keepers, gamblers, criminals, and the thriftless poor of all nationalities. Resenting the sobriety of a staid, industrious community, and having no Irish to boss them, they delighted to follow the jovial pioneer doctor, Albert Alonzo Ames. He was the "good fellow"—a genial, generous reprobate. Devery, Tweed, and many more have exposed in vain this amiable type. "Doc" Ames, tall, straight, and cheerful, attracted men, and they gave him votes for his smiles. He stood for license. There was nothing of the Puritan about him. His father, the sturdy old pioneer, Dr. Alfred Elisha Ames, had a strong strain of it in him, but he moved on with his family of six sons from Garden Prairie, Ill., to Fort Snelling reservation, in 1851, before Minneapolis was founded, and young Albert Alonzo, who then was ten years old, grew up free, easy, and tolerant. He was sent to school, then to college in Chicago, and he returned home a doctor of medicine before he was twenty-one. As the town waxed soberer and richer, "Doc" grew gayer and more and more generous. Skillful as a surgeon, devoted as a physician, and as a man kindly, he increased his practice till he was the best-loved man in the community. He was especially good to the poor. Anybody could summon "Doc" Ames at any hour to any distance. He went, and he gave not only his professional service, but sympathy, and often charity. "Richer men than you will pay your bill" he told the destitute. So there was a basis for his "good-fellowship." There always is; these good fellows are not frauds—not in the beginning.

But there is another side to them sometimes. Ames was sunshine not to the sick and destitute only. To the vicious and the depraved also he was a comfort. If a man was a hard drinker, the good Doctor cheered him with another drink; if he had stolen something, the Doctor helped to get him off. He was naturally vain; popularity developed his love of approbation. His loose life brought disapproval only from the good people, so gradually the Doctor came to enjoy best the society of the barroom and the streets. This society, flattered in turn, worshipped the good Doctor, and, active in politics always, put its physician into the arena.

Had he been wise, or even shrewd, he might have made himself a real power. But he wasn't calculating, only light and frivolous, so he did not organize his forces and run men for office. He sought office himself from the start, and he got most of the small places he wanted by changing his party to seize the opportunity. His floating minority, added to the regular partisan vote, was sufficient ordinarily for his useless victories. As time went on he rose from smaller offices to be a Republican mayor, then twice at intervals to be a Democratic mayor. He was a candidate once for Congress; he stood for governor once on a sort of Populist-Democrat ticket. Ames could not get anything outside of his own town, and after his third term as mayor it was thought he was out of politics altogether. He was getting old, and he was getting worse.

Like many a "good fellow" with hosts of miscellaneous friends down town to whom he was devoted, the good Doctor neglected his own family. From neglect he went on openly to separation from his wife and a second establishment. The climax came not long before the election of 1900. His wife was dying, and his daughter wrote to her father a note saying that her mother wished to see and forgive him. The messenger found him in a saloon. The Doctor read the note, laid it on the bar, and scribbled across it a sentence incredibly obscene. His wife died. The outraged family would not have the father at the funeral, but he appeared, not at the house, but in a carriage on the street. He sat across the way, with his feet up and a cigar in his mouth, till the funeral moved; then he circled around, crossing it and meeting it, and making altogether a scene which might well close any man's career.

It did not end his. The people had just secured the passage of a new primary law to establish direct popular government. There were to be no more nominations by convention. The voters were to ballot for their party candidates. By a slip of some sort, the laws did not specify that Republicans only should vote for Republican candidates, and only Democrats for Democratic candidates. Any voter could vote at either primary. Ames, in disrepute with his own party, the Democratic, bade his followers vote for his nomination for mayor on the Republican ticket. They all voted; not all the Republicans did. He was nominated. Nomination is far from election, and you would say that the trick would not help him. But that was a Presidential year, so the people of Minneapolis had to vote for Ames, the Republican candidate for Mayor. Besides, Ames said he was going to reform; that he was getting old, and wanted to close his career with a good administration. The effective argument, however, was that, since McKinley had to be elected to save the country, Ames must be supported for Mayor of Minneapolis. Why? The great American people cannot be trusted to scratch a ticket.

Well, Minneapolis got its old mayor back, and he was reformed. Up to this time Ames had not been very venal personally. He was a "spender" not a "grafter" and he was guilty of corruption chiefly by proxy; he took the honors and left the spoils to his followers. His administrations were no worse than the worst. Now, however, he set out upon a career of corruption which for deliberateness, invention, and avarice has never been equalled. It was as if he had made up his mind that he had been careless long enough, and meant to enrich his last years. He began early.

Immediately upon his election, before he took office (on January 7th), he organized a cabinet and laid plans to turn the city over to outlaws who were to work under police direction for the profit of his administration. He chose for chief his brother, Colonel Fred W. Ames, who had recently returned under a cloud from service in the Philippines. The Colonel had commanded a Minnesota regiment out there till he proved a coward under fire; he escaped court-martial only on the understanding that he should resign on reaching San Francisco, whither he was immediately shipped. This he did not do, and his brother's influence at Washington saved him to be mustered out with the regiment. But he was a weak vessel for chief of police, and the mayor picked for chief of detectives an abler man, who was to direct the more difficult operations. This was Norman W. King, a former gambler, who knew the criminals needed in the business ahead. King was to invite to Minneapolis thieves, confidence men, pickpockets, and gamblers, and release some that were in the local jail. They were to be organized into groups, according to their profession, and detectives were assigned to assist and direct them. The head of the gambling syndicate was to have charge of the gambling, making the terms and collecting the "graft" just as King and a Captain Hill were to collect from the thieves. The collector for women of the town was to be Irwin A. Gardner, a medical student in the Doctor's office, who was made a special policeman for the purpose. These men looked over the force, selected those men who could be trusted, charged them a price for their retention, and marked for dismissal 107 men out of 225, the 107 being the best policemen in the department from the point of view of the citizens who afterward reorganized the force. John Fitchette, better known as "Coffee John" a Virginian (who served on the Jeff Davis jury), the keeper of a notorious coffee-house, was to be a captain of police, with no duties except to sell places on the police force.

And they did these things that they planned—all and more. The administration opened with the revolution on the police force. They liberated the thieves in the local jail, and made known to the Under World generally that "things were doing" in Minneapolis. The incoming swindlers reported to King or his staff for instructions, and went to work, turning the "swag" over to the detectives in charge. Gambling went on openly, and disorderly houses multiplied under the fostering care of Gardner, the medical student. But all this was not enough. Ames dared to break openly into the municipal system of vice protection.

There was such a thing. Minneapolis, strict in its laws, forbade vices which are inevitable, then regularly permitted them under certain conditions. Legal limits, called "patrol lines" were prescribed, within which saloons might be opened. These ran along the river front, out through part of the business section, with long arms reaching into the Scandinavian quarters, north and south. Gambling also was confined, but more narrowly. And there were limits, also arbitrary, but not always identical with those for gambling, within which the social evil was allowed. But the novel feature of this scheme was that disorderly houses were practically licensed by the city, the women appearing before the clerk of the Municipal Court each month to pay a "fine" of $100. Unable at first to get this "graft" Ames's man Gardner persuaded women to start houses, apartments, and, of all things, candy stores, which sold sweets to children and tobacco to the "lumber Jacks" in front, while a nefarious traffic was carried on in the rear. But they paid Ames, not the city, and that was all the reform administration cared about.

The revenue from all these sources must have been enormous. It only whetted the avarice of the mayor and his Cabinet. They let gambling privileges without restriction to location or "squareness"; the syndicate could cheat and rob as it would. Peddlers and pawnbrokers, formerly licensed by the city, bought permits now instead from "Gardner's father" A. L. Gardner, who was the mayor's agent in this field. Some two hundred slot machines were installed in various parts of the town, with owner's agent and mayor's agent watching and collecting from them enough to pay the mayor $15,000 a year as his share. Auction frauds were instituted. Opium joints and unlicensed saloons, called "blind pigs" were protected. Gardner even had a police baseball team, for whose games tickets were sold to people who had to buy them. But the women were the easiest "graft." They were compelled to buy illustrated biographies of the city officials; they had to give presents of money, jewelry, and gold stars to police officers. But the money they still paid direct to the city in fines, some $35,000 a year, fretted the mayor, and at last he reached for it. He came out with a declaration, in his old character as friend of the oppressed, that $100 a month was too much for these women to pay. They should be required to pay the city fine only once in two months. This puzzled the town till it became generally known that Gardner collected the other month for the mayor. The final outrage in this department, however, was an order of the mayor for the periodic visits to disorderly houses, by the city's physicians, at from $5 to $20 per visit. The two physicians he appointed called when they willed, and more and more frequently, till toward the end the calls became a pure formality, with the collections as the one and only object.

In a general way all this business was known. It did not arouse the citizens, but it did attract criminals, and more and more thieves and swindlers came hurrying to Minneapolis. Some of them saw the police, and made terms. Some were seen by the police and invited to go to work. There was room for all. This astonishing fact that the government of a city asked criminals to rob the people is fully established. The police and the criminals have confessed it separately. Their statements agree in detail. Detective Norbeck made the arrangement, and introduced the swindlers to Gardner, who, over King's head, took the money from them. Here is the story "Billy" Edwards, a "big mitt" man, told under oath of his reception in Minneapolis:

"I had been out to the coast, and hadn't seen Norbeck for some time. After I returned I boarded a Minneapolis car one evening to go down to South Minneapolis to visit a friend. Norbeck and Detective DeLaittre were on the car. When Norbeck saw me he came up and shook hands, and said, 'Hullo, Billy, how goes it?' I said, 'Not very well.' Then he says, 'Things have changed since you went away. Me and Gardner are the whole thing now. Before you left they thought I didn't know anything, but I turned a few tricks, and now I'm It.' 'I'm glad of that, Chris,' I said. He says, 'I've got great things for you. I'm going to fix up a joint for you.' 'That's good,' I said, 'but I don't believe you can do it.' 'Oh, yes, I can,' he replied. 'I'm It now—Gardner and me.' 'Well, if you

can do it,' says I, 'there's money in it.' 'How much can you pay?' he asked. 'Oh, $150 or $200 a week,' says I. 'That settles it,' he said; 'I'll take you down to see Gardner, and we'll fix it up.' Then he made an appointment to meet me the next night, and we went down to Gardner's house together."

There Gardner talked business in general, showed his drawer full of bills, and jokingly asked how Edwards would like to have them. Edwards says:

"I said, 'That looks pretty good to me,' and Gardner told us that he had 'collected' the money from the women he had on his staff, and that he was going to pay it over to the 'old man' when he got back from his hunting trip next morning. Afterward he told me that the mayor had been much pleased with our $500, and that he said everything was all right, and for us to go ahead."

"Link" Crossman, another confidence man who was with Edwards, said that Gardner demanded $1,000 at first, but compromised on $500 for the mayor, $50 for Gardner, and $50 for Norbeck. To the chief, Fred Ames, they gave tips now and then of $25 or $50. "The first week we ran" said Crossman, "I gave Fred $15. Norbeck took me down there. We shook hands, and I handed him an envelope with $15. He pulled out a list of steerers we had sent him, and said he wanted to go over them with me. He asked where the joint was located. At another time I slipped $25 into his hand as he was standing in the hallway of City Hall." But these smaller payments, after the first "opening, $500" are all down on the pages of the "big mitt" ledger, photographs of which illuminate this article. This notorious book, which was kept by Charlie Howard, one of the "big mitt" men, was much talked of at the subsequent trials, but was kept hidden to await the trial of the mayor himself.

The "big mitt" game was swindling by means of a stacked hand at stud poker. "Steerers" and "boosters" met "suckers" on the street, at hotels, and railway stations, won their confidence, and led them to the "joint." Usually the "sucker" was called, by the amount of his loss, "the $102 man" or "the $35 man." Roman Meix alone had the distinction among all the Minneapolis victims of going by his own name. Having lost $775, he became known for his persistent complainings. But they all "kicked" some. To Norbeck at the street door was assigned the duty of hearing their complaints, and "throwing a scare into them." "Oh, so you've been gambling" he would say. "Have you got a license? Well, then, you better get right out of this town." Sometimes he accompanied them to the station and saw them off. If they were not to be put off thus, he directed them to the chief of police. Fred Ames tried to wear them out by keeping them waiting in the anteroom. If they outlasted him, he saw them and frightened them with threats of all sorts of trouble for gambling without a license. Meix wanted to have payment on his check stopped. Ames, who had been a bank clerk, told him so, and then had the effrontery to say that payment on such a check could not be stopped.

Burglaries were common. How many the police planned may never be known. Charles F. Brackett and Fred Malone, police captains and detectives, were active, and one well-established crime of theirs is the robbery of the Pabst Brewing Company office. They persuaded two men, one an employee, to learn the combination of the safe, open and clean it out one night, while the two officers stood guard outside.

The excesses of the municipal administration became so notorious that some of the members of it remonstrated with the others, and certain county officers were genuinely alarmed. No restraint followed their warnings. Sheriff Megaarden, no Puritan himself, felt constrained to interfere, and he made some arrests of gamblers. The Ames people turned upon him in a fury; they accused him of making overcharges in his accounts with the county for fees, and laying the evidence before Governor Van Sant, they had Megaarden removed from office. Ames offered bribes to two county commissioners to appoint Gardner sheriff, so as to be sure of no more trouble in that quarter. This move failed, but the lesson taught Megaarden served to clear the atmosphere, and the spoliation went on as recklessly as ever. It became impossible.

Even lawlessness must be regulated. Dr. Ames, never an organizer, attempted no control, and his followers began to quarrel among themselves. They deceived one another; they robbed the thieves; they robbed Ames himself. His brother became dissatisfied with his share of the spoils, and formed cabals with captains who plotted against the administration and set up disorderly houses, "panel games" and all sorts of "grafts" of their own. The one man loyal to the mayor was Gardner, and Fred Ames, Captain King, and their pals, plotted the fall of the favorite. Now anybody could get anything from the Doctor, if he could have him alone. The Fred Ames clique chose a time when the mayor was at West Baden; they filled him with suspicion of Gardner and the fear of exposure, and induced him to let a creature named "Reddy" Cohen, instead of Gardner, do the collecting, and pay over all the moneys, not directly, but through Fred. Gardner made a touching appeal. "I have been honest. I have paid you all" he said to the mayor. "Fred and the rest will rob you." This was true, but it was of no avail.

Fred Ames was in charge at last, and he himself went about giving notice of the change. Three detectives were with him when he visited the women, and here is the women's story, in the words of one, as it was told again and again in court: "Colonel Ames came in with the detectives. He stepped into a side room and asked me if I had been paying Gardner. I told him I had, and he told me not to pay no more, but to come to his office later, and he would let me know what to do. I went to the City Hall in about three weeks, after Cohen had called and said he was 'the party.' I asked the chief if it was all right to pay Cohen, and he said it was."

The new arrangement did not work so smoothly as the old. Cohen was an oppressive collector, and Fred Ames, appealed to, was weak and lenient. He had no sure hold on the force. His captains, free of Gardner, were undermining the chief. They increased their private operations. Some of the detectives began to drink hard and neglect their work. Norbeck so worried the "big mitt" men by staying away from the joint, that they complained to Fred about him. The chief rebuked Norbeck, and he promised to "do better" but thereafter he was paid, not by the week, but by piece work—so much for each "trimmed sucker" that he ran out of town. Protected swindlers were arrested for operating in the street by "Coffee John's" new policemen who took the places of the negligent detectives. Fred let the indignant prisoners go when they were brought before him, but the arrests were annoying, inconvenient, and disturbed business. The whole system became so demoralized that every man was for himself. There was not left even the traditional honor among thieves.

It was at this juncture, in April, 1902, that the grand jury for the summer term was drawn. An ordinary body of unselected citizens, it received no special instructions from the bench; the county prosecutor offered it only routine work to do. But there was a man among them who was a fighter— the foreman, Hovey C. Clarke. He was of an old New England family. Coming to Minneapolis when a young man, seventeen years before, he had fought for employment, fought with his employers for position, fought with his employees, the lumber-Jacks, for command, fought for his company against competitors; and he had won always, till now he had the habit of command, the impatient, imperious manner of the master, and the assurance of success which begets it. He did not want to be a grand jury-man, he did not want to be a foreman; but since he was both, he wanted to accomplish something.

Why not rip up the Ames gang? Heads shook, hands went up; it was useless to try. The discouragement fired Clarke. That was just what he would do, he said, and he took stock of his jury. Two or three were men with backbone; that he knew, and he quickly had them with him. The rest were all sorts of men. Mr. Clarke won over each man to himself, and interested them all. Then he called for the county prosecutor. The prosecutor was a politician; he knew the Ames crowd; they were too powerful to attack.

"You are excused" said the foreman.

There was a scene; the prosecutor knew his rights.

"Do you think, Mr. Clarke" he cried, "that you can run the grand jury and my office, too?"

"Yes" said Clarke, "I will run your office if I want to; and I want to. You're excused."

Mr. Clarke does not talk much about his doings last summer; he isn't the talking sort. But he does say that all he did was to apply simple business methods to his problem. In action, however, these turned out to be the most approved police methods. He hired a lot of local detectives who, he knew, would talk about what they were doing, and thus would be watched by the police. Having thus thrown a false scent, he hired some other detectives whom nobody knew about. This was expensive; so were many of the other things he did; but he was bound to win, so he paid the price, drawing freely on his own and his colleagues' pockets. (The total cost to the county for a long summer's work by this grand jury was $259.) With his detectives out, he himself went to the jail to get tips from the inside, from criminals who, being there, must have grievances. He made the acquaintance of the jailor, Captain Alexander, and Alexander was a friend of Sheriff Megaarden. Yes, he had some men there who were "sore" and might want to get even.

Now two of these were "big mitt" men who had worked for Gardner. One was "Billy" Edwards, the other "Cheerful Charlie" Howard. I heard too many explanations of their plight to choose any one; this general account will cover the ground: In the Ames mêlée, either by mistake, neglect, or for spite growing out of the network of conflicting interests and gangs, they were arrested, arraigned, not before Fred Ames, but a judge, and held in bail too high for them to furnish. They had paid for an unexpired period of protection, yet could get neither protection nor bail. They were forgotten. "We got the double cross all right" they said, and they bled with their grievance; but squeal, no, sir!—that was "another deal."

But Mr. Clarke had their story, and he was bound to force them to tell it under oath on the stand. If they did, Gardner and Norbeck would be indicted, tried, and probably convicted. In themselves, these men were of no great importance; but they were the key to the situation, and a way up to the mayor. It was worth trying. Mr. Clarke went into the jail with Messrs. Lester Elwood and Willard J. Hield, grand jurors on whom he relied most for delicate work.

They stood by while the foreman talked. And the foreman's way of talking was to smile, swear, threaten, and cajole. "Billy" Edwards told me afterwards that he and Howard were finally persuaded to turn state's evidence, because they believed that Mr. Clarke was the kind of a man to keep his promises and fulfil his threats, "We" he said, meaning criminals generally, "are always stacking up against juries and lawyers who want us to holler. We don't, because we see they ain't wise, and won't get there. They're quitters; they can be pulled off. Clarke has a hard eye. I know men. It's my business to size 'em up, and I took him for a winner, and I played in with him against that whole big bunch of easy things that was running things on the bum." The grand jury was ready at the end of three weeks of hard work to find bills. A prosecutor was needed. The public prosecutor was being ignored, but his first assistant and friend, Al. J. Smith, was taken in hand by Mr. Clarke. Smith hesitated; he knew better even than the foreman the power and resources of the Ames gang. But he came to believe in Mr. Clarke, just as Edwards had; he was sure the foreman would win; so he went over to his side, and, having once decided, he led the open fighting, and, alone in court, won cases against men who had the best lawyers in the State to defend them. His court record is extraordinary. Moreover, he took over the negotiations with criminals for evidence, Messrs. Clarke, Hield, Elwood, and the other jurors providing means and moral support. These were needed. Bribes were offered to Smith; he was threatened; he was called a fool. But so was Clarke, to whom $28,000 was offered to quit, and for whose slaughter a slugger was hired to come from Chicago. What startled the jury most, however, was the character of the citizens who were sent to them to dissuade them from their course. No reform I ever studied has failed to bring out this phenomenon of virtuous cowardice, the baseness of the decent citizen.

Nothing stopped this jury, however. They had courage. They indicted Gardner, Norbeck, Fred Ames, and many lesser persons. But the gang had courage, too, and raised a defence fund to fight Clarke. Mayor Ames was defiant. Once, when Mr. Clarke called at the City Hall, the mayor met and challenged him. The mayor's heelers were all about him, but Clarke faced him.

"Yes, Doc. Ames, I'm after you" he said. "I've been in this town for seventeen years, and all that time you've been a moral leper. I hear you were rotten during the ten years before that. Now I'm going to put you where all contagious things are put—where you cannot contaminate anybody else."

The trial of Gardner came on. Efforts had been made to persuade him to surrender the mayor, but the young man was paid $15,000 "to stand pat" and he went to trial and conviction silent. Other trials followed fast—Norbeck's, Fred Ames's, Chief of Detectives King's. Witnesses who were out of the State were needed, and true testimony from women. There was no county money for extradition, so the grand jurors paid these costs also. They had Meix followed from Michigan down to Mexico and back to Idaho, where they got him, and he was presented in court one day at the trial of Norbeck, who had "steered" him out of town. Norbeck thought Meix was a thousand miles away, and had been bold before. At the sight of him in court he started to his feet, and that night ran away. The jury spent more money in his pursuit, and they caught him. He confessed, but his evidence was not accepted. He was sentenced to three years in state's prison. Men caved all around, but the women were firm, and the first trial of Fred Ames failed. To break the women's faith in the ring, Mayor Ames was indicted for offering the bribe to have Gardner made sheriff—a genuine, but not the best case against him. It brought the women down to the truth, and Fred Ames, retried, was convicted and sentenced to six and a half years in state's prison. King was tried for accessory to felony (helping in the theft of a diamond, which he afterward stole from the thieves), and sentenced to three and a half years in prison. And still the indictments came, with trials following fast. Al. Smith resigned with the consent and thanks of the grand jury; his chief, who was to run for the same office again, wanted to try the rest of the cases, and he did very well.

All men were now on the side of law and order. The panic among the "grafters "was laughable, in spite of its hideous significance. Two heads of departments against whom nothing had been shown suddenly ran away, and thus suggested to the grand jury an in-inquiry which revealed another source of "graft" in the sale of supplies to public institutions and the diversion of great quantities of provisions to the private residences of the mayor and other officials. Mayor Ames, under indictment and heavy bonds for extortion, conspiracy, and bribe-offering, left the State on a night train; a gentleman who knew him by sight saw him sitting up at eleven o'clock in the smoking-room of the sleeping-car, an unlighted cigar in his mouth, his face ashen and drawn, and at six o'clock the next morning he still was sitting there, his cigar still unlighted. He went to West Baden, a health resort in Indiana, a sick and broken man, aging years in a month. The city was without a mayor, the ring was without a leader; cliques ruled, and they pictured one another hanging about the grand-jury room begging leave to turn state's evidence. Tom Brown, the mayor's secretary, was in the mayor's chair; across the hall sat Fred Ames, the chief of police, balancing Brown's light weight. Both were busy forming cliques within the ring. Brown had on his side Coffee John and Police Captain Hill. Ames had Captain "Norm" King (though he had been convicted and had resigned), Captain Krumweide, and Ernest Wheelock, the chief's secretary. Alderman D. Percy Jones, the president of the council, an honorable man, should have taken the chair, but he was in the East; so this unstable equilibrium was all the city had by way of a government.

Then Fred Ames disappeared. The Tom Brown clique had full sway, and took over the police department. This was a shock to everybody, to none more than to the King clique, which joined in the search for Ames. An alderman, Fred M. Powers, who was to run for mayor on the Republican ticket, took charge of the mayor's office, but he was not sure of his authority or clear as to his policy. The grand jury was the real power behind him, and the foreman was telegraphing for Alderman Jones. Meanwhile the cliques were making appeals to Mayor Ames, in West Baden, and each side that saw him received authority to do its will. The Coffee John clique, denied admission to the grand-jury room, turned to Alderman Powers, and were beginning to feel secure, when they heard that Fred Ames was coming back. They rushed around, and obtained an assurance from the exiled mayor that Fred was returning only to resign. Fred—now under conviction—returned, but he did not resign; supported by his friends, he took charge again of the police force. Coffee John besought Alderman Powers to remove the chief, and when the acting mayor proved himself too timid, Coffee John, Tom Brown, and Captain Hill laid a deep plot. They would ask Mayor Ames to remove his brother. This they felt sure they could persuade the "old man" to do. The difficulty was to keep him from changing his mind when the other side should reach his ear. They hit upon a bold expedient. They would urge the "old man" to remove Fred, and then resign himself, so that he could not undo the deed that they wanted done. Coffee John and Captain Hill slipped out of town one night; they reached West Baden on one train and they left for home on the next, with a demand for Fred's resignation in one hand and the mayor's own in the other. Fred Ames did resign, and though the mayor's resignation was laid aside for a while, to avoid the expense of a special election, all looked well for Coffee John and his clique. They had Fred out, and Alderman Powers was to make them great. But Mr. Powers wobbled. No doubt the grand jury spoke to him. At any rate he turned most unexpectedly on both cliques together. He turned out Tom Brown, but he turned out also Coffee John, and he did not make their man chief of police, but another of some one else's selection. A number of resignations was the result, and these the acting mayor accepted, making a clearing of astonished rascals which was very gratifying to the grand jury and to the nervous citizens of Minneapolis.

But the town was not yet easy. The grand jury, which was the actual head of the government, was about to be discharged, and, besides, their work was destructive. A constructive force was now needed, and Alderman Jones was pelted with telegrams from home bidding him hurry back. He did hurry, and when he arrived, the situation was instantly in control. The grand jury prepared to report, for the city had a mind and a will of its own once more. The criminals found it out last.

Percy Jones, as his friends call him, is of the second generation of his family in Minneapolis. His father started him well-to-do, and he went on from where he was started. College graduate and business man, he has a conscience which, however, he has brains enough to question. He is not the fighter, but the slow, sure executive. As an alderman he is the result of a movement begun several years ago by some young men who were convinced by an exposure of a corrupt municipal council that they should go into politics. A few did go in; Jones was one of these few.

The acting mayor was confronted at once with all the hardest problems of municipal government. Vice rose right up to tempt or to fight him. He studied the situation deliberately, and by and by began to settle it point by point, slowly but finally, against all sorts of opposition. One of his first acts was to remove all the proved rascals on the force, putting in their places men who had been removed by Mayor Ames. Another important step was the appointment of a church deacon and personal friend to be chief of police, this on the theory that he wanted at the head of his police a man who could have no sympathy with crime, a man whom he could implicitly trust. Disorderly houses, forbidden by law, were permitted, but only within certain patrol lines, and they were to pay nothing, in either blackmail or "fines." The number and the standing and the point of view of the "good people" who opposed this order was a lesson to Mr. Jones in practical government. One very prominent citizen and church member threatened him for driving women out of two flats owned by him; the rent was the surest means of "support for his wife and children." Mr. Jones enforced his order.

Other interests—saloon-keepers, brewers, etc.—gave him trouble enough, but all these were trifles in comparison with his experience with the gamblers. They represented organized crime, and they asked for a hearing. Mr. Jones gave them some six weeks for negotiations. They proposed a solution. They said that if he would let them (a syndicate) open four gambling places down town, they would see that no others ran in any part of the city. Mr. Jones pondered and shook his head, drawing them on. They went away, and came back with a better promise. Though they were not the associates of criminals, they knew that class and their plans. No honest police force, unaided, could deal with crime. Thieves would soon be at work again, and what could Mr. Jones do against them with a police force headed by a church deacon? The gamblers offered to control the criminals for the city.

Mr. Jones, deeply interested, declared he did not believe there was any danger of fresh crimes. The gamblers smiled and went away. By an odd coincidence there happened just after that what the papers called "an epidemic of crime." They were petty thefts, but they occupied the mind of the acting mayor. He wondered at their opportuneness. He wondered how the news of them got out.

The gamblers soon reappeared. Hadn't they told Mr. Jones crime would soon be prevalent in town again? They had, indeed, but the mayor was unmoved; "porch climbers" could not frighten him. But this was only the beginning, the gamblers said: the larger crimes would come next. And they went away again. Sure enough, the large crimes came. One, two, three burglaries of jewelry in the houses of well-known people occurred; then there was a fourth, and the fourth was in the house of a relative of the acting mayor. He was seriously amused. The papers had the news promptly, and not from the police.

The gamblers called again. If they could have the exclusive control of gambling in Minneapolis, they would do all that they had promised before, and, if any large burglaries occurred, they would undertake to recover the "swag" and sometimes catch the thief. Mr. Jones was sceptical of their ability to do all this. The gamblers offered to prove it. How? They would get back for Mr. Jones the jewelry recently reported stolen from four houses in town. Mr. Jones expressed a curiosity to see this done, and the gamblers went away. After a few days the stolen jewelry, parcel by parcel, began to return; with all due police-criminal mystery it was delivered to the chief of police.

When the gamblers called again, they found the acting mayor ready to give his decision on their propositions. It was this: There should be no gambling, with police connivance, in the city of Minneapolis during his term of office.

Mr. Jones told me that if he had before him a long term, he certainly would reconsider this answer. He believed he would decide again as he had already, but he would at least give studious reflection to the question—Can a city be governed without any alliance with crime? It was an open question. He had closed it only for the four months of his emergency administration. Minneapolis should be clean and sweet for a little while at least, and the new administration should begin with a clear deck.

GLOSSARY

autocracy: literally rule by elites or aristocrats; Steffens uses it in the context of rule by the powerful, whose power was often gained by illicit means

boodle town: boodle refers to money gained or used illegally; a "boodle town" would be a city where it was easy to do so, because of government corruption

bosses: the "boss" of a political machine controlled an organization intended to keep a particular party or faction of a party in power

disorderly houses: bordellos or houses of prostitution

Fort Snelling Reservation: the twin cities of St. Paul and Minneapolis grew up around what was at first the Fort Snelling military base or "military reservation"

Document Analysis

"The Shame of Minneapolis" is a narrative of the career of "Doc" Ames, who began as a frontier physician but wound up entering politics in Minneapolis, and the efforts eventually undertaken by reformers to break Ames's power. At the time, Minneapolis was a city of about 200,000 dominated by hardworking people of Scandinavian descent who minded their own business and were content to leave the running of the city to others. This was a pattern that Steffens's publisher, S. S. McClure, believed existed in many cities—people generally ignored city and local government, which opened the door for bosses and political machines to take control behind the scenes. Ames controlled what would be called a political machine, although Steffens does not use that term. A political machine, run by a "boss," was an unofficial political organization that existed to keep one party or a faction of a party in power. Machines often did this by controlling the vote of the poor and recent immigrants; they offered patronage to the poor in return for their votes. The favors and gifts they granted to voters were paid for from the money the machine raised through graft and corruption. Much of the corruption involved in Ames' control of Minneapolis was typical of machine politics, but there also were some unusual features there. Many political bosses did hold elected office like Ames did, but others worked as "the power behind the throne," and dictated policy to whoever happened to hold office. Ames switched from the Democratic to Republican parties when the political situation favored such a move; this is unusual for a machine politician, who usually had firm loyalties to the group that put him in power. Also, the extent to which the police in Minneapolis were complicit in "ordinary" criminal activity was somewhat rare. In many cities controlled by a machine, the police took bribes to turn a blind eye to crime, especially to "vices" such as gambling, prostitution, or illegal liquor sales. But for the police to actually encourage petty crime like burglaries, and even to put the word out to invite criminals to their city, was not typical.

When Ames was elected mayor, at first he turned a blind eye to the corruption of others in city government, although he benefited from that corruption. As Steffens writes, "He was a 'spender,' not a 'grafter,' and he was guilty of corruption chiefly by proxy; he took the honors and left the spoils to his followers." But when he was reelected as mayor in 1900, it seemed as though he was determined to enrich himself from his office. The result was "a career of corruption which for deliberateness, invention, and avarice has never been equalled."

Ames gathered around him a gang of corrupt officials, including his brother, and under this phase of his administration, gamblers, unlicensed saloon keepers, thieves, prostitutes, and opium dealers operated openly with police connivance, all the while sharing their spoils with city officials in exchange for impunity. This was "the shame of Minneapolis." But the city's "rescue and redemption" began in 1902 under the leadership of a grand jury foreman, Hovey C. Clarke, who was determined to use his position to end the corruption. Employing a team of investigators, he gathered information; he and other grand jurors often paid the investigators out of their own pockets. In time, numerous city officials were indicted, tried, and convicted. As the pressure on Ames mounted, he resigned and fled the city. In the power vacuum that followed, city council president D. Percy Jones assumed control and functioned as acting mayor. He replaced the "rascals" in city government and stood up to the criminal elements, determined that "Minneapolis should be clean and sweet for a little while at least, and the new administration should begin with a clear deck." In Steffens's telling, good eventually triumphed over evil.

In his autobiography, Steffens devoted a chapter to the writing of this article, which established his credentials as a "muckraker." Many of the facts he used had been public knowledge for years before he began his research. Steffens was also successful in getting much information from those who were directly involved in the graft and corruption. He found that if he could plant the suggestion that he already knew everything, even the guilty would open up to him, as they believed there was no danger in discussing things he already knew.

The work of Hovey C. Clarke and D. Percy Jones did clean up Minneapolis for a time. But, as in many cities, corruption reemerged over time. Steffens eventually lost confidence in the idea that reform could be brought about simply by replacing bad men with good men. He believed more systematic changes had to be sought, and this led him to move more and more to the left politically as he got older.

Essential Themes

Three trends converged to give rise to the type of article Steffens wrote. The first was improvements in printing technology, which fostered the publication of a large number of relatively inexpensive magazines, like *McClure's*, that kept people abreast of current affairs. *McClure's* became known as one of the leading journals publishing the muckrakers, and the popularity of some of the writers whose works were featured there led other magazines to also provide outlets for muckraking journalists.

The second trend was the rise of Progressive politics under the presidential administration of Theodore Roosevelt; in fact, Roosevelt is credited with coining the term *muckraking* when he referred in a speech to the "Muck-Rake" in John Bunyan's classic novel *Pilgrim's Progress*—a character who was so busy raking in the muck that he would not lift up his eyes to see the glory of heaven. In this climate, muckraking journalists exposed all manner of social ills in their articles: child labor, political corruption, prison conditions, conditions in the meatpacking industry, scandals involving corporations, and the like—often leading to legislation to correct the ills. Steffens became widely known as a muckraker, and was generally thought to be one of the earliest and best practitioners of this genre of investigation and exposure of corruption.

The third trend was the prevalence of political "machines" in urban centers. Bosses like "Doc" Ames controlled cities by using patronage to attract and keep supporters. They ran a highly efficient system that had power over a political party, elections, and the city's purse strings, granting favors in exchange for support and political contributions. Although these machines in some cases functioned for the good—for example, they often provided recent immigrants from a favored ethnic group with a toehold in their new country—they were just as often corrupt. Machines in some simple form had existed since the late 1700s, but they grew to their greatest power as cities grew tremendously in the late nineteenth and early twentieth cities. As cities grew, people in new neighborhoods often lacked the infrastructure needed like sewer lines, water lines, or convenient access to electricity. Also, there usually was no "welfare safety net" to care for people who were truly in need. Machines often worked to meet these needs, but at the price of demanding the vote of the working-class poor and recent immigrants. One of the best known of these machines was Tammany Hall, or the Society of Saint Tammany, which began as a New York City fraternal organization but in the nineteenth century evolved under William March "Boss" Tweed into a machine that often relied on corruption to control the city's politics until the mid-1930s. Steffens wrote articles for *McClure's* on similar machines in several other cities, including Pittsburgh, Philadelphia, Chicago, and New York City, and two articles on St. Louis. In 1904, these articles were put together as a book entitled, *The Shame of the Cities*, which sold widely.

An immediate impact of "The Shame of Minneapolis" was the establishment of Steffens as a major writer in the genre of exposé journalism that would be termed "muckraking" a few years later. In the same issue of *McClure's* in which Steffens's article appeared (January 1903), two other writers who would also become prominent muckrakers also had important piece—Ida Tarbell published some of her research on Standard Oil's questionable business practices, and Ray Baker wrote about corruption among union officials. The issue sold faster than any previous issue of *McClure's*, and was entirely sold out in three days. The success of *McClure's* stable of muckrakers prompted similar articles in other leading magazines of the time.

Of course, the fact that there was corruption in many city governments was not a groundbreaking revelation. But what Steffens and others did was provide detailed evidence and specific naming of names. The work of the muckrakers did lead to reforms in several cities around the nation aimed at limiting the power of political machines. One such reform was the creation of a city council or commission. In this system, most real power in city government was put in the hands of an elected council or commission; the mayor was only an administrator or figurehead. The theory was that a group of commissioners would be harder for machine politicians to control than a single mayor. A further development of this plan was the commission-city manager form, where citizens elect the commission, and the commission then hires a city manager. This was an example of the Progressive era's belief in efficiency and expertise—the city manager would usually be a person with a graduate degree in urban administration or some related field. The Progressives believed the people, through their vote, should decide the goals or ends of public policy, and expert, trained professionals, would figure out how to implement these goals.

City government reform did clean up machine politics in many cities, at least temporarily. But machines had a nagging habit of coming back, eventually, or a new machine would replace the old one. Steffens himself, in his later years, lost faith in such modest efforts at reform and came to believe that revolutionary change was needed.

—Mark S. Joy, Michael J. O'Neal

Bibliography and Additional Reading

Brasch, Walter M. *Forerunners of the Revolution: Muckrakers and the American Social Conscience.* Lanham, MD: University Press of America, 1990.

Goodwin, Doris Kearns. *The Bully Pulpit: Theodore Roosevelt, William Howard Taft, and the Golden Age of Journalism.* New York: Simon and Schuster, 2013.

Graham, Jr., Otis L. *An Encore for Reform: The Old Progressives and the New Deal.* New York: Oxford University Press, 1967.

Hartshorn, Peter. *I Have Seen the Future: A Life of Lincoln Steffens.* Berkeley, CA: Counterpoint, 2011.

Hofstadter, Richard. *The Age of Reform; From Bryan to F.D.R.* New York: Vintage Books, 1955.

Steffens, Lincoln. *The Autobiography of Lincoln Steffens.* New York: Harcourt, Brace, and World, 1931.

Wilson, Harold. *McClure's Magazine and the Muckrakers.* Princeton, NJ: Princeton University Press, 1970.

■ From *The Jungle*

Date: 1906
Author: Upton Sinclair
Genre: Nonfiction (excerpt)

Summary Overview

In the 1906 novel *The Jungle*, novelist and journalist Upton Sinclair describes the success of Chicago's meatpacking industry in hiding unsanitary factory conditions, as well as the dangers of working in such facilities. Sinclair also comments on the political forces at play, telling the story of a Chicago meatpacker's union that helps decrease the political influence of the factory owners by voting sympathetic candidates into power. The novel was based on Sinclair's own experiences investigating Chicago's meatpacking industry, and his findings would inspire the passage of new food safety laws in the United States.

Defining Moment

Throughout the nineteenth century, the meatpacking industry was one of the largest employers in the Midwest. In the years leading up to the Civil War, this industry employed thousands of Americans, most of whom were located in Cincinnati, Ohio, and other parts of the Ohio River Valley. During and after the Civil War, the meatpacking industry shifted to Chicago, Illinois, a hub of the nation's growing railway system.

In 1865, the establishment of the Union Stock Yards, a meatpacking district just south of Chicago, bolstered Chicago's position as the nation's leader in meatpacking. The stockyards were tremendous, using fifteen miles of railway track to deliver livestock to the slaughterhouses and transport the final products throughout the nation. They also relied on the Chicago River for water, using 500,000 gallons per day, and sent contaminated wastewater back into a river fork. By the beginning of the twentieth century, the Union Stock Yards covered 475 acres, with fifty miles of roads and 130 miles of railway track servicing them.

The industry was highly lucrative, with a growing service area. During the Civil War era, the Cincinnati- and Chicago-based industries were focused on servicing the Midwest. However, the advent of the refrigerated boxcar made it possible to send fresh meat throughout the country, and even around the world. By 1900, the Union Stock Yards employed more than 25,000 people. The meatpacking companies wielded tremendous political and financial influence over the areas in which they operated, and government oversight was limited.

In light of the high degree of economic prosperity the Union Stock Yards brought to the Chicago area, as well as the insular manner in which the meatpacking industry managed itself, few people outside of the industry knew the realities of working at that massive complex. The thousands of workers there, mainly Eastern European immigrants, worked exceptionally long hours in unsanitary and highly dangerous conditions. It was not until the beginning of the twentieth century, when novelist and social activist Upton Sinclair published his novel *The Jungle*, that the nation as a whole began to pay attention to the harsh and unsanitary environment that was the meatpacking industry. The novel inspired the passage of the Federal Food and Drugs Act of 1906, which regulated the manufacture and sale of various foods and medicinal products.

Author Biography

Upton Beall Sinclair was born on September 20, 1878, in Baltimore, Maryland. He and his parents moved to New York City when he was ten. At the age of eighteen, he graduated from what is now the City University of New York and continued his education at Columbia University. Having developed an interest in writing as a teenager, Sinclair published short stories and dime novels throughout his time in college and continued to publish fiction after completing his education. He also became a socialist, and in 1904, embarked on an investigation of the meatpacking industry for the socialist newspaper *Appeal to Reason*. Sinclair traveled to Chicago and remained there for several weeks, observing the life of meatpacking workers and the conditions that surrounded them. These observations became the basis for *The Jungle*, serialized in *Appeal to Reason* in 1905 and published in book form in 1906. Sinclair wrote numerous novels after *The Jungle*, some of which, including the 1927 novel *Oil!*, also proved influential. In 1934, Sinclair unsuccessfully ran for governor of California. Afterward he returned to the private sector, writing a number of historical novels. He died on November 25, 1968, at the age of ninety.

Men walking on wooden rails between cattle pens in the Chicago stockyard (1909). The meatpacking district was the focus of Upton Sinclair's book, The Jungle.

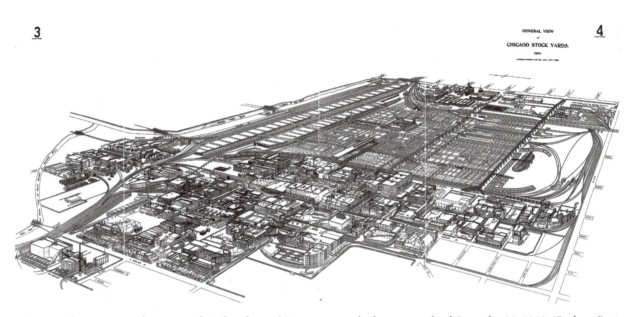

Chicago Packing Houses and Union Stock Yards. Library of Congress copyright deposit entry dated September 30, 1901. (Sanborn-Perris Map Co. Ltd., New York City)

HISTORICAL DOCUMENT

…And then there was the condemned meat industry, with its endless horrors. The people of Chicago saw the government inspectors in Packingtown, and they all took that to mean that they were protected from diseased meat; they did not understand that these hundred and sixty-three inspectors had been appointed at the request of the packers, and that they were paid by the United States government to certify that all the diseased meat was kept in the state. They had no authority beyond that; for the inspection of meat to be sold in the city and state the whole force in Packingtown consisted of three henchmen of the local political machine!…

And then there was "potted game" and "potted grouse," "potted ham," and "deviled ham"—devyled, as the men called it. "De-vyled" ham was made out of the waste ends of smoked beef that were too small to be sliced by the machines; and also tripe, dyed with chemicals so that it would not show white, and trimmings of hams and corned beef, and potatoes, skins and all, and finally the hard cartilaginous gullets of beef, after the tongues had been cut out. All this ingenious mixture was ground up and flavored with spices to make it taste like something. Anybody who could invent a new imitation had been sure of a fortune from old Durham, said Jurgis's informant, but it was hard to think of anything new in a place where so many sharp wits had been at work for so long; where men welcomed tuberculosis in the cattle they were feeding, because it made them fatten more quickly; and where they bought up all the old rancid butter left over in the grocery stores of a continent, and "oxidized" it by a forced-air process, to take away the odor, rechurned it with skim milk, and sold it in bricks in the cities!…

There were the men in the pickle rooms, for instance, where old Antanas had gotten his death; scarce a one of these that had not some spot of horror on his person. Let a man so much as scrape his finger pushing a truck in the pickle rooms, and he might have a sore that would put him out of the world; all the joints of his fingers might be eaten by the acid, one by one. Of the butchers and floorsmen, the beef boners and trimmers, and all those who used knives, you could scarcely find a person who had the use of his thumb; time and time again the base of it had been slashed, till it was a mere lump of flesh against which the man pressed the knife to hold it. The hands of these men would be criss-crossed with cuts, until you could no longer pretend to count them or to trace them. They would have no nails,—they had worn them off pulling hides; their knuckles were swollen so that their fingers spread out like a fan. There were men who worked in the cooking rooms, in the midst of steam and sickening odors, by artificial light; in these rooms the germs of tuberculosis might live for two years, but the supply was renewed every hour. There were the beef luggers, who carried two-hundred-pound quarters into the refrigerator cars, a fearful kind of work, that began at four o'clock in the morning, and that wore out the most powerful men in a few years. There were those who worked in the chilling rooms, and whose special disease was rheumatism; the time limit that a man could work in the chilling rooms was said to be five years. There were the wool pluckers, whose hands went to pieces even sooner than the hands of the pickle men; for the pelts of the sheep had to be painted with acid to loosen the wool, and then the pluckers had to pull out this wool with their bare hands, till the acid had eaten their fingers off. There were those who made the tins for the canned meat, and their hands, too, were a maze of cuts, and each cut represented a chance for blood poisoning. Some worked at the stamping machines, and it was very seldom that one could work long there at the pace that was set, and not give out and forget himself, and have a part of his hand chopped off. There were the "hoisters," as they were called, whose task it was to press the lever which lifted the dead cattle off the floor. They ran along upon a rafter, peering down through the damp and the steam, and as old Durham's architects had not built the killing room for the convenience of the hoisters, at every few feet they would have to stoop under a beam, say four feet above the one they ran on, which got them into the habit of stooping, so that in a few years they would be walking like chimpanzees. Worst of any, however, were the fertilizer men, and those who served in the cooking rooms. These people could not be shown to the visitor—for the odor of a fertilizer man would scare away any ordinary visitor at a hundred yards, and as for the other men, who worked in tank rooms full of steam, and in some of which there were open vats near the level of the floor, their peculiar trouble was that they fell into the vats; and when they were fished out, there was never enough of them left to be worth exhibiting—sometimes they would be over-looked for days, till all but the bones of them had gone out to the world as Durham's Pure Leaf Lard!…

There was never the least attention paid to what was cut up for sausage; there would come all the way back from Europe old sausage that had been rejected, and that was mouldy and white—it would be dosed with borax and glycerine, and dumped into the hoppers, and made over again for home consumption. There would be meat that had tumbled out on the floor, in the dirt and sawdust, where the workers had tramped and spit uncounted billions of consumption germs. There would be meat stored in great piles in rooms; and the water from leaky roofs would drip over it, and thousands of rats would race about on it. It was too dark in these storage places to see well, but a man could run his hand over these piles of meat and sweep off handfuls of the dried dung of rats. These rats were nuisances, and the packers would put poisoned bread out for them, they would die, and then rats, bread, and meat would go into the hoppers together. This is no fairy story and no joke; the meat would be shov-elled into carts, and the man who did the shoveling would not trouble to lift out a rat even when he saw one—there were things that went into the sausage in comparison with which a poisoned rat was a tid-bit. There was no place for the men to wash their hands before they ate their dinner, and so they made a practice of washing them in the water that was to be ladled into the sausage. There were the butt-ends of smoked meat, and the scraps of corned beef, and all the odds and ends of the waste of the plants, that would be dumped into old barrels in the cellar and left there. Under the system of rigid economy which the packers enforced, there were some jobs that it only paid to do once in a long time, and among these was the cleaning out of the waste barrels. Every spring they did it; and in the barrels would be dirt and rust and old nails and stale water—and cart load after cart load of it would be taken up and dumped into the hoppers with fresh meat, and sent out to the public's breakfast. Some of it they would make into "smoked" sausage—but as the smoking took time, and was therefore expensive, they would call upon their chemistry department, and preserve it with borax and color it with gelatine to make it brown. All of their sausage came out of the same bowl, but when they came to wrap it they would stamp some of it "special," and for this they would charge two cents more a pound....

And then the editor wanted to know upon what ground Dr. Schliemann asserted that it might be possible for a society to exist upon an hour's toil by each of its members. "Just what," answered the other, "would be the productive capacity of society if the present resources of science were utilized, we have no means of ascertaining; but we may be sure it would exceed anything that would sound reasonable to minds inured to the ferocious barbarities of Capitalism. After the triumph of the international proletariat, war would of course be inconceivable; and who can figure the cost of war to humanity—not merely the value of the lives and the material that it destroys, not merely the cost of keeping millions of men in idleness, of arming and equipping them for battle and parade, but the drain upon the vital energies of society by the war-attitude and the war-terror, the brutality and ignorance, the drunkenness, prostitution, and crime it entails, the industrial impotence and the moral deadness? Do you think that it would be too much to say that two hours of the working time of every efficient member of a community goes to feed the red fiend of war?"

And then Schliemann went on to outline some of the wastes of competition: the losses of industrial warfare; the ceaseless worry and friction; the vices—such as drink, for instance, the use of which had nearly doubled in twenty years, as a consequence of the intensification of the economic struggle; the idle and unproductive members of the community, the frivolous rich and the pauperized poor; the law and the whole machinery of repression; the wastes of social ostentation, the milliners and tailors, the hairdressers, dancing masters, chefs and lackeys. "You understand," he said, "that in a society dominated by the fact of commercial competition, money is necessarily the test of prowess, and wastefulness the sole criterion of power. So we have, at the present moment, a society with, say, thirty per cent of the population occupied in producing useless articles, and one per cent occupied in destroying them…"

And then there were official returns from the various precincts and wards of the city itself! Whether it was a factory district or one of the "silk-stocking" wards seemed to make no particular difference in the increase; but one of the things which surprised the [Socialist] party leaders most was the tremendous vote that came rolling in from the stockyards. Packingtown comprised three wards of the city, and the vote in the spring of 1903 had been five hundred, and in the fall of the same year, sixteen hundred. Now, only a year later, it was over sixty-three hundred—and the Democratic vote only eighty-eight hundred! There were other wards in which the Democratic vote had been actually surpassed, and in two districts, members of the state legislature had been elected. Thus Chicago now led the country; it had set a new standard for the party, it had shown the workingmen the way!

—So spoke an orator upon the platform; and two thousand pairs of eyes were fixed upon him, and two thousand voices were cheering his every sentence. The orator had been the head of the city's relief bureau in the stockyards, until the sight of misery and corruption had made him sick. He was young, hungry-looking, full of fire; and as he swung his long arms and beat up the crowd, to Jurgis he seemed the very spirit of the revolution. "Organize! Organize! Organize!"—that was his cry. He was afraid of this tremendous vote, which his party had not expected, and which it had not earned. "These men are not Socialists!" he cried. "This election will pass, and the excitement will die, and people will forget about it; and if you forget about it, too, if you sink back and rest upon your oars, we shall lose this vote that we have polled today, and our enemies will laugh us to scorn! It rests with you to take your resolution—now, in the flush of victory, to find these men who have voted for us, and bring them to our meetings, and organize them and bind them to us! We shall not find all our campaigns as easy as this one. Everywhere in the country tonight the old party politicians are studying this vote, and setting their sails by it; and nowhere will they be quicker or more cunning than here in our own city. Fifty thousand Socialist votes in Chicago means a municipal-ownership Democracy in the spring! And then they will fool the voters once more, and all the powers of plunder and corruption will be swept into office again! But whatever they may do when they get in, there is one thing they will not do, and that will be the thing for which they were elected! They will not give the people of our city municipal ownership—they will not mean to do it, they will not try to do it; all that they will do is give our party in Chicago the greatest opportunity that has ever come to Socialism in America! We shall have the sham reformers self-stultified and self-convicted; we shall have the radical Democracy left without a lie with which to cover its nakedness! And then will begin the rush that will never be checked, the tide that will never turn till it has reached its flood—that will be irresistible, overwhelming—the rallying of the outraged workingmen of Chicago to our standard! And we shall organize them, we shall drill them, we shall marshal them for the victory! We shall bear down the opposition, we shall sweep it before us—and Chicago will be ours! Chicago will be ours! CHICAGO WILL BE OURS!"

GLOSSARY

borax: a white, crystalline powder (hydrated sodium borate) used as a cleaning agent

tripe: the stomach lining of a cow or ox, used as food

Document Analysis

The Jungle tells the story of a Lithuanian immigrant, Jurgis Rudkus, who arrives in Chicago in search of work. He and his family settle in an area known as Packingtown, where they experience a wide range of hardships. Jurgis finds work in the meatpacking industry but continues to struggle with poverty and crime in addition to the physical dangers of his work environment. He eventually becomes interested in socialism and labor unions, seeing them as a possible solution to the rampant corruption of the meatpacking industry. Though *The Jungle* is a work of fiction, the novel is a thinly veiled commentary on life at the Union Stock Yards and expresses Sinclair's positive views of unionization and socialist ideals.

Throughout *The Jungle*, Jurgis witnesses firsthand many of the unsanitary conditions and unhealthy products being assembled in Packingtown. Some departments within the facility in which he works use dye and other chemicals, parts of older and unused meat segments, and even diseased animal corpses in the creation of household food products. The production of sausage continues even after rat droppings as well as cleaning chemicals, dirt, and sawdust have fallen into the openly stored piles of meat. Sinclair's descriptions of these unhygienic conditions are graphic and clearly demonstrate that meat products produced in such conditions are unfit for human consumption.

Sinclair likewise uses the novel to draw attention to the corruption of the meatpacking industry as well as its human cost. Government inspectors visit Packingtown but accomplish little, as the companies pay or otherwise influence the inspectors to sign off on their unsanitary practices. Workers, such as Jurgis, are unable to improve the sanitary conditions of their work environment; in fact, the plants of Packingtown are even said to lack hand-washing facilities. Workers returning home carry germs and harmful substances on their hands and clothes, exposing their families to those environmental conditions as well. Furthermore, Sinclair, through Jurgis, emphasizes the extreme dangers associated with working in Packingtown. Picklers, boners, butchers, and other workers are said to be at constant risk of injury, and thanks to the unsanitary working conditions and numerous hazardous substances around them, even the smallest cut has the potential to develop a terrible infection. Other workers, such as those responsible for operating hoisting machinery, spend so much time bent over that they walk around "like chimpanzees."

After experiencing the hardships of meatpacking work, Jurgis eventually meets Dr. Nicholas Schliemann, a Swiss native whose socialist views appear to provide a solution. Schliemann convinces Jurgis of the value of unions, which could allow the meatpackers to unite and speak with one voice. Jurgis realizes that unionization could empower the people of Packingtown and give them the ability to take control of Chicago politics and put an end to the harmful and exploitative practices of the meatpacking industry.

Essential Themes

In *The Jungle*, Jurgis Rudkus arrives in the United States in search of opportunity, but he instead encounters hardship, crime, corruption, and danger in a large system of slaughterhouses known as Packingtown. The story is fictional, but Sinclair's novel is heavily based on his experiences and observations at the very real Union Stock Yards outside of Chicago. Sinclair believed that the secrets of the meatpacking industry—then hidden from the prying eyes of critics, activists, and the public at large—needed to be revealed to all Americans, and the novel form allowed him to do so in an accessible manner, presenting a depiction of the meatpacking industry that resonated with readers on several levels.

In the novel, it is common for workers to be injured, maimed, or even killed while working in Packingtown. Death can be immediate, Jurgis learns, or it can be long and painful due to infection. Sinclair calls attention to the terrible human cost of the meatpacking industry, presenting in unflinching detail the amputations, mutilations, and deaths that commonly occur in a work environment that favors production over worker safety. In addition, the meatpacking industry is shown to use extremely unsanitary and unhealthy practices in the production of its products. Chemicals, animal waste, and other foreign substances are commonly dumped into the meat, and expired and even rancid byproducts are packaged and sold to customers. The government is shown to monitor these practices, but, as Jurgis learns, government inspectors are on site as a service to the companies themselves rather than the public. By describing the unsanitary production of food products in detail, Sinclair made it clear to his readers that poor working conditions in meatpacking facilities affected not only the people who worked there, but also the unsuspecting consumers who ate the contaminated products—perhaps including the readers themselves.

—*Michael P. Auerbach*

Bibliography and Additional Reading

Barrett, James R. *Work and Community in the Jungle: Chicago's Packinghouse Workers, 1894–1922.* Champaign: U of Illinois P, 1990. Print.

Halpern, Rick. *Down on the Killing Floor: Black and White Workers in Chicago's Packinghouses, 1904–1954.* Urbana: U of Illinois P, 1997. Print.

Stromquist, Shelton, and Marvin Bergman. *Unionizing the Jungles: Labor and Community in the Twentieth-Century Meatpacking Industry.* Iowa City: U of Iowa P, 1997. Print.

Warren, Wilson J. *Tied to the Great Packing Machine: The Midwest and Meatpacking.* Iowa City: U of Iowa P, 2007. Print.

■ Jane Addams: "Passing of the War Virtues"

Date: 1907
Author: Jane Addams
Genre: Nonfiction (excerpt)

Summary Overview

Jane Addams was part of the Progressive movement, a broad and diverse middle-class coalition that, at the turn of the twentieth century, tried to reform American society and reconcile democracy with capitalism. The steady industrialization and urbanization of the 1880s and 1890s had deeply transformed American society, spurring harsh conflicts between labor and management. The middle class had supported the process of industrialization by espousing the Victorian values of laissez-faire individualism, domesticity, and self-control. Yet by the 1890s it was apparent that these values had trapped the middle class between the warring demands of big business and the working classes. Growing consumerism, a new wave of immigration, and tensions between the sexes further challenged bourgeois existence. In the face of these confrontations, the Progressives tried to reform the American capitalist system and its institutions from within, seeking to strike a compromise between radical demands and the preservation of established interests. Addams's concern with the major issues of Progressivism and her own agenda for social reform clearly emerge in a variety of her essays and speeches. In chapter 8 of her book *Newer Ideals of Peace* (1907), entitled "Passing of the War Virtues" she makes clear, for example, her condemnation of military ideals in the conception of an effective model of social control and efficient management of economic and political institutions.

Defining Moment

In the essay titled "Passing of the War Virtues" Addams was reaching out to like-minded Progressive thinkers who were already sympathetic to the movement. Individuals who favored social change, particularly in terms of equality for women, and pacifists were likely a targeted audience. However, in a fashion that was typical of Addams, she was also attempting to reach out to more conservative members of society who might be persuaded to consider her point of view on the issue of progressive social change. Addams realized in order to see true change in the nation there had to be constructive action that could only be achieved through the coming together of individuals who did not

necessarily share the same worldview. Therefore, this essay was an attempt to appeal to a base of supporters already in place while recruiting new members to the Progressive movement.

Author Biography

Jane Addams, the eighth of nine children, was born on September 6, 1860, in Cedarville, Illinois, into a wealthy family of Quaker background. Addams was a member of the first generation of American women to attend college. She graduated in 1881 from Rockford Female Seminary, in Illinois, which the following year became Rockford College for Women, allowing Addams to obtain her bachelor's degree. In the 1880s Addams began studying medicine at the Women's Medical College of Philadelphia, but she had to suspend her studies because of poor health. Throughout the decade Addams also suffered from depression owing to her father's sudden death in 1881. Her physical and mental conditions, however, did not prevent her from traveling extensively in Europe. During one of her voyages, Addams visited London's original settlement house of Toynbee Hall, established in 1884, with her companion, Ellen Gates Starr. The visit led the two women to establish the Chicago settlement house of Hull House in 1889, the second such house to be established in America. (Dr. Stanton Coit and Charles B. Stover had founded the first American settlement house, the Neighborhood Guild of New York City, in 1886.) Through Hull House, Addams found a vocation for her adult life, overcoming the sense of uselessness that had besieged her for most of the 1880s.

Addams campaigned for every major reform issue of her era, such as fairer workplace conditions for men and women, tenement regulation, juvenile-court law, women's suffrage, and women's rights. She worked closely with social workers, politicians, and labor and immigrant groups to achieve her purposes, and she was not afraid to take controversial stances, as when she decided to campaign against U.S. entry into World War I. While in the first part of her life Addams was mainly involved in social work in Hull House, in the twentieth century she used her notoriety to advance political causes and became a well-known public figure. In 1910 she was the first woman president of the National Conference of Social Work, and in 1912 she actively campaigned for the Progressive presidential candidate, Theodore Roosevelt, becoming the first woman to give a nominating speech at a party convention. Addams was also a founding member of the National Association for the Advancement of Colored People.

In conjunction with her antiwar efforts, she became the president of the Woman's Peace Party in 1915 and chaired the International Women's Congress for Peace and Freedom at The Hague, Netherlands. That congress led to the foundation of the Women's International League for Peace and Freedom, which Addams chaired until 1929, when she was made honorary president for the remainder of her life. Americans were not unanimous in their praise for Addams's campaigning for peace. On the contrary, she was bitterly attacked by the press and was expelled from the Daughters of the American Revolution. In 1931, however, Addams's antiwar efforts won her the Nobel Peace Prize, which she shared with Nicholas Murray Butler. Because of her declining health, she was unable to collect the prize in person. Addams died in Chicago on May 21, 1935, three days after being diagnosed with cancer.

Addams's life, speeches, and writings are typical of middle-class reformers at the turn of the century. She was widely acknowledged as a pioneer social worker, and she spoke vigorously in favor of social reform. Her addresses and public interventions show her to have been idealistic yet committed to concrete action. Like other Progressive thinkers, such as John Dewey, Herbert Croly, Walter Lippmann, and Charlotte Perkins Gilman, Addams was deeply concerned with the changing nature of human ties and the meaning of community in an increasingly industrialized and urbanized world. Taking a critical stance toward the laissez-faire capitalism that had characterized the

Sociologist, suffragette, social worker, philosopher, and Nobel Peace Prize winner Jane Addams, in 1924 or 1926. (Bain News Service; Restoration by Adam Cuerden)

Gilded Age, a period of excessive displays of wealth in the late nineteenth century, Progressives like Addams expanded the authority to solve private and public problems to include not only the individual but also the government. They charged the state with the task of intervening in social and economic matters when appropriate, to defeat self-interest in the name of the common good.

THE BIG FOUR AT THE
TWO CHICAGO CONVENTIONS

1912 cartoon, showing the "Big Four at the Two Chicago Conventions". Front row (Progressive or "Bull Moose" party): Theodore Roosevelt, Jane Addams, Hiram Johnson, Albert Beveridge; Back row (Republican party): Boies Penrose, William Barnes, Jr., Winthrop M. Crane, Elihu Root. (It was a little out of the ordinary for a woman to be considered a political power figure in 1912.)

HISTORICAL DOCUMENT

Let us by all means acknowledge and preserve that which has been good in warfare and in the spirit of warfare; let us gather it together and incorporate it in our national fibre. Let us, however, not be guilty for a moment of shutting our eyes to that which for many centuries must have been disquieting to the moral sense, but which is gradually becoming impossible, not only because of our increasing sensibilities, but because great constructive plans and humanized interests have captured our hopes and we are finding that war is an implement too clumsy and barbaric to subserve our purpose. We have come to realize that the great task of pushing forward social justice could be enormously accelerated if primitive methods as well as primitive weapons were once for all abolished....

Warfare in the past has done much to bring men together. A sense of common anger and the stirring appeal to action for a common purpose, easily open the channels of sympathy through which we partake of the life about us. But there are certainly other methods of opening those channels. A social life to be healthy must be consciously and fully adjusted to the march of social needs, and as we may easily make a mistake by forgetting that enlarged opportunities are ever demanding an enlarged morality, so we will fail in the task of substitution if we do not demand social sympathy in a larger measure and of a quality better adapted to the contemporaneous situation. Perhaps the one point at which this undertaking is most needed is in regard to our conception of patriotism, which, although as genuine as ever before, is too much dressed in the trappings of the past and continually carries us back to its beginnings in military prowess and defence....

Unless our conception of patriotism is progressive, it cannot hope to embody the real affection and the real interest of the nation. We know full well that the patriotism of common descent is the mere patriotism of the clan—the early patriotism of the tribe—and that, while the possession of a like territory is an advance upon that first conception, both of them are unworthy to be the patriotism of a great cosmopolitan nation. We shall not have made any genuine advance until we have grown impatient of a patriotism founded upon military prowess and defence, because this really gets in the way and prevents the growth of that beneficent and progressive patriotism which we need for the understanding and healing of our current national difficulties....

We come at last to the practical question as to how these substitutes for the war virtues may be found. How may we, the children of an industrial and commercial age, find the courage and sacrifice which belong to our industrialism. We may begin with August Comte's assertion that man seeks to improve his position ... by the destruction of obstacles and by the construction of means, or, designated by their most obvious social results, if his contention is correct, by military action and by industrial action....

Then we find ourselves asking what may be done to make more picturesque those lives which are spent in a monotonous and wearing toil, compared to which the camp is exciting and the barracks comfortable. How shall it be made to seem as magnificent patiently to correct the wrongs of industrialism as to do battle for the rights of the nation? This transition ought not to be so difficult in America, for to begin with, our national life in America has been largely founded upon our success in invention and engineering, in manufacturing and commerce. Our prosperity has rested upon constructive labor and material progress, both of them in striking contrast to warfare....

We ignore the fact that war so readily throws back the ideals which the young are nourishing into the mold of those which the old should be outgrowing. It lures young men not to develop, but to exploit; it turns them from the courage and toil of industry to the bravery and endurance of war, and leads them to forget that civilization is the substitution of law for war....

It remains to be seen whether or not democratic rule will diminish war. Immoderate and uncontrolled desires are at the root of most national as well as of most individual crimes, and a large number of persons may be moved by unworthy ambitions quite as easily as a few. If the electorate of a democracy accustom themselves to take the commercial view of life, to consider the extension of trade as the test of a national prosperity, it becomes comparatively easy for mere extension of commercial opportunity to assume a moral aspect and to receive the moral sanction. Unrestricted commercialism is an excellent preparation for governmental aggression. The nation which is accustomed to condone the questionable business methods of a rich man because of his success, will find no difficulty in obscuring the moral issues involved in any undertaking that is successful. It becomes easy to deny the moral basis of self-government and to substitute militarism....

The advance of constructive labor and the subsidence and disappearance of destructive warfare is a genuine line of progression....

To some of us it seems clear that marked manifestations of [the] movement [for world peace] are found in the immigrant quarters of American cities. The ... survey of the immigrant situation would indicate that all the peoples of the world have become part of the American tribunal, and that their sense of pity, their clamor for personal kindness, their insistence upon the right to join in our progress, can no longer be disregarded. The burdens and sorrows of men have unexpectedly become intelligent and urgent to this nation, and it is only by accepting them with some magnanimità that we can develop the larger sense of justice which is becoming world-wide and is lying in ambush, as it were, to manifest itself in governmental relations. Men of all nations are determining upon the abolition of degrading poverty, disease, and intellectual weakness, with their resulting industrial inefficiency, and are making a determined effort to conserve even the feeblest citizen to the State. To join in this determined effort is to break through national bonds and to unlock the latent fellowship between man and man.... It is but necessary to make this fellowship wider, to extend its scope without lowering its intensity. Those emotions which stir the spirit to deeds of self-surrender and to high enthusiasm, are among the world's most precious assets. That this emotion has so often become associated with war, by no means proves that it cannot be used for other ends. There is something active and tangible in this new internationalism, although it is difficult to make it clear, and in our striving for a new word with which to express this new and important sentiment, we are driven to the rather absurd phrase of "cosmic patriotism." Whatever it may be called, it may yet be strong enough to move masses of men out of their narrow national considerations and cautions into new reaches of human effort and affection....

The International Peace Conference held in Boston in 1904 was opened by a huge meeting in which men of influence and modern thought from four continents, gave reasons for their belief in the passing of war. But none was so modern, so fundamental and so trenchant, as the address which was read from the prophet Isaiah.... He contended that peace could be secured only as men abstained from the gains of oppression and responded to the cause of the poor; that swords would finally be beaten into plowshares and pruning-hooks, not because men resolved to be peaceful, but because all the metal of the earth would be turned to its proper use when the poor and their children should be abundantly fed. It was as if the ancient prophet foresaw that under an enlightened industrialism peace would no longer be an absence of war, but the unfolding of world-wide processes making for the nurture of human life. He predicted the moment which has come to us now that peace is no longer an abstract dogma but has become a rising tide of moral enthusiasm slowly engulfing all pride of conquest and making war impossible.

GLOSSARY

American tribunal: a court of law, but here suggesting a larger and more informal community of shared ideals

camp: the military life

Comte, Auguste: French social philosopher and reformer (1798–1857)

conserve: preserve the existence of

enlarged morality: a matured and maturing sense of right and wrong

intelligent: understood

Isaiah: Israelite prophet of the 700s BCE for whom one of the most significant books in the Old Testament is named

magnanimità: Italian version of the word magnanimity, meaning generosity of spirit

march: changing nature

patriotism of common descent: loyalty to one's nation that comes simply from having been born there, as opposed to loyalty based on principles

Document Analysis

One of the chief concerns of Progressives was the establishment of effective institutions that could replace the notions of individualism and unrestrained commercialism that had characterized the Gilded Age. In chapter 8 of her book *Newer Ideals of Peace* (1907), entitled "Passing of the War Virtues" Addams claims that a fairer society can be achieved only if the older military values that are considered founding virtues of the American social order are replaced by "the growth of that beneficent and progressive patriotism which we need for the understanding and healing of our current national difficulties." The chapter is a logical anticipation of Addams's involvement in the movement against U.S. entry into World War I. Although Addams credits the war spirit of the past with having brought men together, she claims that the changing times require a new type of spirit, one that seeks "the construction of means" by "industrial action" rather than "the destruction of obstacles" by "military action."

In an effort to appeal also to the most conservative sector of American society, Addams states that the quintessentially American faith in material progress itself discords with military virtues. American prosperity, she asserts, rests on "constructive labor and material progress, both of them in striking contrast to warfare."

Military values lead to the establishment of an exploitative society and encourage younger people to "forget that civilization is the substitution of law for war." Addams is careful not to espouse a vision of society based merely on the accumulation of wealth, however. Consistent with the Progressive tenets that the government should intervene in social and economic affairs and that forms of social control are needed to protect the common good, Addams claims that one should be wary of "unrestricted commercialism" which is "an excellent preparation for governmental aggression." This line of thought is typical of Addams's strategy to mediate between those with more radical demands and those who want to preserve society as is. She begins by expressing her faith in the American ideal of material progress, yet she leads the reader to question the individualistic notions that hard work necessarily translates into economic success and that the poor have only themselves to blame.

Addams cites the urban poor and the immigrant as examples of citizens who are helping to develop the world peace movement: "Their sense of pity, their clamor for personal kindness, their insistence upon the right to join in our progress, can no longer be disregarded." The fight against poverty can stimulate "the latent fellowship between man and man"; thus, the quest for a fairer society can replace the war virtues to unite human beings across national borders. Like other Progressive reformers, Addams also stresses the importance of efficient industrial management. She holds that the fight against "degrading poverty, disease and intellectual weakness" will result in the improvement of industrial efficiency. Addams thus frames the replacement of military values and the fight against poverty within the Progressives' quest for proficient administration in economic, social, and political institutions. "Passing of the War Virtues" is revealing of Addams's beliefs that the present system of government was inadequate in a complex industrial age and that public officials should eliminate inefficiency and exploitation.

Another important dimension of the fight against poverty in this era was its international significance. Addams clearly emphasizes the importance of extending human fellowship beyond national interests, stating that the fight against social injustices can become a common element for nations. In accordance with its international dimension, the chapter ends with a description of the International Peace Conference held in Boston in 1904. Addams refers to it as a "huge meeting" at which influential thinkers from all over the world "gave reasons for their belief in the passing of war." Citing "the address which was read from the prophet Isaiah" Addams speaks of the prophet's vision of peace as being attainable only if men forsake "the gains of oppression" and respond "to the cause of the poor." She ends her chapter affirming that "an enlightened industrialism" would help to define peace not only in negative terms as "an absence of war" but also as "the unfolding of worldwide processes making for the nurture of human life." Once again Addams tries to strike a compromise between the demands of labor and management; the phrase "enlightened industrialism" positions the author, like the majority of the Progressives, as functioning within the capitalist economy. Addams's reformist creed did not target the system to overthrow it; on the contrary, it sought to prevent conflicts and promote a more harmonious society.

Essential Themes

Around the time Addams's essay was written women were engaged in the struggle for equal rights, and even though some states had granted women the right to vote by 1907 there were still significant barriers in place preventing women from being equal to men in society and under the law. Regardless of the progress some states were seeing in terms of women's suffrage, some powerful political forces and certain portions of the male population were not in favor of the advancement of women in society. Because of this, attempts to become more civically engaged were becoming a top priority for many women. Due to industrialization, men were more frequently drawn away from the home for work, and women began to focus on public welfare and improving their own position within society. Many women believed their job was to take care of the home, and for these women home referred to the surrounding communities in which they lived. These women believed they had an obligation to not only make advancements for themselves both socially and politically, but many felt they had a responsibility to look out for the welfare of children and poverty-stricken individuals in society. Women in this time period were in need of a role model and leader, many of whom looked to Jane Addams to fill this role.

Jane Addams was viewed as a charismatic leader of the Progressive party, and was nationally revered as a woman to be respected. Her social work was highly regarded, and her dedication to women's equality was unquestionable. In this period of time when men were dominant in politics and some of these men were dedicated to keeping women oppressed and unequal, Addams's focus never faltered. Addams managed to become a prominent fixture in the political realm, as evidenced by her 1912 endorsement of Roosevelt's presidential nomination on behalf of all American women. While her political agenda was evident, her focus extended well beyond the scope of electoral politics, as she wrote prolifically about issues such as peace, education, faith, and prostitution. She was involved with the peace movement during World War I, and encouraged others to embrace a pacifist ideology. Her tireless efforts to aid the plight of women, children, and those in need, as well as her work towards causing social change and encouraging peace positioned Addams to become a heroine to many.

The work of Jane Addams had a tremendously positive impact on the fight for women's equality, and the promotion of Progressive ideals and values. While Addams was certainly not the only women fighting for these principles, she was successful in capturing the nation's attention, which proved to be a valuable resource in the struggle for social change. By gaining national attention and earning the support and respect of those who also wished to see social change, many found themselves in improved social, economic, and political situations. Addams and those who agreed with, and supported her efforts, found themselves able to influence the government to intervene in the lives of individuals to make positive changes. While it will never be completely possible to know exactly the degree to which Addams influenced societal change, it is clear that her efforts helped many embrace the idea of Progressive reforms in this country.

—*Luca Prono, Amber R. Dickinson*

Bibliography and Additional Reading

Conway, Jill. "Jane Addams: An American Heroine." *Daedalus* 93, no. 2 (1964): 761–80.

Miller, Grant. "Women's Suffrage, Political Responsiveness, and Child Survival in American History." *The Quarterly Journal of Economics* 123, no. 3 (2008): 1287–1327.

Seigfried, Charlene Haddock. "The Social Self in Jane Addams' Prefaces and Introductions." *Transactions of the Charles S. Peirce Society: A Quarterly Journal in American Philosophy* 49, no. 2 (2013): 127–56.

■ Eugene V. Debs: Antiwar Speech

Date: 1918
Author: Eugene V. Debs
Genre: Speech

Summary Overview

The American trade union leader, orator, and Socialist Party activist Eugene Debs was a master at making what might today look like radical political ideas seem as American as apple pie. A student of history as well as politics, Debs regularly invoked the memory of the Founding Fathers to make his policy suggestions seem more acceptable. Motivated by an unyielding sense of justice, he often tried to shame authorities to do what he thought was right. Whether addressing audiences at a labor rally or on the campaign trail, Debs invariably came back to a sharp critique of the American political system, touting the virtues of his brand of Socialism. His goal as a politician was not necessarily to win elections but instead to inspire listeners by his own example and to win converts to the Socialist cause. In a country with no Socialist legacy—unlike many European countries where Socialism was established—it is really quite remarkable that Debs had any success at all as a politician. That success was due in no small part to the power of Debs's oratory and prose. In his 1918 Antiwar Speech, Debs associates military warfare with class warfare.

Defining Moment

Notions built around socialist utopianism first developed in the United States in the early 1800s, but it wasn't until after the Civil War, following a large wave of European, especially German immigration, did modern, Marxist-inspired socialism first take root. Several socialist parties were established in the 1870s, including the Social Democratic Party of North America, the Workingmen's Party of the United States, and the Socialist Labor Party. Although socialist sentiment was strong throughout the rapidly industrializing United States, few workers wanted to abandon the Democratic or Republican parties for groups, often negatively associated with anarchism and immigration. Many American socialists instead began to work actively in trade unionism, founding organizations such as the American Federation of Labor in 1886. Although activists did support the aims of organized labor, they objected to its strategies, and this, along with the overwhelmingly German makeup of the socialist parties, and strong nativist and antisocialist sentiment

throughout the nation, created a division among the various leftist workers groups. It wasn't until 1901 that the disparate socialist groups and organized labor began to come together under the leadership of Eugene V. Debs and his newly formed Socialist Party of America.

Debs, a native-born worker who had battled fiercely against the railroads at the tailend of the nineteenth century, was a fiery and passionate orator, who although controversial, was able to appeal to a broader swath of American workers, effectively reinventing the socialist movement away from its origins as a mainly immigrant phenomenon. Drawing on American symbolism and history, Debs argued for a wholly American socialism, one that placed social and economic justice as central to the promise of the nation's founding. With Debs as the new face of the movement, socialist leaders drew ever greater ties to the union movement, often helping to fund and organize strikes and work stoppages. With the rise of socialism in Europe and ongoing labor unrest at home, many leading capitalists and politicians began to view the American socialist movement as a threat and began to take ever greater steps to curb its growth. Things came to a head with America's entry into World War I, as socialists, Debs among them, took a strong antidraft and antiwar position. For socialist leaders, the Great War was just another struggle begun by the master classes for which the powerless were to give their lives. As socialists staged antiwar demonstrations, the United States government passed laws meant to treat such protests as a form of treason.

As with most of his speeches, Debs' antiwar address is directed primarily at industrial workers, those most likely to toil away in factories to build what Franklin Roosevelt would one day call the "arsenal for democracy," or to be sent to fight and die in the trenches of Europe. On the one hand, Debs was attempting to stoke the fires of Socialist revolution, by rallying workers and the poor against what he saw as the exploitation of the powerless by a callous capitalist elite. On the other hand, he was trying to shift the American political system to be more inclusive and democratic by challenging the near universal presupposition that the Great War was a just war. For Debs, only Socialism offered an escape from the

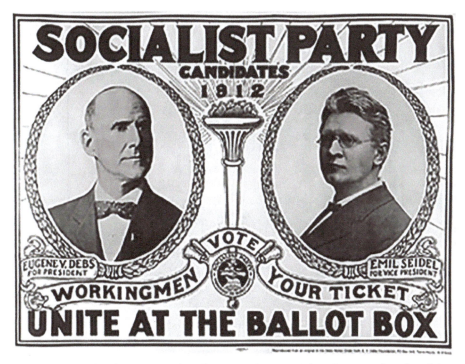

Campaign poster from his 1912 presidential campaign featuring Debs and vice presidential candidate, Emil Seidel.

Debs speaking in Canton, Ohio, in 1918. He was arrested for sedition shortly thereafter.

Cartoon showing U.S. Socialist Presidential candidate, who ran from in prison in the 1920 election. This cartoon depicts Eugene V. Debs and his quest for the presidency. Debs campaigned while in jail saying: "Anyhow, there are worse places than a front porch!" (a reference to Warren G. Harding's "front porch campaign"). A sign reads: Yours for The Presidency Eugene V. Debs ("Yours for the Presidency" echoes "Yours for the Revolution," a popular sign-off within Socialist circles of the period.) In his pocket, Debs has a paper marked "Speech" (Cartoon by Clifford K. Berryman)

Eugene V. Debs, Max Eastman, and Rose Pastor Stokes in 1918.

endless cycle of war and exploitation, and only socialism offered the powerless true equality within the state.

Author Biography

Eugene Victor Debs was a trade union leader, orator, and frequent Socialist Party candidate for the presidency of the United States. He was born in Terre Haute, Indiana, in 1855. While working his way up through the hierarchy of the Brotherhood of Locomotive Firemen, an important railroad union, he was elected city clerk in Terre Haute in 1879. He also served one term in the Indiana state legislature in 1885. In 1893 Debs cofounded the American Railway Union (ARU), an industrial union that, unlike most exclusive railroad brotherhoods of the era, admitted railroad workers of all skill levels. As the leader of that organization, Debs led the infamous Pullman strike of 1894.

The Pullman strike was an effort to organize workers at the Pullman Palace Car Company of Pullman, Illinois. As part of the strike, ARU members nationwide decided to boycott all trains that carried the company's famous sleeping cars in an effort to force them to recognize the union. As a result, rail traffic stopped nationwide. In response, railroad companies deliberately placed mail cars on trains with Pullman Palace Cars in order to encourage government intervention in the dispute. The legal injunction issued by a federal judge in response to the boycott essentially shut down the strike and destroyed the union. In 1895, Debs was convicted of interfering with the mail as a result of his refusal to abide by that injunction. Debs's political views were greatly affected by the Socialist literature he read during his short stay in jail. Indeed, this incarceration would prove to be the pivotal point of his entire life.

Upon his release, Debs announced his conversion to Socialism. He also changed career paths from being a trade union leader to being a political leader. Debs would serve as a Socialist Party presidential candidate five times: 1900, 1904, 1908, 1912, and 1920. His best showing occurred in 1912 when he came close to garnering a million votes. That was 6 percent of the total votes cast in that election. In 1918, Debs was convicted of sedition for a speech he had given in Canton, Ohio, earlier that year. Debs had to run his final campaign for president as a protest candidate from his jail cell. A famous campaign button from 1920 read "For President—Convict No. 9653." Between elections Debs toured the country giving speeches and writing articles that critiqued the American capitalist system and championed the cause of Socialism. Debs died in 1926 at the age of seventy.

Debs represented a vision of Socialism in America that got lost in the anti-Communist hysteria of the Cold War era. His political beliefs, though Socialist, were grounded in American ideals like justice, equal rights, and Christianity. Debs's willingness to go to prison for the causes he championed greatly increased his appeal and the popularity of his ideas. While many other figures in American socialism were immigrants from European countries like Germany, where Socialism was more in the mainstream, Debs attracted native-born Americans to the Socialist cause. His success as a politician came as the result of hundreds of thousands of Americans entertaining the possibility of radical change in American life in an era when the adverse effects of industrialization had made them unhappy with the existing political system.

HISTORICAL DOCUMENT

Comrades, friends and fellow-workers, for this very cordial greeting, this very hearty reception, I thank you all with the fullest appreciation of your interest in and your devotion to the cause for which I am to speak to you this afternoon.

To speak for labor; to plead the cause of the men and women and children who toil; to serve the working class, has always been to me a high privilege; a duty of love....

I realize that, in speaking to you this afternoon, there are certain limitations placed upon the right of free speech. I must be exceedingly careful, prudent, as to what I say, and even more careful and prudent as to how I say it. I may not be able to say all I think; but I am not going to say anything that I do not think. I would rather a thousand times be a free soul in jail than to be a sycophant and coward in the streets....

If it had not been for the men and women who, in the past, have had the moral courage to go to jail, we would still be in the jungles....

There is but one thing you have to be concerned about, and that is that you keep foursquare with the principles of the international Socialist movement. It is only when you begin to compromise that trouble begins. So far as I am concerned, it does not matter what others may say, or think, or do, as long as I am sure that I am right with myself and the cause. There are so many who seek refuge in the popular side of a great question. As a Socialist, I have long since learned how to stand alone. For the last month I have been traveling over the Hoosier State; and, let me say to you, that, in all my connection with the Socialist movement, I have never seen such meetings, such enthusiasm, such unity of purpose; never have I seen such a promising outlook as there is today, notwithstanding the statement published repeatedly that our leaders have deserted us. Well, for myself, I never had much faith in leaders. I am willing to be charged with almost anything, rather than to be charged with being a leader. I am suspicious of leaders, and especially of the intellectual variety. Give me the rank and file every day in the week. If you go to the city of Washington, and you examine the pages of the Congressional Directory, you will find that almost all of those corporation lawyers and cowardly politicians, members of Congress, and misrepresentatives of the masses—you will find that almost all of them claim, in glowing terms, that they have risen from the ranks to places of eminence and distinction. I am very glad I cannot make that claim for myself. I would be ashamed to admit that I had risen from the ranks. When I rise it will be with the ranks, and not from the ranks....

They tell us that we live in a great free republic; that our institutions are democratic; that we are a free and self-governing people. This is too much, even for a joke. But it is not a subject for levity; it is an exceedingly serious matter....

Wars throughout history have been waged for conquest and plunder. In the Middle Ages when the feudal lords who inhabited the castles whose towers may still be seen along the Rhine concluded to enlarge their domains, to increase their power, their prestige and their wealth they declared war upon one another. But they themselves did not go to war any more than the modern feudal lords, the barons of Wall Street go to war. The feudal barons of the Middle Ages, the economic predecessors of the capitalists of our day, declared all wars. And their miserable serfs fought all the battles. The poor, ignorant serfs had been taught to revere their masters; to believe that when their masters declared war upon one another, it was their patriotic duty to fall upon one another and to cut one another's throats for the profit and glory of the lords and barons who held them in contempt. And that is war in a nutshell. The master class has always declared the wars; the subject class has always fought the battles. The master class has had all to gain and nothing to lose, while the subject class has had nothing to gain and all to lose—especially their lives.

They have always taught and trained you to believe it to be your patriotic duty to go to war and to have yourselves slaughtered at their command. But in all the history of the world you, the people, have never had a voice in declaring war, and strange as it certainly appears, no war by any nation in any age has ever been declared by the people.

And here let me emphasize the fact—and it cannot be repeated too often—that the working class who fight all the battles, the working class who make the supreme sacrifices, the working class who freely shed their blood and furnish the corpses, have never yet had a voice in either declaring war or making peace. It is the ruling class that invariably does both. They alone declare war and they alone make peace....

If war is right let it be declared by the people. You who have your lives to lose, you certainly above all others have the right to decide the momentous issue of war or peace....

The heart of the international Socialist never beats a retreat.

They are pressing forward, here, there and everywhere, in all the zones that girdle the globe. Everywhere these awakening workers, these class-conscious proletarians, these hardy sons and daughters of honest toil are proclaiming the glad tidings of the coming emancipation, everywhere their hearts are attuned to the most sacred cause that ever challenged men and women to action in all the history of the world. Everywhere they are moving toward democracy and the dawn; marching toward the sunrise, their faces all aglow with the light of the coming day. These are the Socialists, the most zealous and enthusiastic crusaders the world has ever known. They are making history that will light up the horizon of coming generations, for their mission is the emancipation of the human race. They have been reviled; they have been ridiculed, persecuted, imprisoned and have suffered death, but they have been sufficient to themselves and their cause, and their final triumph is but a question of time.

Do you wish to hasten the day of victory? Join the Socialist Party! Don't wait for the morrow. Join now! Enroll your name without fear and take your place where you belong. You cannot do your duty by proxy. You have got to do it yourself and do it squarely and then as you look yourself in the face you will have no occasion to blush. You will know what it is to be a real man or woman. You will lose nothing; you will gain everything. Not only will you lose nothing but you will find something of infinite value, and that something will be yourself. And that is your supreme need—to find yourself—to really know yourself and your purpose in life.

You need at this time especially to know that you are fit for something better than slavery and cannon fodder. You need to know that you were not created to work and produce and impoverish yourself to enrich an idle exploiter. You need to know that you have a mind to improve, a soul to develop, and a manhood to sustain....

To turn your back on the corrupt Republican Party and the still more corrupt Democratic Party—the gold-dust lackeys of the ruling class—counts for still more after you have stepped out of those popular and corrupt capitalist parties to join a minority party that has an ideal, that stands for a principle, and fights for a cause. This will be the most important change you have ever made and the time will come when you will thank me for having made the suggestion....

There are few men who have the courage to say a word in favor of the I.W.W. I have. Let me say here that I have great respect for the I.W.W. Far greater than I have for their infamous detractors.... It is only necessary to label a man "I.W.W." to have him lynched as they did Praeger, an absolutely innocent man. He was a Socialist and bore a German name, and that was his crime. A rumor was started that he was disloyal and he was promptly seized and lynched by the cowardly mob of so-called "patriots."

War makes possible all such crimes and outrages. And war comes in spite of the people. When Wall Street says war the press says war and the pulpit promptly follows with its Amen. In every age the pulpit has been on the side of the rulers and not on the side of the people. That is one reason why the preachers so fiercely denounce the I.W.W....

Political action and industrial action must supplement and sustain each other. You will never vote the Socialist republic into existence. You will have to lay its foundations in industrial organization. The industrial union is the forerunner of industrial democracy. In the shop where the workers are associated is where industrial democracy has its beginning. Organize according to your industries! Get together in every department of industrial service! United and acting together for the common good your power is invincible.

When you have organized industrially you will soon learn that you can manage as well as operate industry. You will soon realize that you do not need the idle masters and exploiters. They are simply parasites. They do not employ you as you imagine but you employ them to take from you what you produce, and that is how they function in industry. You can certainly dispense with them in that capacity. You do not need them to depend upon for your jobs. You can never be free while you work and live by their sufferance. You must own your own tools and then you will control your own jobs, enjoy the products of your own labor and be free men instead of industrial slaves.

Organize industrially and make your organization complete. Then unite in the Socialist Party. Vote as you strike and strike as you vote.

Your union and your party embrace the working class. The Socialist Party expresses the interests, hopes and aspirations of the toilers of all the world.

GLOSSARY

bore a German name, and that was his crime: reference to the widespread paranoia of the time regarding Germans and eastern Europeans, seen by many to be terrorists and spies

class-conscious: aware of one's role in what Debs saw as the historic struggle between the workers and the capitalists

comrades: a term used at the time by a wide spectrum on the far left to indicate brotherhood in the international workers' movement

industrial democracy: a system of government whereby the workers act as a single union and thereby effectively control the government

proletarians: industrial workers

sycophant: a submissive flatterer; someone who plays up to the rich and powerful for personal gain

SUPPLEMENTAL HISTORICAL DOCUMENT

E. V. Debs

Statement to the Court Upon Being Convicted of Violating the Sedition Act

Delivered: September 18, 1918

September 18, 1918

Your Honor, years ago I recognized my kinship with all living beings, and I made up my mind that I was not one bit better than the meanest on earth. I said then, and I say now, that while there is a lower class, I am in it, and while there is a criminal element I am of it, and while there is a soul in prison, I am not free.

I listened to all that was said in this court in support and justification of this prosecution, but my mind remains unchanged. I look upon the Espionage Law as a despotic enactment in flagrant conflict with democratic principles and with the spirit of free institutions…

Your Honor, I have stated in this court that I am opposed to the social system in which we live; that I believe in a fundamental change—but if possible by peaceable and orderly means…

Standing here this morning, I recall my boyhood. At fourteen I went to work in a railroad shop; at sixteen I was firing a freight engine on a railroad.

I remember all the hardships and privations of that earlier day, and from that time until now my heart has been with the working class. I could have been in Congress long ago. I have preferred to go to prison…

I am thinking this morning of the men in the mills and the factories; of the men in the mines and on the railroads. I am thinking of the women who for a paltry wage are compelled to work out their barren lives; of the little children who in this system are robbed of their childhood and in their tender years are seized in the remorseless grasp of Mammon and forced into the industrial dungeons, there to feed the monster machines while they themselves are being starved and stunted, body and soul. I see them dwarfed and diseased and their little lives broken and blasted because in this high noon of Christian civilization money is still so much more important than the flesh and blood of childhood. In very truth gold is god today and rules with pitiless sway in the affairs of men.

In this country—the most favored beneath the bending skies—we have vast areas of the richest and most fertile soil, material resources in inexhaustible abundance, the most marvelous productive machinery on earth, and millions of eager workers ready to apply their labor to that machinery to produce in abundance for every man, woman, and child—and if there are still vast numbers of our people who are the victims of poverty and whose lives are an unceasing struggle all the way from youth to old age, until at last death comes to their rescue and lulls these hapless victims to dreamless sleep, it is not the fault of the Almighty: it cannot be charged to nature, but it is due entirely to the outgrown social system in which we live that ought to be abolished not only in the interest of the toiling masses but in the higher interest of all humanity…

I believe, Your Honor, in common with all Socialists, that this nation ought to own and control its own industries. I believe, as all Socialists do, that all things that are jointly needed and used ought to be jointly owned—that industry, the basis of our social life, instead of being the private property of a few and operated for their enrichment, ought to be the common property of all, democratically administered in the interest of all…

I am opposing a social order in which it is possible for one man who does absolutely nothing that is useful to amass a fortune of hundreds of millions of dollars, while millions of men and women who work all the days of their lives secure barely enough for a wretched existence.

This order of things cannot always endure. I have registered my protest against it. I recognize the feebleness of my effort, but, fortunately, I am not alone. There are multiplied thousands of others who, like myself, have come to realize that before we may truly enjoy the blessings of civilized life, we must reorganize society upon a mutual and cooperative basis; and to this end we have organized a great economic and political movement that spreads over the face of all the earth.

There are today upwards of sixty millions of Socialists, loyal, devoted adherents to this cause, regardless of nationality, race, creed, color, or sex. They are all making common cause. They are spreading with tireless energy the propaganda of the new social order. They are waiting, watching, and working hopefully through all the hours of the day and the night. They are still in a minority. But they have learned how to be patient and to bide their time. The feel—they know, indeed—that the time is coming, in spite of all opposition, all persecution, when this emancipating gospel will spread among all the peoples, and when this minority will become the triumphant majority and, sweeping into power, inaugurate the greatest social and economic change in history.

In that day we shall have the universal commonwealth—the harmonious cooperation of every nation with every other nation on earth…

Your Honor, I ask no mercy and I plead for no immunity. I realize that finally the right must prevail. I never so clearly comprehended as now the great struggle between the powers of greed and exploitation on the one hand and upon the other the rising hosts of industrial freedom and social justice.

I can see the dawn of the better day for humanity. The people are awakening. In due time they will and must come to their own.

When the mariner, sailing over tropic seas, looks for relief from his weary watch, he turns his eyes toward the southern cross, burning luridly above the tempest-vexed ocean. As the midnight approaches, the southern cross begins to bend, the whirling worlds change their places, and with starry fingerpoints the Almighty marks the passage of time upon the dial of the universe, and though no bell may beat the glad tidings, the lookout knows that the midnight is passing and that relief and rest are close at hand. Let the people everywhere take heart of hope, for the cross is bending, the midnight is passing, and joy cometh with the morning.

Source: *Marxists Internet Archive*

Document Analysis

Debs began a speaking tour because the Socialist press that he had depended upon to distribute his writings was wiped out by government censorship. In 1917 and 1918 America passed the Espionage and Sedition Acts, which made expressing spoken and written opposition to both the war and the government that waged it a federal crime. Debs knew he was risking his already failing health and his freedom by speaking out. He toured anyway. The words that Debs spoke at Nimisilla Park in Canton, Ohio, before twelve hundred people were little different from the ones he had spoken at earlier stops on his tour. What made this speech different was the presence of a government stenographer and the willingness of the local U.S. attorney, E. S. Wertz, to prosecute Debs (against the advice of Wertz's superiors) for what he said.

Much of the speech deals with specific controversies, like the case of the jailed trade unionist Tom Mooney, which do not resonate down to this day, but there are many passages in the text that demonstrate Debs's ability to inspire. For example, near the beginning of the speech, Debs jokes openly about the possibility of getting arrested. Indeed, he suggests that he would rather be arrested than remain silent about the injustice around him. His willingness to speak under threat of arrest was undoubtedly as important in inspiring his listeners as any particular phrase he spoke that day. Notably, much of the speech is devoted to attacks not just on the government but also on Wall Street. He attacks Wall Street for greed and shortsightedness in the exploitation of its employees. Debs is arguing that the worse conditions get, the better Socialism will do. In fact, Debs suggests that the triumph of Socialism in America is near, an argument that might have seemed strange at a time when Socialists and Socialism had been largely silenced by government repression.

In the speech, Debs repeats his long-standing critique of the two-party system. He calls both the Democratic and Republican parties corrupt, presumably because of their mutual embrace of the war. He recommends organizing along industrial lines, meaning workers from all skill levels, just as the American Railway Union (ARU) had done. He then suggests that joining the Socialist Party is the political equivalent of industrial organization. If your union embraces the working class, he suggests, your political party should too. While the positions of the Socialist Party were unpopular at the time, Debs argues that a brighter day would come as long as his listeners remained true to themselves.

It is also worth noting that Debs defended the Industrial Workers of the World (IWW) during his speech, despite his differences with the organization. "Let me say here that I have great respect for the I.W.W.," he told the crowd. "Far greater than I have for their infamous detractors." This is an excellent illustration of how the Left came together in the face of a common enemy, in this case the Wilson administration. In September 1917, months before Debs spoke, the U.S. Justice Department had simultaneously raided forty-eight IWW meeting halls across the country, arresting 165 leaders. While this did not destroy the organization entirely, it certainly rendered it incapable of effectively opposing the war. The example of the Wobblies could not have been far from Debs's mind when he spoke in Canton. That Debs spoke there (and elsewhere beforehand) is a testament to his courage.

In his two-hour speech, Debs made no direct reference to World War I, which raged in Europe at the time. Instead, he attacks war in general, most notably in this famous passage: "The master class has always declared the wars; the subject class has always fought the battles. The master class has had all to gain and nothing to lose, while the subject class has had nothing to gain and all to lose—especially their lives." That quotation is nothing but an eloquent way of associating military warfare with class warfare, a point that has been made many times since. Unfortunately for Debs, the government and much of the public were unwilling to accept any public opposition to a conflict that was, in fact, fairly unpopular compared with other wars throughout American history. Simply pointing out that different social classes are affected differently by war was enough to get Debs arrested.

As was the case after the Pullman strike, Debs did not deny the charges against him. "I wish to admit the truth of all that has been testified to in this proceeding," he told the jury that eventually convicted him. "I would not retract a word that I have uttered that I believe to be true to save myself from going to the penitentiary for the rest of my days." Indeed, Debs refused to mount any defense at all. Although he was convicted, he did not die in prison or even serve his entire ten-year sentence. Combat in World War I ended in 1918, but the United States did not sign a peace treaty to end the war formally until after Warren Harding became president in 1921. With peace officially at hand, Harding pardoned Debs and other political prisoners who had opposed the war, effective that Christmas. Debs was in poor health before he ever went to jail. His time in prison undoubtedly accelerated his decline.

Essential Themes

After delivering his two-hour speech against the war, Eugene Debs was promptly arrested for violation of the Espionage Act. In the trial that followed not long after, Debs offered no defense beyond an opening and closing statement in which he described his opposition to all war and stated, famously, "While there is a lower class, I am in it; while there is a criminal element, I am of it; while there is a soul in prison, I am not free." Debs was sentenced to ten years in prison, and although he was pardoned by Warren G. Harding after thirty-two months, the confinement took its toll. Already in poor health before the sentence, once he was freed he was never the same again. In 1924 Debs was nominated for the Nobel Peace Prize, but by that point had largely receded from public life. He died in 1926. Much like Debs himself, his Socialist movement also did not fully recover. Weakened by opposition to the war, and demonized by the inherent associations to Soviet Communism, American socialism, although resurgent with the New Deal and with the rise of the New Left in the 1960s, never became the force that leaders such as Debs had hoped. However, Debs himself became an inspiration to millions, his words echoed by politicians and activists to this present day. While Debs' attack on the two party system can be heard in the arguments of third parties across the political spectrum, his positions on social welfare and economic justice have become major planks in the modern Democratic Party, most clearly exemplified by the 2016 candidacy of Senator Bernie Sanders of Vermont. Although the place of Socialism and Socialist parties within the framework of American politics remains dubious, the ideas that Socialism, and Eugene V. Debs, inspired continue to resonate and motivate into the present day.

—*KP Dawes, Jonathan Rees*

Bibliography and Additional Reading

Chace, James. *Wilson, Roosevelt, Taft and Debs—The Election that Changed the Country*. New York: Simon and Schuster, 2009.

Debs, Eugene V. *Writings of Eugene V Debs: A Collection of Essays by America's Most Famous Socialist*. St. Petersburg, FL: Red and Black Publishers, 2009.

Debs, Eugene V. *Gentle Rebel: Letters of Eugene V. Debs*. Champaign: University of Illinois Press, 1995.

Freeberg, Ernest. *Democracy's Prisoner*. Cambridge, MA: Harvard University Press, 2009.

Ginger, Ray. *The Bending Cross: A Biography of Eugene Victor Debs*. Chicago: Haymarket Books, 2007.

Salvatore, Nick. *Eugene V. Debs: Citizen and Socialist*. Champaign: University of Illinois Press, 1984.

THIS man subjected himself to imprisonment and probably to being shot or hanged

THE prisoner used language tending to discourage men from enlisting in the United States Army

IT is proven and indeed admitted that among his incendiary statements were—

THOU shalt not kill

and

BLESSED are the peacemakers

Blessed are the Peacemakers *by George Bellows. Antiwar cartoon depicting Jesus with a halo in prison stripes alongside a list of his seditious crimes. First published in* The Masses *in 1917.*

■ Remarks by Scott Nearing at His Trial

Date: April 1918
Author: Scott Nearing
Genre: Testimony; speech; address

Summary Overview

This document is a speech concerning one man's right to free speech and the written word, made to publicize his point of view safely and lawfully. Scott Nearing was charged with hindering military service, insubordination, mutiny, and refusing to do his duty within the military. He was charged with these crimes because he produced a pamphlet promoting his own radical pacifist ideals during wartime, specifically during American involvement in World War I. This speech is his defense to the charges laid against him by the government of the United States. These charges all fell under the Espionage Act of 1917. Sometime after his trial, the Supreme Court stated that this act does not extend to or interfere with a person's right to free speech; Nearing's successful defense against such charges shows that, while his opinion may have been unpopular, he was still allowed to publish it according to his First Amendment rights.

Defining Moment

The Espionage Act of 1917 was passed on June 15, 1917 in response to the United States' entrance into World War I or The Great War, as it was called at the time. The act was created during the administration of President Woodrow Wilson and made any interference with soldiers or the war effort a crime. Even those suspected of such interference, such as passing along information to the enemies of the United States, could be prosecuted. In the case of Scott Nearing, he was prosecuted because he was an outspoken member of the pacifist community who printed and distributed pamphlets speaking out against the war and the government that had involved Americans in the struggle. Nearing was acquitted because he never overtly acted against the country; he simply made his own opinions public. But many times throughout history, the very act of speaking against the government has been seen as an act of sedition, and, therefore, a punishable offense. Fortunately in this case, Nearing was protected by the First Amendment and allowed to continue with his work.

This document shows how one man defended himself in the tense and troubling times of war against his own government, which feared that some of its own people might be working against its interests. There may have been good reason to pass the Espionage Act, as there were in fact German spies and their allies working within the United States in an effort to create disruptions that would lessen America's impact on the war. And, as with many such fears, innocent people began to fall within the sights of the men in charge of securing national safety. Furthermore, pacifists, as well as socialists, were becoming more and more vocal, especially those, such as Scott Nearing, who spoke publicly dozens of times a year. Pacifism and the war effort were mutually exclusive. This resulted in many pacifists, especially those with large followings, being viewed as detrimental to the war effort and seditious in their actions. Possibly the most famous case during this time was that of Eugene Debs, an outspoken Socialist, who was found guilty of sedition after giving speeches calling on people to resist the draft. Unlike Nearing, who simply promoted his own ideas, Debs attempted to organize others to work against the government and the war effort, resulting in his arrest and imprisonment.

Author Biography

Scott Nearing was born in 1883 in Pennsylvania and spent most of his life on the radical side of politics and economics, publishing his beliefs, and those of the many groups with which he was involved, in books and pamphlets. Nearing was a university professor, an extreme pacifist and a Socialist, before moving to Communism later in his life. He was a founding member of The People's Council of America for Democracy and Peace and also an active member of the Socialist Party of America. His ability to speak publicly and his desire for peace led him to speak against the American government on many occasions and continue his activism throughout both World Wars and the Cold War. Such staunch pacifism and his noncapitalist economic beliefs kept him at odds with the U.S. government, especially since he was not afraid to voice his opinions, having been known to write many letters to sitting presidents with his thoughts and opinions on world events. He continued such work until his death in 1983, just days after his one-hundredth birthday.

HISTORICAL DOCUMENT

Gentlemen, I am on trial here before you, charged with obstructing the recruiting and enlistment service to the detriment of the service, and with attempting and causing insubordination, disloyalty, mutiny and the refusal of duty within the military and naval forces….

The prosecution has not been able to show a single instance in which recruiting was obstructed. They have not been able to show a single instance in which insubordination, disloyalty, and refusal of duty were caused.

It has been seventeen or eighteen months since this pamphlet was published. During that time there have been about nineteen thousand copies of it loose in the country, and the prosecution was unable to bring before you a single instance where these things have actually occurred.

How then, do they seek to make out their case? Mr. Barnes said, in his opening:

> It is not necessary for the Government to show that there was an actual obstruction in the sense of a physical obstruction; it was not necessary for the Government to show actual mutiny and disloyalty, but the publication of this book in itself is sufficient to result in a conviction.

In other words, the Government maintains that the publication of this book, and the intent showed by the publication of the book, and by their surrounding evidence is sufficient to warrant a conviction….

I am charged, furthermore, with expressing further and other opinions in the pamphlet on militarism and in certain other ways, so that the whole crime of which I am supposed to be—according to the prosecution's case—guilty, the whole crime consists in my expression of opinion….

So that by convicting me for writing this book you convict me for public discussion, and you draw my intent from my discussion. On the same ground I think all of the opponents of any administration during the war might be convicted for opposing in any way the administration….

All through my life, I have been interested in preserving the institutions of democracy. That has been one of the things, as I tried to point out on the witness stand, that seem to me fundamentally important. I believe that democracy is a better form of social organization than aristocracy, or monarchy or any other form of Government that the world has ever known. Discussion is one of the purposes of democracy. Democracy means that a people talking a question over, thinking it out and reaching a decision upon it, may then register that decision.

The only way to have intelligent public opinion is to have discussion, and the moment you check discussion you destroy democracy….

The District Attorney was at considerable pains to prove to you that I am a Socialist. He asked me questions about the Socialist Party Platform; many questions, in order to prove that I am a Socialist. I am a Socialist.

I want to tell you something about what that means: in the first place, I am an internationalist; that is, I believe in the brotherhood of all men. In the language of the Declaration of Independence, I believe that all men are created equal, that they have certain rights to life, liberty and the pursuit of happiness. That holds true of the man that lives next door to me, and it holds true of the man that lives in South Africa, and the man that lives way over in Asia. I believe in the Brotherhood of Man …

During war, we ask people to go out and deliberately injure their fellows. We ask a man to go out and maim or kill another man against whom he has not a solitary thing in the world,—a man who may be a good farmer, a good husband, a good son, and a good worker, and a good citizen. Another man comes out and shoots him down; that is, he goes out and raises his hand against his neighbor to do his neighbor damage. That is the way society is destroyed.

I have been a student of public affairs. I am a Socialist. I am a pacifist. But I am not charged with any of these things as offenses. On the other hand I believe that as an American citizen I have a right to discuss public questions ... I have a right to oppose the passage of a law ... I have a right under the law, after the law is passed, to agitate for a development of public sentiment that will result in a repeal of that law.

In other words ... in a democracy, if we are to have a democracy, as a student of public affairs and as a Socialist and as a pacifist, I have a right to express my opinions. I may be wrong, utterly wrong, and nobody listen to me, nobody pay any attention to me. I have a right to express my opinions.

I am an American, my ancestors have been Americans for more than 200 years. As an American I have certain rights and certain duties. Among my rights under the First Amendment to the Constitution are the rights of free speech and the free press; the right to speak and print the convictions that I have. It was for those rights that our ancestors left Europe and came here. It is for those rights that some of us are contending today.

I do not care for the prosperity of this country if we are going to have gag laws. I care not for the wealth of this country if we are going to be forbidden to have free speech, and an opportunity for expressing our minds and expressing our opinions and discussing the great issues that are before us.... In America we want liberty. And I believe that as an American citizen, that is the dearest possession for which I can contend. That is my right constitutionally and legally. But if there were no constitution and no law, it would be my right as a member of a democratic society.

...Citizenship involves duties as well as rights.... When I believe that our country is in danger, our common life and our common liberties are in peril, then it is my duty to warn you, it is my duty to speak out and continue to speak out as long as I have an opportunity to do so....

Gentlemen, I want to say to you that I want to see America free. I want to see liberty, opportunity and democracy here, as well as in every other country on earth. As long as America is not free, you are not free and I am not free....

I have expressed my hopes, my ideals, my ambitions for liberty in America, and for brotherhood and peace among all people of the world. I have done what I could, and for the time being the matter is in your hands.

GLOSSARY

detriment: loss, damage, disadvantage, or injury

maim: to deprive of the use of some part of the body; cripple

mutiny: revolt or rebellion against constituted authority

Socialism: a theory or system of social organization that advocates the investing of ownership and control of production and distribution of capital, land, etc., in the community as a whole

Document Analysis

The bulk of this document is a man defending his right to free speech, a right guaranteed by the First Amendment of the Constitution of the United States of America. So the question becomes: If this is a right that is guaranteed, why was Scott Nearing put on trial? The answer to this question lies in the inherent tension between the individual and the government during a war. Nearing's defense lays out the charges, the evidence that the government has against him, and then explains his view about his rights and why the ability to speak his mind is central to democracy and should not be taken away because of fear during war.

Nearing openly admits that he published a pacifist pamphlet that called for Americans to abstain from the war effort. But that was the extent of his crime. Unlike other activists, Nearing contained his actions to the printing of reading material. The most interesting thing about the beginning of his defense is that he actually uses the prosecutor's, Mr. Barnes, own words against him. This was not simply to emphasize his case, but to show that government itself knew it had no real evidence. "[I]t was not necessary for the Government to show actual mutiny and disloyalty, but the publication of this book in itself is sufficient." This statement places the case directly in the realm of a fight over the First Amendment and what actions it protects in a wartime setting. As Nearing argues, "the whole crime consists in my expression of opinions." As Nearing and the judge and jury see it, this prosecution rests entirely on the idea that because someone expresses an opinion that stands in opposition to the government and its actions, that person is subject to punishment. If Nearing had, like Eugene Debs, accompanied his words with actions that directly hindered some aspect of the war, he would have been liable to lawful retribution. But this was not the case.

Nearing moves from speaking directly about his right to express his opinion to the broader topic of what it means to be an American and live in a democratic society. He speaks passionately and persuasively about many of the ideas that the founding fathers wished to protect when they created the Constitution. In order to continually better society, discussion must be not only allowed, but encouraged; otherwise it will stagnate and eventually waste away. Nearing also openly admits to being a Socialist, which was not a crime, although it was considered in a negative light. But Nearing owns his party affiliation and explains that he believes in people, in their equality and that such beliefs stand in direct opposition to war. To him, war is not a part of society, but the end of it. Furthermore, even though it is an unpopular opinion to hold during a war, it is still his right as an American to express this opinion. The beauty and most difficult part of the First Amendment is that no one has to agree with another person's opinion, but an individual is still allowed to speak, no matter how disagreeable his opinion. Nearing believed in this and his speech concludes elegantly by asking the members of the jury, and everyone in court, to uphold the rights guaranteed to Americans and to protect liberty in America.

Essential Themes

The most obvious short-term impact of this defense was Scott Nearing's acquittal and consequent return to regular life. But the effects were also more widely felt, as the Espionage Act would be used in many subsequent cases in order to secure the country from threats during wartime. Eventually, elements of the Espionage Act came to make up part of a federal code, which is still enforced today. This case, and cases like it, sparked debates concerning the extent of First Amendment rights and how people were allowed to express themselves when they were opposing the government and governmental actions. What is it to be a citizen? What are the responsibilities of a citizen? How far is the government allowed to go when prosecuting a citizen for expressing his or her opinions? Where is the line between expressing opinions and actively working against the government? These questions may seem familiar, as they are still debated today.

In the long term, this case is just one of decades' worth of cases that involve the Espionage Act, although it has now been altered and amended several times. These cases continue to come before courts, and understanding of the First Amendment continues to be redefined. Especially during war, when threats to the country and its citizens emerge, freedom becomes susceptible to harm, sometimes by the very government that is supposed to protect it. Speeches like Scott Nearing's serve as a reminder to readers that even though Nearing's own fight took place nearly one hundred years ago, he was dealing with many of the same issues we now confront, such as finding the balance between protecting people and oppressing them. Democracy is a fragile system, with both the people and the government having to work to check each other so that neither gains nor loses too much control. Figures such as Nearing provide examples of how that can be done, and Nearing's own speech reminds us that there are those who are willing to fight against their own government for the benefit of their country.

—*Anna Accettola*

Bibliography and Additional Reading

Carroll, Thomas F. "Freedom of Speech and of the Press in War Time: The Espionage Act." *The Michigan Law Review* 17 (1919): 621–665.

Chatfield, Charles. "World War I and the Liberal Pacifist in the United States." *The American Historical Review* 75 (1970): 1920–1937.

Nearing, Scott. *The Making of a Radical: A Political Autobiography.* Vermont: Chelsea Green Publishing, 2000.

Sherman, Steve, ed. *A Scott Nearing Reader: The Good Life in Bad Times.* Lanham, MD: Scarecrow Press, 1989.

■ The Sedition Act of 1918

Date: May 16, 1918
Author: Sixty-fifth U.S. Congress
Genre: Legislation

Summary Overview

When World War I broke out in Europe in 1914, the United States attempted to maintain its neutrality, but as the growing conflict threatened U.S. interests, President Woodrow Wilson petitioned Congress to strengthen the laws designed to protect national security. In 1917, Congress passed the Espionage Act, which enumerated a broad list of prohibited activities and imposed fines, imprisonment, and even death for individuals who willfully violated its provisions. Then in 1918, the legislature extended the Espionage Act by passing the Sedition Act, which further restricted speech and press in matters deemed related to national security and allowed the postmaster general to refuse delivery of any mail believed to violate the act's provisions. By the early 1920s, Congress had repealed many of the provisions within both acts, but not before the government prosecuted, jailed, or deported hundreds of individuals under those provisions.

Defining Moment

Shortly after the United States declared war on Germany in April 1917, the legislature passed the Espionage Act, authorizing harsh punishments for any actions, speech, or writings that willfully jeopardized national security or endangered the war effort. But as the war unfolded and fear of socialist and communist influence grew, the government felt growing pressure to further control any public expressions of antiwar sentiment. Passed in May 1918, the Sedition Act greatly expanded the prohibitions established by the Espionage Act, seemingly to include any speech or writing even vaguely antipatriotic.

The federal government prosecuted numerous leaders and antiwar activists under provisions of the Espionage Act and Sedition Act. Eugene V. Debs, a member of the Socialist Party who ran for U.S. president in 1904, 1908, and 1912, was arrested and prosecuted for the antiwar sentiments expressed in his June 16, 1818, speech in Canton, Ohio. He was convicted on the grounds that the speech obstructed military recruiting, and he was then sentenced to ten years in prison. He served nearly three of those years before President Warren G. Harding intervened to reduce his sentence and secure his release in December 1921. Additionally, a key provision of the Sedition Act allowed the postmaster general to refuse delivery of any mail believed to violate any provision of the act. This not only prevented antiwar and antidraft activists from sharing their message via mailed newsletters and pamphlets, but it also placed the creators of these messages in danger of prosecution and imprisonment.

Debate ensued over the sweeping provisions of both the Espionage Act and the Sedition Act, particularly those provisions that appeared to contradict the First Amendment's guarantee of free speech. However, the U.S. Supreme Court upheld the Sedition Act in the 1919 case *Abrams v. United States*. The defendants in *Abrams* had distributed leaflets criticizing the war and U.S. interference in the Russian Revolution, and they advocated a general strike among workers producing military goods. They were convicted under the Sedition Act for advocating "curtailment of production" of materials necessary for the war effort. Writing for the court, Justice John Hessin Clarke held that the conviction did not violate the defendants' First Amendment rights to free speech, because Congress deemed such activity to pose imminent danger to the United States. He cited Justice Oliver Wendall Holmes's opinion in the earlier *Schenck v. United States* to support this conclusion; however, Justice Holmes dissented in *Abrams*, arguing that the actions of the defendants in *Abrams* did not pose the same "clear and present danger" as did the *Schenck* defendants, and thus the conviction should not stand.

By March 1919, U.S. Attorney General Thomas Watt Gregory recommended that President Wilson pardon nearly two hundred prisoners who had been convicted under both the Espionage Act and the Sedition Act. Congress officially repealed the Sedition Act an

On July 20, 1917, Secretary of War Newton D. Baker, blindfolded, drew the first draft number in the lottery to be called up: Number 258. Those drafted were to serve in the American forces during World War I.

parts of the Espionage Act on December 13, 1920; other parts of the Espionage Act still exist in modified form, and the U.S. government continues to prosecute individuals under its provisions nearly one hundred years after its initial passing.

Author Biography

The Sixty-fifth U.S. Congress passed the Sedition Act on May 16, 1918. This Congress sat from March 4, 1917 until March 4, 1919, and oversaw significant legislation, including declaring war against Germany, establishing Liberty Bonds to finance the war, and passing both the Espionage Act and the Sedition Act.

Even before the United States joined World War I, President Woodrow Wilson encouraged the legislature to strengthen laws designed to protect national security. Shortly after the country declared war on Germany, the Sixty-fifth Congress passed the Espionage Act on June 15, 1917. Eleven months later, on May 16, 1918, it passed the Sedition Act, which amended the Espionage Act to prohibit an even broader array of activities that could jeopardize national security.

The Sedition Act was repealed in 1921, more than two years after the end of World War I and after numerous antiwar activists and suspected communist sympathizers were convicted, imprisoned, and sometimes deported under its provisions.

HISTORICAL DOCUMENT

Be it enacted, That section three of the [Espionage] Act ... approved June 15, 1917, be ... amended so as to read as follows:

Sec. 3. Whoever, when the United States is at war, shall willfully make or convey false reports or false statements with intent to interfere with the operation or success of the military or naval forces of the United States, or to promote the success of its enemies, or shall willfully make or convey false reports or false statements, or say or do anything except by way of bona fide and not disloyal advice to an investor or investors, with intent to obstruct the sale by the United States of bonds or other securities of the United States or the making of loans by or to the United States, and whoever when the United States is at war, shall willfully cause or attempt to cause, or incite or attempt to incite, insubordination, disloyalty, mutiny, or refusal of duty, in the military or naval forces of the United States, or shall willfully obstruct or attempt to obstruct the recruiting or enlistment services of the United States, and whoever, when the United States is at war, shall willfully utter, print, write or publish any disloyal, profane, scurrilous, or abusive language about the form of government of the United States or the Constitution of the United States, or the military or naval forces of the United States, or the flag of the United States, or the uniform of the Army or Navy of the United States into contempt, scorn, contumely, or disrepute, or shall willfully utter, print, write, or publish any language intended to incite, provoke, or encourage resistance to the United States, or to promote the cause of its enemies, or shall willfully display the flag of any foreign enemy, or shall willfully by utterance, writing, printing, publication, or language spoken, urge, incite, or advocate any curtailment of production in this country of any thing or things, product or products, necessary or essential to the prosecution of the war in which the United States may be engaged, with intent by such curtailment to cripple or hinder the United States in the prosecution of war, and whoever shall willfully advocate, teach, defend, or suggest the doing of any of the acts or things in this section enumerated, and whoever shall by word or act support or favor the cause of any country with which the United States is at war or by word or act oppose the cause of the United States therein, shall be punished by a fine of not more than $10,000 or the imprisonment for not more than twenty years, or both: Provided, That any employee or official of the United States Government who commits any disloyal act or utters any unpatriotic or disloyal language, or who, in an abusive and violent manner criticizes the Army or Navy or the flag of the United States shall be at once dismissed from the service....

Sec. 4. When the United States is at war, the Postmaster General may, upon evidence satisfactory to him that any person or concern is using the mails in violation of any of the provisions of this Act, instruct the postmaster at any post office at which mail is received addressed to such person or concern to return to the postmaster at the office at which they were originally mailed all letters or other matter so addressed, with the words "Mail to this address undeliverable under Espionage" plainly written or stamped upon the outside thereof, and all such letters or other matter so returned to such postmasters shall be by them returned to the senders thereof under such regulations as the Postmaster General may prescribe.

Document Analysis

Section 3 of the Sedition Act expands the prohibitions defined in Section 3 of the Espionage Act of 1917. Like the Espionage Act, the Sedition Act authorizes fines of up to $10,000 and imprisonment for up to twenty years for individuals who during times of war make false reports with intent to interfere with U.S. military operations, cause (or attempt to cause) insubordination within the military, or obstruct (or attempt to obstruct) military recruitment activity.

The Sedition Act also expanded the list of provisions to punish those who make false statements to obstruct the sale of U.S. bonds or securities; speak or print any "disloyal" language about the U.S. government, Constitution, military, military uniforms, or flag; display the flag of any foreign enemy; speak or print anything advocating the curtailment, with intent to hinder the U.S. success in the war, of the production of war materials; or advocate, teach, defend, or suggest that others do any of these prohibited acts. Even more broadly, this section allows for punishment of individuals who, by word or act, "support or favor the cause of any country with which the United States is at war" or who "oppose the cause of the United States therein."

Finally, Section 3 provides that any employee or official of the U.S. government who commits "any disloyal act or utters any unpatriotic or disloyal language," including criticizing the Army, Navy, or the U.S. flag, will be immediately dismissed from service.

Section 4 grants the postmaster general authority to refuse postal service access to anyone suspected of violating the Sedition Act. In conjunction with the local postmasters, the postmaster general can return any mail to its sender conspicuously marked with "Mail to this address undeliverable under the Espionage Act" if there is suspicion that its contents or its recipient might be in violation of any provision of the Sedition Act or its predecessor, the Espionage Act.

Essential Themes

Passed in April 1917, shortly after the United States declared war on Germany, the Espionage Act authorized harsh punishments for actions, speech, and writings deemed a threat to U.S. interests or national security. However, as fear of socialist and communist influences grew in the general public, vigilante citizen groups reacted to perceived threats and insufficient patriotism with increasing violence. To maintain control over the rapidly escalating situation, the federal government sought to expand its authority to intervene in matters it believed could pose a threat not just to national security, but also to public calm and welfare.

As a result, the following year, the legislature passed the Sedition Act, which greatly extended the prohibitions of the Espionage Act to include nearly any act,

utterance, or writing that even vaguely criticized the U.S. government or the war efforts. Expressing one's opinion about the unfairness of the draft could result in a decade-long prison sentence; even criticizing the U.S. military's uniforms could result in prosecution under the Sedition Act. These amendments did successfully extend the government's reach to prosecute any undesirable behavior or critical sentiments, but they also further fueled public fear and the persecution of suspected socialist and communist sympathizers— the first episode to become known as the Red Scare.

Additionally, Postmaster General Albert S. Burleson applied with gusto the new authority granted by Section 4: Working with the postmasters of several major cities, he blocked the mailing of several major socialist publications and facilitated the prosecution of their editors and writers. Initially, the Wilson administration encouraged his enthusiasm, as he successfully prevented dissemination of ideas that were critical of the war and used his nationwide network of postmasters to track and pursue dissenters. However, Burleson's enthusiastic efforts fell out of favor with President Wilson when Burleson began targeting some of the administration's supporters.

Despite the enthusiasm with which the federal government incarcerated and deported antiwar advocates and suspected communist sympathizers under its provisions, the Sedition Act was repealed on December 13, 1920.

—*Tracey M. DiLascio*

Bibliography and Additional Reading

Doenecke, Justus D. *Nothing Less Than War: A New History of America's Entry into World War I*. Lexington: University Press of Kentucky, 2011.

Holborn, Mark, and Hilary Roberts. *The Great War: A Photographic Narrative*. New York: Knopf, 2013.

Meyer, G. J. A World Undone: *The Story of the Great War, 1914–1918*. New York: Bantam, 2006.

Stevenson, David. *With Our Backs to the Wall: Victory and Defeat in 1918*. Cambridge: Harvard University Press, 2011.

■ *Schenck v. United States*

Date: 1919
Author: Oliver Wendell Holmes Jr.
Genre: Court opinion

Summary Overview

Oliver Wendell Holmes Jr., remains one of the most influential of American legal philosophers. His formulation of the "clear and present danger" test regarding the right to free speech in his opinion in *Schenck v. United States*, which was further refined in his dissent in *Abrams v. United States*, set the stage for the development of free speech law in America. Charles Schenck, secretary-general of the Socialist Party of America, had been charged with printing and distributing antidraft literature, thus violating the Espionage Act of 1917. He appealed his conviction on First Amendment grounds, but the court upheld the constitutionality of the Espionage Act and rejected the First Amendment protection of free speech—judging the legality of speech according to its tendency to provoke illegal acts.

Defining Moment

Because the First Amendment to the Constitution guarantees free speech rights to all people who are either born or become American citizens, the court's opinion in the Schenck case was applicable to all U.S. citizens. The ruling in this case would become the law of the land, and had the potential to impact free speech issues for many years following the decision. The court's "clear and present danger" test used in the Schenck case would ultimately be replaced in the court's decision-making process, but the ruling would nonetheless effectively place limits on an individual's First Amendment rights in the early 1900s. The right of free speech has long been regarded as one of the most valued rights citizens are granted, and the decision to either limit or extend speech rights has always been of significant interest to people throughout America. In more current times, the ruling in this case is significant to those who are interested in tracking the evolution of free speech rights in America and how that evolution, including the ruling in *Schenck v. United States*, plays a part in current free speech rights.

Author Biography

Oliver Wendell Holmes Jr., like many before him, believed John Marshall, the "Great Chief Justice," to be the one person who best embodied American law. But Holmes, for his part, so profoundly influenced American law during his own lifetime that many others, like the noted court historian Bernard Schwartz, believe that "it was Holmes, more than any other legal thinker, who set the agenda for modern Supreme Court jurisprudence."

Born in 1841 into what Oliver Wendell Holmes Sr.—himself a celebrated physician and writer—called "the Brahmin caste of New England," the younger Holmes spent much of his life struggling to free himself from the large shadow cast by his father. The Civil War presented him with an opportunity both to leave home and to distinguish himself in an endeavor outside his father's sphere. Holmes served with great distinction in the Union army. Seriously wounded three times, he was discharged after three years with the rank of brevet lieutenant colonel. He then returned to his father's home and, against the elder Holmes's wishes, enrolled in law school at Harvard University.

Holmes continued to live under his father's roof even after marrying at the relatively advanced age of thirty-one. During that period, Holmes assiduously applied himself to gaining distinction in the legal field, practicing as a litigator while at the same time pursuing legal scholarship as coeditor of the *American Law Review*. With the successful publication of his newly edited twelfth edition of James Kent's *Commentaries on American Law* in 1873, Holmes and his wife, Fanny, were finally able to move into a home of their own. Invited to deliver the prestigious Lowell Institute lectures in 1880, Holmes published them to great acclaim the following year as *The Common Law*, earning him such renown that he was soon invited to teach at Harvard Law School.

Holmes had been lecturing at Harvard for less than a year when he abruptly tendered his resignation. He had been appointed to the Supreme Judicial Court of Massachusetts a month earlier, but his university colleagues and students learned of his new position only upon reading about it in the newspapers. Holmes served as an associate justice of the state's highest tribunal for

ASSERT YOUR RIGHTS!

Article 6, Section 2, of the Constitution of the United States says: "This Constitution shall be the *supreme law of the Land*."

Article 1 (Amendment) says: "Congress shall make no law respecting an establishment of religion, or *prohibiting the free exercise thereof*."

Article 9 (Amendment) says: "The enumeration in the Constitution of certain rights, shall not be construed to deny or disparge others retained by the people:"

The Socialist Party says that any individual or officers of the law entrusted with the administration of conscription regulations, violate the provisions of the United States Constitution, the Supreme Law of the Land, when they refuse to recognize your right to assert your opposition to the draft.

If you are conscientiously opposed to war, if you believe in the commandment "thou shalt not kill," then that is your religion, and you shall not be prohibited from the free exercise thereof.

In exempting clergymen and members of the Society of Friends (popularly called Quakers) from active military service, the examination boards have discriminated against you.

If you do not assert and support your rights, you are helping to "deny or disparage rights" which it is the solemn duty of all citizens and residents of the United States to retain.

Here in this city of Philadelphia was signed the immortal Declaration of Independence. As a citizen of "the cradle of American Liberty" you are doubly charged with the duty of upholding the rights of the people.

Will you let cunning politicians and a mercenary capitalist press wrongly and untruthfully mould your thoughts? Do not forget your right to elect officials who are opposed to conscription.

In lending tacit or silent consent to the conscription law, in neglecting to assert your rights, you are (whether unknowingly or not) helping to condone and support a most infamous and insidious conspiracy to abridge and destroy the sacred and cherished rights of a free people. You are a citizen, not a subject! You delegate your power to the officers of the law to be used for your good and welfare, not against you.

They are your servants. Not your masters. Their wages come from the expenses of government which you pay. Will you allow them to unjustly rule you? The fathers who fought and bled to establish a free and independent nation here in America were so opposed to the militarism of the old world from which they had escaped; so keenly alive to the dangers and hardships they had undergone in fleeing from political, religious and military oppression, that they handed down to us "certain rights which must be retained by the people."

They held the spirit of militarism in such abhorrence and hate, they were so apprehensive of the formation of a military machine that would insidiously and secretly advocate the invasion of other lands, that they limited the power of Congress over the militia in providing only for the calling forth of "the militia to execute laws of the Union, suppress insurrections and repel invasions." (See general powers of Congress, Article 1, Section 8, Paragraph 15.)

No power was delegated to send our citizens away to foreign shores to shoot up the people of other lands, no matter what may be their internal or international disputes.

The people of this country did not vote in favor of war. At the last election they voted against war.

To draw this country into the horrors of the present war in Europe, to force the youth of our land into the shambles and bloody trenches of war-crazy nations, would be a crime the magnitude of which defies description. Words could not express the condemnation such cold-blooded ruthlessness deserves.

Will you stand idly by and see the Moloch of Militarism reach forth across the sea and fasten its tentacles upon this continent? Are you willing to submit to the degradation of having the Constitution of the United States treated as a "mere scrap of paper?"

Do you know that patriotism means a love for your country and not hate for others?

Will you be led astray by a propaganda of jingoism masquerading under the guise of patriotism?

No specious or plausible pleas about a "war for democracy" can becloud the issue. Democracy cannot be shot into a nation. It must come spontaneously and purely from within.

Democracy must come through liberal education. Upholders of military ideas are unfit teachers.

To advocate the persecution of other peoples through the prosecution of war is an insult to every good and wholesome American tradition.

"These are the times that try men's souls."

"Eternal vigilance is the price of liberty."

You are responsible. You must do your share to maintain, support and uphold the rights of the people of this country.

In this world crisis where do you stand? Are you with the forces of liberty and light or war and darkness?

(OVER)

Supreme Court of the United States Record, Schenck v. United States, Nos. 437–38 (S. Ct. May 3, 1918). The first page of the pamphlet at issue in the case.

LONG LIVE THE CONSTITUTION OF THE UNITED STATES

Wake Up, America! Your Liberties Are in Danger!

The 13th Amendment, Section 1, of the Constitution of the United States says: "Neither slavery nor involuntary servitude, except as a punishment for crime whereof the party shall have been duly convicted, shall exist within the United States, or any place subject to their jurisdiction.

The Constitution of the United States is one of the greatest bulwarks of political liberty. It was born after a long, stubborn battle between king-rule and democracy. (We see little or no difference between arbitrary power under the name of a king and under a few misnamed "representatives.") In this battle the people of the United States established the principle that freedom of the individual and personal liberty are the most sacred things in life. Without them we become slaves.

For this principle the fathers fought and died. The establishment of this principle they sealed with their own blood. Do you want to see this principle abolished? Do you want to see despotism substituted in its stead? Shall we prove degenerate sons of illustrious sires?

The Thirteenth Amendment to the Constitution of the United States, quoted above, embodies this sacred idea. The Socialist Party says that this idea is violated by the Conscription Act. When you conscript a man and compel him to go abroad to fight against his will, you violate the most sacred right of personal liberty, and substitute for it what Daniel Webster called "despotism in its worst form."

A conscript is little better than a convict. He is deprived of his liberty and of his right to think and act as a free man. A conscripted citizen is forced to surrender his right as a citizen and become a subject. He is forced into involuntary servitude. He is deprived of the protection given him by the Constitution of the United States. He is deprived of all freedom of conscience in being forced to kill against his will.

Are you one who is opposed to war, and were you misled by the venal capitalist newspapers, or intimidated or deceived by gang politicians and registrars into believing that you would not be allowed to register your objection to conscription? Do you know that many citizens of Philadelphia insisted on their right to answer the famous question twelve, and went on record with their honest opinion of opposition to war, notwithstanding the deceitful efforts of our rulers and the newspaper press to prevent them from doing so? Shall it be said that the citizens of Philadelphia, the cradle of American liberty, are so lost to a sense of right and justice that they will let such monstrous wrongs against humanity go unchallenged?

In a democratic country each man must have the right to say whether he is willing to join the army. Only in countries where uncontrolled power rules can a despot force his subjects to fight. Such a man or men have no place in a democratic republic. This is tyrannical power in its worst form. It gives control over the life and death of the individual to a few men. There is no man good enough to be given such power.

Conscription laws belong to a bygone age. Even the people of Germany, long suffering under the yoke of militarism, are beginning to demand the abolition of conscription. Do you think it has a place in the United States? Do you want to see unlimited power handed over to Wall Street's chosen few in America? If you do not, join the Socialist Party in its campaign for the repeal of the Conscription Act. Write to your congressman and tell him you want the law repealed. Do not submit to intimidation. You have a right to demand the repeal of any law. Exercise your rights of free speech, peaceful assemblage and petitioning the government for a redress of grievances. Come to the headquarters of the Socialist Party, 1326 Arch street, and sign a petition to congress for the repeal of the Conscription Act. Help us wipe out this stain upon the Constitution!

Help us re-establish democracy in America.
Remember, "eternal vigilance is the price of liberty.
Down with autocracy!
Long live the Constitution of the United States! Long live the Republic!

Books on Socialism for Sale at

SOCIALIST PARTY BOOK STORE AND HEADQUARTERS

1326 ARCH ST. Phone, Filbert 3121

(OVER)

25

Supreme Court of the United States Record, Schenck v. United States, *Nos. 437–38 (S. Ct. May 3, 1918).*
The second page of the pamphlet at issue in the case.

the next sixteen years. During much of that period he found the work trivial and repetitive, but he used the time to hone his style into the taut, epigrammatic form that would eventually earn him a place in the American legal pantheon. He also delivered a number of important public speeches, the most significant of which, "The Path of the Law" (1897) and "Law in Science and Science in Law" (1899), cemented his position as a pathbreaking legal realist who believed that law should be based on experience rather than on abstract principles and logic. In July 1899, when the chief justice of the Massachusetts Supreme Court died, Holmes was tapped to be his successor.

Holmes was not universally popular. His personal style was often characterized as combative, and in 1896 he had issued a notorious dissenting opinion in *Vegelahn v. Guntner*, arguing that furniture workers had a right to strike for better wages and hours, even at the expense of their employer, so long as they did so peacefully and without malice. Holmes's "actual malice" standard would later become a cornerstone of First Amendment law, but in 1902 his *Vegelahn* dissent threatened to derail a possible appointment to the U.S. Supreme Court. Finally, however, President Theodore Roosevelt overcame his qualms, and in August of that year, Holmes was nominated to succeed Horace Gray (who, like Holmes, had previously served on the Massachusetts Supreme Court) in occupying the court's "Massachusetts seat." Once again, Holmes declined to resign his previous post until the eleventh hour.

Holmes would serve on the court for thirty years, during which he authored 873 opinions—more than any other Supreme Court justice has written to date. The number of Holmes's dissents was proportionately low, but they were so eloquently and powerfully written that they have led to his being dubbed the "Great Dissenter." In what is perhaps his most celebrated opinion, his dissent in *Lochner v. New York* (1905), Holmes, joined by the maverick John Marshall Harlan, voted against the court's long-standing deference to the doctrine of substantive due process, arguing for New York State's right to enact legislation limiting work hours and against unbridled freedom of contract. Writing for the majority in *Schenck v. United States* (1919), Holmes declared that the right of free speech was not absolute, but that same year he refined his restrictive "clear and present danger" standard in his dissenting opinion in *Abrams v. United States*, excluding most political dissent from government suppression.

Holmes's reputation is not unblemished. He was farsighted, to be sure, but he was also very much a creature of his times. A disciple of social Darwinism—a theory adapted to human society from Charles Darwin's "survival of the fittest" theory of evolution—he also absorbed principles of eugenics, popular in his day. He may have believed that jurists were obliged to set personal prejudices aside when deciding cases, but all indications are that Holmes contentedly upheld, in *Buck v. Bell* (1927), the Virginia statute mandating the sterilization of "feeble-minded" individuals.

In April 1929, Holmes's wife of fifty-seven years died. Holmes stayed on the court, publicly celebrating his ninetieth birthday two years later, but then began to fail. Colleagues and friends hinted that it was time for him to leave, and on January 11, 1932, he did so, announcing only, "I won't be in tomorrow;" he submitted his resignation the following day. In 1935, two days before his ninety-fourth birthday, Holmes died of pneumonia in his home.

HISTORICAL DOCUMENT

The document in question, upon its first printed side, recited the first section of the Thirteenth Amendment, said that the idea embodied in it was violated by the Conscription Act, and that a conscript is little better than a convict. In impassioned language, it intimated that conscription was despotism in its worst form, and a monstrous wrong against humanity in the interest of Wall Street's chosen few. It said "Do not submit to intimidation," but in form, at least, confined itself to peaceful measures such as a petition for the repeal of the act. The other and later printed side of the sheet was headed "Assert Your Rights." It stated reasons for alleging that anyone violated the Constitution when he refused to recognize "your right to assert your opposition to the draft," and went on "If you do not assert and support your rights, you are helping to deny or disparage rights which it is the solemn duty of all citizens and residents of the United States to retain."

It described the arguments on the other side as coming from cunning politicians and a mercenary capitalist press, and even silent consent to the conscription law as helping to support an infamous conspiracy. It denied the power to send our citizens away to foreign shores to shoot up the people of other lands, and added that words could not express the condemnation such cold-blooded ruthlessness deserves,… winding up, "You must do your share to maintain, support and uphold the rights of the people of this country." Of course, the document would not have been sent unless it had been intended to have some effect, and we do not see what effect it could be expected to have upon persons subject to the draft except to influence them to obstruct the carrying of it out. The defendants do not deny that the jury might find against them on this point.

But it is said, suppose that that was the tendency of this circular, it is protected by the First Amendment to the Constitution. Two of the strongest expressions are said to be quoted respectively from well-known public men. It well may be that the prohibition of laws abridging the freedom of speech is not confined to previous restraints,

although to prevent them may have been the main purpose, as intimated in *Patterson v. Colorado*…. We admit that in many places and in ordinary times the defendants in saying all that was said in the circular would have been within their constitutional rights. But the character of every act depends upon the circumstances in which it is done…. The most stringent protection of free speech would not protect a man in falsely shouting fire in a theatre and causing a panic. It does not even protect a man from an injunction against uttering words that may have all the effect of force…. The question in every case is whether the words used are used in such circumstances and are of such a nature as to create a clear and present danger that they will bring about the substantive evils that Congress has a right to prevent. It is a question of proximity and degree. When a nation is at war many things that might be said in time of peace are such a hindrance to its effort that their utterance will not be endured so long as men fight and that no Court could regard them as protected by any constitutional right. It seems to be admitted that if an actual obstruction of the recruiting service were proved, liability for words that produced that effect might be enforced. The statute of 1917 in section 4 … punishes conspiracies to obstruct as well as actual obstruction. If the act, (speaking, or circulating a paper,) its tendency and the intent with which it is done are the same, we perceive no ground for saying that success alone warrants making the act a crime…. Indeed that case might be said to dispose of the present contention if the precedent covers all media concludendi. But as the right to free speech was not referred to specially, we have thought fit to add a few words.

It was not argued that a conspiracy to obstruct the draft was not within the words of the Act of 1917. The words are "obstruct the recruiting or enlistment service," and it might be suggested that they refer only to making it hard to get volunteers. Recruiting heretofore usually having been accomplished by getting volunteers, the word is apt to call up that method only in our minds. But recruiting is gaining fresh supplies for the forces, as well by draft

as otherwise. It is put as an alternative to enlistment or voluntary enrollment in this act.

GLOSSARY

media concludendi: grounds for asserting a right

Wall Street: a street in New York City where the New York Stock Exchange is located; more generally, the investment industry as a whole

Document Analysis

Charles Schenck, secretary-general of the Socialist Party of America, was charged with printing and distributing literature urging American men to resist the draft during World War I. A federal district court found Schenck guilty of having violated the 1917 Espionage Act, which outlawed interference with conscription. Schenck appealed his criminal conviction to the U.S. Supreme Court, questioning the constitutionality of the Espionage Act on First Amendment grounds. There was, he argued, a tradition in Anglo-American law of distinguishing between opinion and incitement to illegal action. His leaflet was a reflection of the debate then raging in American society about the justness of the war and, as such, was an expression of opinion. Rather than violence, it urged that those subject to the draft assert their rights by signing an anticonscription petition that would be forwarded to Congress.

Writing for a unanimous court, Justice Holmes upheld the constitutionality of the Espionage Act and Schenck's conviction. In considering First Amendment protection for any speech, he states, the court must consider not only the content of the speech but also its context. Whereas in some circumstances banning speech such as Schenck's leaflet might amount to prohibited prior restraint, in the context of wartime, such speech is akin to shouting "fire" in a crowded theater. In distributing his leaflets Schenck plainly intended to interfere with the draft, and such interference plainly violates the nation's settled right to draft citizens during time of war. Furthermore, the Espionage Act plainly applies to conspiracies as well as to actual obstruction of military activities; the intended action need not have actually succeeded to be prohibited. The test, Holmes memorably declares, is whether the words at issue

present a "clear and present danger" of provoking "substantive evils" that Congress is empowered to prevent.

Decided in 1919, *Schenck* was the court's first significant attempt to define what constitutes free speech under the First Amendment. Two schools of thought about the subject grew directly out of this case: Absolutists hold that the framers meant, literally, that "Congress shall make no law … abridging the freedom of speech," while others believe that an individual's right to be left alone must be balanced against compelling public necessity. For his part, Holmes's subsequent refinement of the "clear and present danger" test seems to indicate that his use of the phrase in *Schenck* had been casual. In two companion unanimous decisions to *Schenck*, *Frohwerk v. United States*, and *Debs v. United States*, Holmes used the same traditional "bad tendency" test—judging the legality of speech according to its tendency to provoke illegal acts—that he had employed in earlier free speech cases. It is arguable, then, that in *Schenck* he intended to equate the "clear and present danger" test with the "bad tendency" test. Within a few months, however, Holmes, together with Justice Louis D. Brandeis, would begin the process of refining the "clear and present danger" test in *Abrams v. United States* so that it would reflect his intention of providing greater legal latitude for dissident speech.

Essential Themes

In the early 1900s, there was significant opposition to efforts made by the government to draft soldiers for war efforts. Some people simply did not want to involuntarily fight in a war, but the government was committed to enforcing not only the draft, but the efforts created to enforce the draft and promote loyalty and obedience among American soldiers. This widespread opposition to the draft led Congress to create the Espionage Act, designed to punish those who were successful in their efforts to evade the draft. Over 2,000 individuals were charged with violating tenants of the act, and around 900 citizens served jail time for disobeying the law. The sentiments Schenck was promoting in his flier were not uncommon among the population at the time, as many felt the draft was a violation of their rights. Regardless of this, the government felt the promotion of the idea to protest the draft were a threat to the law established in the Espionage Act. Perhaps in a time of peace the government's response would have been different, and while Schenck's document was not a violent call to action it was the fact that America was in the middle of a war that made Schenck's actions so inflammatory.

For most citizens at the time, there was an assumption that because of the right to free speech outlined in the First Amendment a person had the ability to say anything they felt like saying. This case would challenge that misconception and introduce serious parameters to what is actually meant by a person's inherent right to free speech. Schenck's actions and the court's decision in the case firmly established that if a person's actions violated a law, the speech was not permissible regardless of what is stated in the Bill of Rights. Because Schenck's call to action, albeit peaceful, challenged the Espionage Act, Schenck's right to speak freely about his opposition to the draft was limited. The "clear and present danger" test used to make the decision in this case was later replaced by the language "imminent lawless action", meaning speech could be restricted if it was likely to result in actions violating laws.

As American citizens, we often assume we have an inherent right to say whatever we want to say, whenever we want to say it. The ruling in this case proves that is not necessarily so, and there are times when parameters may be placed on free speech rights. The Supreme Court's ruling in the Schenck case clearly places limitations on the right of free speech as guaranteed in the First Amendment to the Constitution. In this specific instance, the court found that Schenck's actions were not permissible because they took place during wartime. Had Schenck's ideas been presented during a time of peace, perhaps the tenants of the Espionage Act would not have been violated and therefore the information in the flier would not have been as inflammatory as the court found it to be. The court's ruling determined that a citizen's speech is not limitless, and the context of the times and the circumstances surrounding a person's speech may come into play when determining if certain types of speech will be allowed. This court ruling, and similar rulings that would follow, have established the precedent that while free speech is still a highly regarded and fiercely protected right, American citizens are subject to certain speech limitations.

—*Amber R. Dickinson, Lisa Paddock*

Bibliography and Additional Reading

Goodman, Mark. "First Amendment Tension: Advocacy and Clear and Present Danger." *Communication Law Review*, 2015.

Irons, Peter. *A People's History of the Supreme Court*. New York: Penguin Books, 1999.

Linde, Hans A. "Clear and Present Danger Reexamined: Dissonance in the Brandenburg Concerto." *Stanford Law Review*, 1970.

Strong, Frank R. "Fifty Years of "Clear and Present Danger": From Schenck to Brandenburg and Beyond." *The Supreme Court Review*, 1969.

■ *Abrams v. United States*

Date: Decided Nov. 10, 1919
Author: Justice Oliver Wendell Holmes
Genre: Court opinion

Summary Overview

As World War I was declining, a group of Russians living in America created and distributed pamphlets regarding the United States' involvement with the Russian Revolution. The pamphlets called out the actions of an "abusive President Wilson," denounced sending American troops to Russia, and called for Russian workers to strike. Two pamphlets were distributed by means of being thrown out of an open window. This distribution of information happened at a time when the government had placed stringent restrictions on civil liberties in America, with freedom of speech being specifically limited. The individuals, including Jacob Abrams, were detained, charged, and convicted for inciting resistance to the war efforts, which came with a sentence of around 20 years in prison. Regardless of the fact there was little evidence to suggest the pamphlets had been effective in their intent, the defendants were facing a serious punishment for their crime. In a 7–2 vote the court upheld the convictions of Abrams and the other defendants. Justice Clarke, writing for the majority, echoed Holmes' sentiments in earlier cases of the same nature. Shortly thereafter, Justice Holmes reconsidered his stance on First Amendment rights and wrote a passionate and eloquent dissent in defense of freedom of speech.

Defining Moment

Jacob Abrams was a Russian immigrant and anarchist living in New York City, where, amid the clamor of debate over U.S. involvement in World War I, he was arrested in August 1918. Abrams and several associates were charged with violating the Sedition Act of 1918 (an amendment to the 1917 Espionage Act) by writing, printing, and distributing two leaflets—one in English, one in Yiddish—denouncing President Woodrow Wilson for sending troops to fight in Soviet Russia. The Yiddish version also included a call for a general strike to protest U.S. interventionist policy. At trial in federal court, the leaflets were found to violate the Sedition Act's ban against language abusive to the government as well as its prohibition of speech intended to curtail the production of materials essential to the prosecution of the war.

Upon appeal, a seven-member majority of the U.S. Supreme Court voted to uphold Abrams's criminal conviction. Justice John H. Clarke, writing for the court, cited the "clear and present danger" test that Holmes had announced only months before in his opinion for the unanimous court in *Schenck v. United States*. But during the intervening period, Holmes had modified his perception of his own test, as spurred by the persecution of dissidents during the "red scare" that followed World War I as well as by a *Harvard Law Review* article. The article in question, by Zechariah Chafee, Jr., mistakenly claimed that Holmes had intended his new test to make punishment for the "bad tendency" of words to be impossible; but Holmes, in turn, used Chafee's argument to buttress his refinement of what constitutes a "clear and present danger" in his *Abrams* dissent, in which he was joined by Justice Brandeis.

Author Biography

Oliver Wendell Holmes Jr., like many before him, believed John Marshall, the "Great Chief Justice," to be the one person who best embodied American law. But Holmes, for his part, so profoundly influenced American law during his own lifetime that many others, like the noted court historian Bernard Schwartz, believe that "it was Holmes, more than any other legal thinker, who set the agenda for modern Supreme Court jurisprudence."

Born in 1841 into what Oliver Wendell Holmes Sr.—himself a celebrated physician and writer—called "the Brahmin caste of New England," the younger Holmes spent much of his life struggling to free himself from the large shadow cast by his father. The Civil War presented him with an opportunity both to leave home and to distinguish himself in an endeavor outside his father's sphere. Holmes served with great distinction in the Union army. Seriously wounded three times, he was discharged after three years with the rank of brevet lieutenant colonel. He then returned to his father's home and, against the elder Holmes's wishes, enrolled in law school at Harvard University.

Holmes continued to live under his father's roof even after marrying at the relatively advanced age of thirty-one. During that period, Holmes assiduously applied himself to gaining distinction in the legal field, practicing as a litigator while at the same time pursuing legal scholarship as coeditor of the *American Law Review*. With the successful publication of his newly edited twelfth edition of James Kent's *Commentaries on American Law* in 1873, Holmes and his wife, Fanny, were finally able to move into a home of their own. Invited to deliver the prestigious Lowell Institute lectures in 1880, Holmes published them to great acclaim the following year as *The Common Law*, earning him such renown that he was soon invited to teach at Harvard Law School.

Holmes had been lecturing at Harvard for less than a year when he abruptly tendered his resignation. He had been appointed to the Supreme Judicial Court of Massachusetts a month earlier, but his university colleagues and students learned of his new position only upon reading about it in the newspapers. Holmes served as an associate justice of the state's highest tribunal for the next sixteen years. During much of that period he found the work trivial and repetitive, but he used the time to hone his style into the taut, epigrammatic form that would eventually earn him a place in the American legal pantheon. He also delivered a number of important public speeches, the most significant of which, "The Path of the Law" (1897) and "Law in Science and Science in Law" (1899), cemented his position as a path-breaking legal realist who believed that law should be based on experience rather than on abstract principles and logic. In July 1899, when the chief justice of the Massachusetts Supreme Court died, Holmes was tapped to be his successor.

Holmes was not universally popular. His personal style was often characterized as combative, and in 1896 he had issued a notorious dissenting opinion in *Vegelahn v. Guntner*, arguing that furniture workers had a right to strike for better wages and hours, even at the expense of their employer, so long as they did so peacefully and without malice. Holmes's "actual malice" standard would later become a cornerstone of First Amendment law, but in 1902 his *Vegelahn* dissent threatened to derail a possible appointment to

the U.S. Supreme Court. Finally, however, President Theodore Roosevelt overcame his qualms, and in August of that year, Holmes was nominated to succeed Horace Gray (who, like Holmes, had previously served on the Massachusetts Supreme Court) in occupying the court's "Massachusetts seat." Once again, Holmes declined to resign his previous post until the eleventh hour.

Holmes would serve on the court for thirty years, during which he authored 873 opinions—more than any other Supreme Court justice has yet to write. The number of his dissents was proportionately low, but they were so eloquently and powerfully written that they have led to Holmes being dubbed the "Great Dissenter." In what is perhaps his most celebrated opinion, his dissent in *Lochner v. New York* (1905), Holmes, joined by the maverick John Marshall Harlan, voted against the court's long-standing deference to the doctrine of substantive due process, arguing for New York State's right to enact legislation limiting work hours and against unbridled freedom of contract. Writing for the majority in *Schenck v. United States* (1919), Holmes declared that the right of free speech was not absolute, but that same year he refined his restrictive "clear and present danger" standard in his dissenting opinion in *Abrams v. United States*, excluding most political dissent from government suppression.

Holmes's reputation is not unblemished. He was far-sighted, to be sure, but he was also very much a creature of his times. A disciple of social Darwinism—a theory adapted to human society from Charles Darwin's "survival of the fittest" theory of evolution—he also absorbed principles of eugenics, popular in his day. He may have believed that jurists were obliged to set personal prejudices aside when deciding cases, but all indications are that Holmes contentedly upheld, in *Buck v. Bell* (1927), the Virginia statute mandating the sterilization of "feeble-minded" individuals.

In April 1929, Holmes's wife of fifty-seven years died. Holmes stayed on the court, publicly celebrating his ninetieth birthday two years later, but then began to fail. Colleagues and friends hinted that it was time for him to leave, and on January 11, 1932, he did so, announcing only, "I won't be in tomorrow"; he submitted his resignation the following day. In 1935, two days before his ninety-fourth birthday, Holmes died of pneumonia in his home.

American troops parading in Vladivostok, August 1918. (National Archives)

HISTORICAL DOCUMENT

(Holmes dissent)

I am aware, of course, that the word intent as vaguely used in ordinary legal discussion means no more than knowledge at the time of the act that the consequences said to be intended will ensue. Even less than that will satisfy the general principle of civil and criminal liability. A man may have to pay damages, may be sent to prison, at common law might be hanged, if, at the time of his act, he knew facts from which common experience showed that the consequences would follow, whether he individually could foresee them or not. But, when words are used exactly, a deed is not done with intent to produce a consequence unless that consequence is the aim of the deed. It may be obvious, and obvious to the actor, that the consequence will follow, and he may be liable for it even if he regrets it, but he does not do the act with intent to produce it unless the aim to produce it is the proximate motive of the specific act, although there may be some deeper motive behind.

It seems to me that this statute must be taken to use its words in a strict and accurate sense. They would be absurd in any other. A patriot might think that we were wasting money on aeroplanes, or making more cannon of a certain kind than we needed, and might advocate curtailment with success, yet, even if it turned out that the curtailment hindered and was thought by other minds to have been obviously likely to hinder the United States in the prosecution of the war, no one would hold such conduct a crime. I admit that my illustration does not answer all that might be said, but it is enough to show what I think, and to let me pass to a more important aspect of the case. I refer to the First Amendment to the Constitution, that Congress shall make no law abridging the freedom of speech.

I never have seen any reason to doubt that the questions of law that alone were before this Court in the Cases of Schenck, Frohwerk, and Debs were rightly decided. I do not doubt for a moment that by the same reasoning that would justify punishing persuasion to murder, the United States constitutionally may punish speech that produces or is intended to produce a clear and imminent danger that it will bring about forthwith certain substantive evils that the United States constitutionally may seek to prevent. The power undoubtedly is greater in time of war than in time of peace because war opens dangers that do not exist at other times.

But as against dangers peculiar to war, as against others, the principle of the right to free speech is always the same. It is only the present danger of immediate evil or an intent to bring it about that warrants Congress in setting a limit to the expression of opinion where private rights are not concerned. Congress certainly cannot forbid all effort to change the mind of the country. Now nobody can suppose that the surreptitious publishing of a silly leaflet by an unknown man, without more, would present any immediate danger that its opinions would hinder the success of the government arms or have any appreciable tendency to do so. Publishing those opinions for the very purpose of obstructing, however, might indicate a greater danger and at any rate would have the quality of an attempt. So I assume that the second leaflet if published for the purposes alleged in the fourth count might be punishable. But it seems pretty clear to me that nothing less than that would bring these papers within the scope of this law. An actual intent in the sense that I have explained is necessary to constitute an attempt, where a further act of the same individual is required to complete the substantive crime.... It is necessary where the success of the attempt depends upon others because if that intent is not present the actor's aim may be accomplished without bringing about the evils sought to be checked....

In this case sentences of twenty years imprisonment have been imposed for the publishing of two leaflets that I believe the defendants had as much right to publish as the Government has to publish the Constitution of the United States now vainly invoked by them. Even if I am technically wrong and enough can be squeezed from these poor and puny anonymities to turn the color of legal litmus paper; I will add, even if what I think the necessary intent were shown; the most nominal punishment seems to me all that possibly could be inflicted, unless the defendants are to be made to suffer not for what the indictment alleges but for the creed that they avow....

Persecution for the expression of opinions seems to me perfectly logical. If you have no doubt of your premises or your power and want a certain result with all your heart you naturally express your wishes in law and sweep away all opposition. To allow opposition by speech seems to indicate that you think the speech impotent, as when a man says that he has squared the circle, or that you do not care whole heartedly for the result, or that you doubt either your power or your premises. But when men have realized that time has upset many fighting faiths, they may come to believe even more than they believe the very foundations of their own conduct that the ultimate good desired is better reached by free trade in ideas—that the best test of truth is the power of the thought to get itself accepted in the competition of the market, and that truth is the only ground upon which their wishes safely can be carried out. That at any rate is the theory of our Constitution. It is an experiment, as all life is an experiment. Every year if not every day we have to wager our salvation upon some prophecy based upon imperfect knowledge. While that experiment is part of our system I think that we should be eternally vigilant against attempts to check the expression of opinions that we loathe and believe to be fraught with death, unless they so imminently threaten immediate interference with the lawful and pressing purposes of the law that an immediate check is required to save the country. I wholly disagree with the argument of the Government that the First Amendment left the common law as to seditious libel in force. History seems to me against the notion. I had conceived that the United States through many years had shown its repentance for the Sedition Act of 1798, by repaying fines that it imposed. Only the emergency that makes it immediately dangerous to leave the correction of evil counsels to time warrants making any exception to the sweeping command, "Congress shall make no law abridging the freedom of speech." Of course I am speaking only of expressions of opinion and exhortations, which were all that were uttered here, but I regret that I cannot put into more impressive words my belief that in their conviction upon this indictment the defendants were deprived of their rights under the Constitution of the United States.

GLOSSARY

Debs: Eugene V. Debs, a Socialist American labor leader who was imprisoned for antiwar statements during World War I

Frohwerk: Jacob Frohwerk, who was fined and imprisoned for helping to prepare antidraft articles during World War I and whose appeal was denied in *Frohwerk v. United States*

litmus paper: paper that turns various colors to indicate the acidity or baseness of a substance

Document Analysis

Although the questions of law presented in *Schenck* were rightly decided, Holmes asserts, the basic principle of free speech is the same during war as it is in times of peace: Congress can prohibit speech only when it threatens to provoke immediate danger. In this case, "the surreptitious publishing of a silly leaflet by an unknown man" cannot be construed as threatening immediate danger—even in wartime, when the government does have, of necessity, greater latitude in prohibiting certain kinds of speech. The Sedition Act, meanwhile, requires that the same party responsible for performing a prohibited act also be responsible for forming the criminal intent behind the act; the kind of conspiracy of words outlawed in *Abrams* under the original Espionage Act cannot be a consideration here. Holmes goes on to say that persecution for the expression of opinion may make sense logically, but history has undone many "fighting faiths," and society has come to understand that the validity of any belief can best be tested by free exchange in the marketplace of ideas. This, he says, is the theory behind the nation's very Constitution, which is itself a grand experiment. Holmes concludes that the First Amendment trumps common law with respect to seditious libel, such that neither expression of belief nor mere exhortation to action qualifies as criminal offense. In other words, there must be a clear connection between an act of speech leading to a real crime being committed. Holmes was confident Justice Clarke had manipulated the interpretation of the First Amendment in a way that was not sound, and Holmes wrote his dissent in an attempt to provide a more accurate interpretation and therefore repair the damage his earlier court opinions may have caused. Holmes firmly asserted the facts of the *Abrams* case did, in no way, justify the convictions and punishments received.

Essential Themes

For the next decade, Holmes and Brandeis continued to develop their notion of what would constitute a clear and present danger sufficient to allow government prohibition of speech. The extremely rigorous standard established in Holmes' dissent was never completely adopted by the court, however his dissent is credited with paving the way for movement towards freer speech in the country. The "clear and present danger" test was used until 1969, when a direct incitement standard was implemented through the *Brandenburg v. Ohio* decision. The court eventually adopted their libertarian view of First Amendment protection for political dissent, and many aspects of the "clear and present danger" test remain at the heart of First Amendment law today. Without Holmes' dissent, it is unclear what the fate of free speech might have been in the United States, and as such the *Abrams* dissent is generally considered to be one of Justice Holmes' most influential opinions. While the prosecution of Adams and his peers seems unthinkable in today's world, there was a time when free speech was a truly limited freedom. Holmes' decision to admit he was wrong, and to establish a more rigid standard by which we should examine speech rights, has offered up the protection of one of our most prized liberties.

—*Amber R. Dickinson*

Bibliography and Additional Reading

Irons, Peter. *A People's History of the Supreme Court*. New York: Penguin, 1999.

Pollock, Frederick. "Abrams v. United States." *Law Quarterly Review* 36.4, 1920.

Wigmore, John H. "*Abrams v. U.S.*: Freedom of Speech and Freedom of Thuggery in War-Time and Peace-Time." *Illinois Law Review* 14.8, 1919.

■ *Gitlow v. New York*

Date: June 8, 1925
Author: U.S. Supreme Court
Genre: Court opinion

Summary

Although the Supreme Court upheld the conviction of a left-wing activist for writing and distributing a socialist pamphlet, it also ruled that the First Amendment's guarantee of freedom of speech is so fundamental to the notion of due process of law in the Fourteenth Amendment that it must be made applicable to the states under the incorporation doctrine.

In 1902, following President William McKinley's assassination, New York enacted a Criminal Anarchy Law that made it a felony to advocate "that organized government should be overthrown by force or violence, or by assassination of the executive head or of any of the executive officials of government, or by any unlawful means." The statute, originally enacted in response to the anarchist movement, was applied against Benjamin Gitlow, publisher of the *Left Wing Manifesto*, which paraphrased Karl Marx's *Communist Manifesto*, calling for "revolutionary mass action" to bring about "annihilation of the parliamentary state." However, the only specific action the *Manifesto* called for was a series of mass political strikes. There was no evidence that Gitlow's speeches and activities had resulted in any kind of illegal action. In 1920, nevertheless, he was found guilty of violating the 1902 statute, and was sentenced to spend from 5 to 10 years in prison.

Justice Edward T. Sanford wrote the opinion for the 7–2 majority that upheld both the guilty verdict and the sentence. Sanford warned that Gitlow's writings were dangerous because "a single revolutionary spark may kindle a fire that, smoldering for a time, may burst into a sweeping and destructive conflagration." Sanford's opinion allowed a state to forbid both speech and publication if they had a tendency to result in action dangerous to public security, even though such utterances might create no clear and present danger. This rationale by the Court's majority has sometimes been called the "dangerous tendency" test.

The most significant aspect of the *Gitlow* decision was Justice Sanford's declaration: "For present purposes we may and do assume that freedom of speech and of the press—which are protected by the First Amendment from abridgment by Congress—are among the fundamental personal rights and 'liberties' protected by the due process clause of the Fourteenth Amendment from impairment by the States." The effect of this statement was that the free speech and free press clauses of the First Amendment would henceforth be incorporated into the Fourteenth Amendment, thereby making the clauses binding on state and local governments—to be supervised by the U.S. Supreme Court's because of its established power of judicial review.

In a dissenting opinion, Justice Oliver Wendell Holmes insisted that Gitlow's pamphlet was not likely to incite any dangerous action. Quoting his earlier statement in *Schenck v. United States* (1919), Holmes argued that restrictions on free speech should be assessed according to the clear and present danger test, and he found that "it is manifest that there was no present danger of an attempt to overthrow the government by force on the part of the admittedly small minority who shared the defendant's views." Justice Louis D. Brandeis joined Holmes's dissent.

Gitlow remained a theoretical issue until the Supreme Court invalidated a state law for violating the First Amendment's protection of free speech in *Stromberg v. California* (1931).

HISTORICAL DOCUMENT

U.S. Supreme Court

Gitlow v. People, 268 U.S. 652 (1925)

Gitlow v. People

No.19

Argued April 12, 1923

Reargued November 23, 1923

Decided June 8, 1925

268 U.S. 652

MR. JUSTICE SANFORD delivered the opinion of the Court.

Benjamin Gitlow was indicted in the Supreme Court of New York, with three others, for the statutory crime of criminal anarchy. New York Penal Laws, §§ 160, 161.[1] He was separately tried, convicted, and sentenced to imprisonment. The judgment was affirmed by the Appellate Division and by the Court of Appeals. The case is here on writ of error to the Supreme Court, to which the record was remitted. 260 U.S. 703.

The contention here is that the statute, by its terms and as applied in this case, is repugnant to the due process clause of the Fourteenth Amendment. Its material provisions are:

"§ 160. *Criminal anarchy defined.* Criminal anarchy is the doctrine that organized government should be overthrown by force or violence, or by assassination of the executive head or of any of the executive officials of government, or by any unlawful means. The advocacy of such doctrine either by word of mouth or writing is a felony."

"§ 161. *Advocacy of criminal anarchy.* Any person who:"

"1. By word of mouth or writing advocates, advises or teaches the duty, necessity or propriety of overthrowing or overturning organized government by force or violence, or by assassination of the executive head or of any of the executive officials of government, or by any unlawful means; or,"

"2. Prints, publishes, edits, issues or knowingly circulates, sells, distributes or publicly displays any book, paper, document, or written or printed matter in any form, containing or advocating, advising or teaching the doctrine that organized government should be overthrown by force, violence or any unlawful means is guilty of a felony and punishable" by imprisonment or fine, or both.

The indictment was in two counts. The first charged that the defendant had advocated, advised and taught the duty, necessity and propriety of overthrowing and overturning organized government by force, violence and unlawful means, by certain writings therein set forth entitled "The Left Wing Manifesto"; the second, that he had printed, published and knowingly circulated and distributed a certain paper called "The Revolutionary Age," containing the writings set forth in the first count advocating, advising and teaching the doctrine that organized government should be overthrown by force, violence and unlawful means.

The following facts were established on the trial by undisputed evidence and admissions: the defendant is a member of the Left Wing Section of the Socialist Party, a dissenting branch or faction of that party formed in opposition to its dominant policy of "moderate Socialism." Membership in both is open to aliens as well as citizens. The Left Wing Section was organized nationally at a conference in New York City in June, 1919, attended by ninety delegates from twenty different States. The conference elected a National Council, of which the defendant was a member, and left to it the adoption of a "Manifesto." This was published in The Revolutionary Age, the official organ of the Left Wing. The defendant was on the board of managers

---

1 Laws of 1909, ch. 88; Consol.Laws, 1909, ch. 40. This statute was originally enacted in 1902. Laws of 1902, ch. 371.

of the paper, and was its business manager. He arranged for the printing of the paper, and took to the printer the manuscript of the first issue which contained the Left Wing Manifesto, and also a Communist Program and a Program of the Left Wing that had been adopted by the conference. Sixteen thousand copies were printed, which were delivered at the premises in New York City used as the office of the Revolutionary Age and the headquarters of the Left Wing, and occupied by the defendant and other officials. These copies were paid for by the defendant, as business manager of the paper. Employees at this office wrapped and mailed out copies of the paper under the defendant's direction, and copies were sold from this office. It was admitted that the defendant signed a card subscribing to the Manifesto and Program of the Left Wing, which all applicants were required to sign

before being admitted to membership; that he went to different parts of the State to speak to branches of the Socialist Party about the principles of the Left Wing and advocated their adoption, and that he was responsible for the Manifesto as it appeared, that "he knew of the publication, in a general way, and he knew of its publication afterwards, and is responsible for its circulation."

There was no evidence of any effect resulting from the publication and circulation of the Manifesto.

No witnesses were offered in behalf of the defendant.

Extracts from the Manifesto are set forth in the margin.[2] Coupled with a review of the rise of Socialism, it condemned the dominant "moderate Socialism" for its recognition of the necessity of the democratic parliamentary state; repudiated its policy of introducing Socialism by legislative

---

2 Italics are given as in the original, but the paragraphing is omitted.

"The Left Wing Manifesto"

"Issued on Authority of the Conference by the "National Council of the Left Wing"

"The world is in crisis. Capitalism, the prevailing system of society, is in process of disintegration and collapse.... Humanity can be saved from its last excesses only by the Communist Revolution. There can now be only the Socialism which is one in temper and purpose with the proletarian revolutionary struggle.... The class struggle is the heart of Socialism. Without strict conformity to the class struggle, in its revolutionary implications, Socialism becomes either sheer Utopianism, or a method of reaction.... The dominant Socialism united with the capitalist governments to prevent a revolution. The Russian Revolution was the first act of the proletariat against the war and Imperialism.... [The] proletariat, urging on the poorer peasantry, conquered power. It accomplished a proletarian revolution by means of the Bolshevik policy of 'all power to the Soviets,'—organizing the new transitional state of proletarian dictatorship.... Moderate Socialism affirms that the bourgeois, democratic parliamentary state is the necessary basis for the introduction of Socialism.... Revolutionary Socialism, on the contrary, insists that the democratic parliamentary state can never be the basis for the introduction of Socialism; that it is necessary to destroy

the parliamentary state, and construct a new state of the organized producers, which will deprive the bourgeoisie of political power, and function as a revolutionary dictatorship of the proletariat.... Revolutionary Socialism alone is capable of mobilizing the proletariat for Socialism, for the conquest of the power of the state, by means of revolutionary mass action and proletarian dictatorship.... Imperialism is dominant in the United States, which is now a world power.... The war has aggrandized American Capitalism, instead of weakening it as in Europe.... These conditions modify our immediate task, but do not alter its general character; this is not the moment of revolution, but it is the moment of revolutionary struggle.... Strikes are developing which verge on revolutionary action, and in which the suggestion of proletarian dictatorship is apparent, the striker-workers trying to usurp functions of municipal government, as in Seattle and Winnipeg. The mass struggle of the proletariat is coming into being.... These strikes will constitute the determining feature of proletarian action in the days to come. Revolutionary Socialism must use these mass industrial revolts to broaden the strike, to make it general and militant; use the strike for political objectives, and, finally, develop the mass political strike against Capitalism and the state. Revolutionary Socialism must base itself on the mass struggles of the proletariat, engage directly in these struggles while emphasizing the revolutionary purposes of Socialism and the proletarian movement. The mass strikes of the American proletariat provide measures, and advocated, in plain and unequivocal language, the necessity of accomplishing the "Communist Revolution" by a militant and "revolutionary Socialism", based on "the class struggle" and mobilizing the "power of the proletariat in action," through mass industrial revolts developing into mass

political strikes and "revolutionary mass action", for the purpose of conquering and destroying the parliamentary state and establishing in its place, through a "revolutionary dictatorship of the proletariat", the system of Communist Socialism. The then recent strikes in Seattle and Winnipeg[3] were cited as

the material basis out of which to develop the concepts and action of revolutionary Socialism.... Our "task ... is to articulate and organize the mass of the unorganized industrial proletariat, which constitutes the basis for a militant Socialism. The struggle for the revolutionary industrial unionism of the proletariat becomes an indispensable phase of revolutionary Socialism, on the basis of which to broaden and deepen the action of the militant proletariat, developing reserves for the ultimate conquest of power.... Revolutionary Socialism adheres to the class struggle because through the class struggle alone—the mass struggle—can the industrial proletariat secure immediate concessions and finally conquer power by organizing the industrial government of the working class. The class struggle is a political struggle ... in the sense that its objective is political—the overthrow of the political organization upon which capitalistic exploitation depends, and the introduction of a new social system. The direct objective is the conquest by the proletariat of the power of the state. Revolutionary Socialism does not propose to "capture" the bourgeois parliamentary state, but to conquer and destroy it. Revolutionary Socialism, accordingly, repudiates the policy of introducing Socialism by means of legislative measures on the basis of the bourgeois state.... It proposes to conquer by means of political action ... in the revolutionary Marxian sense, which does not simply mean parliamentarism, but the *class action* of the proletariat *in any form* having as its objective the conquest of the power of the state.... Parliamentary action which emphasizes the implacable character of the class struggle is an indispensable means of agitation.... But parliamentarism cannot conquer the power of the state for the proletariat.... It is accomplished not by the legislative representatives of the proletariat, but by *the mass power of the proletariat in action*. The supreme power of the proletariat inheres in the *political mass strike,* in using the industrial mass power of the proletariat for political objectives. Revolutionary Socialism, accordingly, recognizes that the supreme form of proletarian political action is *the political mass strike....* The power of the proletariat lies fundamentally in its control of the industrial process. The mobilization of this

control in action against the bourgeois state and Capitalism means the end of Capitalism, the initial form of the revolutionary mass action that will conquer the power of the state.... The revolution starts with strikes of protest, developing into mass political strikes and then into revolutionary mass action for the conquest of the power of the state. Mass action becomes political in purpose while extra-parliamentary in form; it is equally a process of revolution and the revolution itself in operation. The final objective of mass action is the conquest of the power of the state, the annihilation of the bourgeois parliamentary state and the introduction of the transition proletarian state, functioning as a revolutionary dictatorship of the proletariat.... The bourgeois parliamentary state is the organ of the bourgeoisie for the coercion of the proletariat. The revolutionary proletariat must, accordingly, destroy this state.... It is therefore necessary that the proletariat organize its own state *for the coercion and suppression of the bourgeoisie....* Proletarian dictatorship is a recognition of the necessity for a revolutionary state to coerce and suppress the bourgeoisie; it is equally a recognition of the fact that, in the Communist reconstruction of society, the proletariat as a class alone counts.... The old machinery of the state cannot be used by the revolutionary proletariat. It must be destroyed. The proletariat creates a new state, based directly upon the industrially organized producers, upon the industrial unions or Soviets, or a combination of both. It is this state alone, functioning as a dictatorship of the proletariat, that can realize Socialism.... While the dictatorship of the proletariat performs its negative task of crushing the old order, it performs the positive task of constructing the new. Together with the government of the proletarian dictatorship, there is developed a new "government," which is no longer government in the old sense, since it concerns itself with the management of production, and not with the government of persons. Out of workers' control of industry, introduced by the proletarian dictatorship, there develops the complete structure of Communist Socialism—industrial self-government of the communistically organized producers. When this structure is completed, which implies the complete instances of a development already verging on revolutionary action and suggestive of proletarian dictatorship, in which the strike-workers were "trying to usurp the functions of municipal government", and revolutionary Socialism, it was urged, must use these mass industrial revolts to broaden the strike, make it general and militant, and develop it into mass political strikes and revolutionary mass action for the annihilation of the parliamentary state.

At the outset of the trial, the defendant's counsel objected to the introduction of any evidence under the indictment on the grounds that, as a matter of law, the Manifesto "is not in contravention of the statute," and that "the statute is in contravention of" the due process clause of the Fourteenth Amendment. This objection was denied. They also moved, at the close of the evidence, to dismiss the indictment and direct an acquittal "on the grounds stated in the first objection to evidence." and again on the grounds that "the indictment does not charge an offense" and the evidence "does not show an offense." These motions were also denied.

The court, among other things, charged the jury, in substance, that they must determine what was the intent, purpose and fair meaning of the Manifesto; that its words must be taken in their ordinary meaning, as they would be understood by people whom it might reach; that a mere statement or analysis of social and economic facts and historical incidents, in the nature of an essay, accompanied by prophecy as to the future course of events, but with no teaching, advice or advocacy of action, would not constitute the advocacy, advice or teaching of a doctrine for the overthrow of government within the meaning of the statute; that a mere statement that unlawful acts might accomplish such a purpose would be insufficient, unless there was a teaching, advising and advocacy of employing such unlawful acts for the purpose of overthrowing government, and that, if the jury had a reasonable doubt that the Manifesto did teach, advocate or advise the duty, necessity or propriety of using unlawful means for the overthrowing of organized government, the defendant was entitled to an acquittal.

The defendant's counsel submitted two requests to charge which embodied in substance the statement that to constitute criminal anarchy within the meaning of the statute it was necessary that the language used or published should advocate, teach or advise the duty, necessity or propriety of doing "some definite or immediate act or acts" of force, violence or unlawfulness directed toward the overthrowing of organized government. These were denied further than had been charged. Two other requests to charge embodied in substance the statement that, to constitute guilt, the language used or published must be "reasonably and ordinarily calculated to incite certain persons" to acts of force, violence or unlawfulness, with the object of overthrowing organized government. These were also denied.

* * * * *

The precise question presented, and the only question which we can consider under this writ of error, then is whether the statute, as construed

---

expropriation of the bourgeoisie economically and politically, the dictatorship of the proletariat ends, in its place coming the full and free social and individual autonomy of the Communist order.... It is not a problem of immediate revolution. It is a problem of the immediate revolutionary struggle. The revolutionary epoch of the final struggle against Capitalism may last for years and tens of years; but the Communist International offers a policy and program immediate and ultimate in scope, that provides for the immediate class struggle against Capitalism, in its revolutionary implications, and for the final act of the conquest of power. The old order is in decay. Civilization is in collapse. The proletarian revolution and the Communist reconstruction of society—the struggle for these—is now indispensable. This is the message of the Communist International to the workers of the world. The Communist International calls the proletariat of the world to the final struggle!

3 There was testimony at the trial that

> "there was an extended strike at Winnipeg commencing May 15, 1919, during which the production and supply of necessities, transportation, postal and telegraphic communication and fire and sanitary protection were suspended or seriously curtailed."

and applied in this case by the state courts, deprived the defendant of his liberty of expression in violation of the due process clause of the Fourteenth Amendment.

The statute does not penalize the utterance or publication of abstract "doctrine" or academic discussion having no quality of incitement to any concrete action. It is not aimed against mere historical or philosophical essays. It does not restrain the advocacy of changes in the form of government by constitutional and lawful means. What it prohibits is language advocating, advising or teaching the overthrow of organized government by unlawful means. These words imply urging to action. Advocacy is defined in the Century Dictionary as: "1. The act of pleading for, supporting, or recommending; active espousal." It is not the abstract "doctrine" of overthrowing organized government by unlawful means which is denounced by the statute, but the advocacy of action for the accomplishment of that purpose. It was so construed and applied by the trial judge, who specifically charged the jury that:

> "A mere grouping of historical events and a prophetic deduction from them would neither constitute advocacy, advice or teaching of a doctrine for the overthrow of government by force, violence or unlawful means. [And] if it were a mere essay on the subject, as suggested by counsel, based upon deductions from alleged historical events, with no teaching, advice or advocacy of action, it would not constitute a violation of the statute...."

The Manifesto, plainly, is neither the statement of abstract doctrine nor, as suggested by counsel, mere prediction that industrial disturbances and revolutionary mass strikes will result spontaneously in an inevitable process of evolution in the economic system. It advocates and urges in fervent language mass action which shall progressively foment industrial disturbances and, through political mass strikes and revolutionary mass action, overthrow and destroy organized parliamentary government. It concludes with a call to action in these words:

> "The proletariat revolution and the Communist reconstruction of society—*the struggle for these*—is now indispensable.... The Communist International calls the proletariat of the world to the final struggle!"

This is not the expression of philosophical abstraction, the mere prediction of future events; it is the language of direct incitement....

For present purposes, we may and do assume that freedom of speech and of the press which are protected by the First Amendment from abridgment by Congress are among the fundamental personal rights and "liberties" protected by the due process clause of the Fourteenth Amendment from impairment by the States. We do not regard the incidental statement in *Prudential Ins. Co. v. Cheek*, that the Fourteenth Amendment imposes no restrictions on the States concerning freedom of speech, as determinative of this question.

It is a fundamental principle, long established, that the freedom of speech and of the press which is secured by the Constitution does not confer an absolute right to speak or publish, without responsibility, whatever one may choose, or an unrestricted and unbridled license that gives immunity for every possible use of language and prevents the punishment of those who abuse this freedom.... Reasonably limited, it was said by Story in the passage cited, this freedom is an inestimable privilege in a free government; without such limitation, it might become the scourge of the republic.

That a State in the exercise of its police power may punish those who abuse this freedom by utterances inimical to the public welfare, tending to corrupt public morals, incite to crime, or disturb the public peace, is not open to question.... Thus, it was held by this Court in the *Fox* Case that a State may punish publications advocating and encouraging a breach of its criminal laws; and, in the *Gilbert* Case, that a State may punish utterances teaching or advocating that its citizens should not assist the United States in prosecuting or carrying on war with its public enemies.

And, for yet more imperative reasons, a State may punish utterances endangering the foundations of organized government and threatening its overthrow by unlawful means. These imperil its own existence as a constitutional State. Freedom of speech and press, said Story (*supra*) does not protect disturbances to the public peace or the attempt to subvert the government. It does not protect publications or teachings which tend to subvert or imperil the government or to impede or hinder it in the performance of its governmental duties. *State v. Holm*. It does not protect publications prompting the overthrow of government by force; the punishment of those who publish articles which tend to destroy organized society being essential to the security of freedom and the stability of the State. *People v. Most*. And a State may penalize utterances which openly advocate the overthrow of the representative and constitutional form of government of the United States and the several States, by violence or other unlawful means. *People v. Lloyd. See also State v. Tachin*, and *People v. Steelik*. In short, this freedom does not deprive a State of the primary and essential right of self-preservation, which, so long as human governments endure, they cannot be denied.…

By enacting the present statute, the State has determined, through its legislative body, that utterances advocating the overthrow of organized government by force, violence and unlawful means are so inimical to the general welfare and involve such danger of substantive evil that they may be penalized in the exercise of its police power. That determination must be given great weight. Every presumption is to be indulged in favor of the validity of the statute. *Mugler v. Kansas*. And the case is to be considered "in the light of the principle that the State is primarily the judge of regulations required in the interest of public safety and welfare;" and that its police

> "statutes may only be declared unconstitutional where they are arbitrary or unreasonable attempts to exercise authority vested in the State in the public interest."

Great Northern Ry. v. Clara City. That utterances inciting to the overthrow of organized government by unlawful means present a sufficient danger of substantive evil to bring their punishment within the range of legislative discretion is clear. Such utterances, by their very nature, involve danger to the public peace and to the security of the State. They threaten breaches of the peace, and ultimate revolution. And the immediate danger is none the less real and substantial because the effect of a given utterance cannot be accurately foreseen. The State cannot reasonably be required to measure the danger from every such utterance in the nice balance of a jeweler's scale. A single revolutionary spark may kindle a fire that, smouldering for a time, may burst into a sweeping and destructive conflagration. It cannot be said that the State is acting arbitrarily or unreasonably when, in the exercise of its judgment as to the measures necessary to protect the public peace and safety, it seeks to extinguish the spark without waiting until it has enkindled the flame or blazed into the conflagration. It cannot reasonably be required to defer the adoption of measures for its own peace and safety until the revolutionary utterances lead to actual disturbances of the public peace or imminent and immediate danger of its own destruction; but it may, in the exercise of its judgment, suppress the threatened danger in its incipiency. In *People v. Lloyd*, it was aptly said:

> "Manifestly, the legislature has authority to forbid the advocacy of a doctrine designed and intended to overthrow the government without waiting until there is a present and imminent danger of the success of the plan advocated. If the State were compelled to wait until the apprehended danger became certain, then its right to protect itself would come into being simultaneously with the overthrow of the government, when there would be neither prosecuting officers nor courts for the enforcement of the law."

We cannot hold that the present statute is an arbitrary or unreasonable exercise of the police power of the State unwarrantably infringing the freedom of speech or press, and we must and do sustain its constitutionality.

This being so, it may be applied to every utterance—not too trivial to be beneath the notice of the law—which is of such a character and used with such intent and purpose as to bring it within the prohibition of the statute. This principle is illustrated in *Fox v. Washington; Abrams v. United States*; *Schaefer v. United States*; *Pierce v. United States*; and *Gilbert v. Minnesota*. In other words, when the legislative body has determined generally, in the constitutional exercise of its discretion, that utterances of a certain kind involve such danger of substantive evil that they may be punished, the question whether any specific utterance coming within the prohibited class is likely, in and of itself, to bring about the substantive evil is not open to consideration. It is sufficient that the statute itself be constitutional and that the use of the language comes within its prohibition.

It is clear that the question in such cases is entirely different from that involved in those cases where the statute merely prohibits certain acts involving the danger of substantive evil, without any reference to language itself, and it is sought to apply its provisions to language used by the defendant for the purpose of bringing about the prohibited results. There, if it be contended that the statute cannot be applied to the language used by the defendant because of its protection by the freedom of speech or press, it must necessarily be found, as an original question, without any previous determination by the legislative body, whether the specific language used involved such likelihood of bringing about the substantive evil as to deprive it of the constitutional protection. In such cases, it has been held that the general provisions of the statute may be constitutionally applied to the specific utterance of the defendant if its natural tendency and probable effect was to bring about the substantive evil which the legislative body might prevent. *Schenck v. United States, Debs v. United States*. And the general statement in the *Schenck* Case that the

> "question in every case is whether the words are used in such circumstances and

are of such a nature as to create a clear and present danger that they will bring about the substantive evils"

—upon which great reliance is placed in the defendant's argument—was manifestly intended, as shown by the context, to apply only in cases of this class, and has no application to those like the present, where the legislative body itself has previously determined the danger of substantive evil arising from utterances of a specified character.

The defendant's brief does not separately discuss any of the rulings of the trial court. It is only necessary to say that, applying the general rules already stated, we find that none of them involved any invasion of the constitutional rights of the defendant. It was not necessary, within the meaning of the statute, that the defendant should have advocated "some definite or immediate act or acts" of force, violence or unlawfulness. It was sufficient if such acts were advocated in general terms, and it was not essential that their immediate execution should have been advocated. Nor was it necessary that the language should have been "reasonably and ordinarily calculated to incite certain persons" to acts of force, violence or unlawfulness. The advocacy need not be addressed to specific persons. Thus, the publication and circulation of a newspaper article may be an encouragement or endeavor to persuade to murder, although not addressed to any person in particular. *Queen v. Most, L.R.,* 7 Q.B.D. 244.

We need not enter upon a consideration of the English common law rule of seditious libel or the Federal Sedition Act of 1798, to which reference is made in the defendant's brief. These are so unlike the present statute that we think the decisions under them cast no helpful light upon the questions here.

And finding, for the reasons stated, that the statute is not, in itself, unconstitutional, and that it has not been applied in the present case in derogation of any constitutional right, the judgment of the Court of Appeals is *Affirmed*.

SUPPLEMENTAL HISTORICAL DOCUMENT

AMENDMENT XIV

Section 1.

All persons born or naturalized in the United States, and subject to the jurisdiction thereof, are citizens of the United States and of the State wherein they reside. No State shall make or enforce any law which shall abridge the privileges or immunities of citizens of the United States; nor shall any State deprive any person of life, liberty, or property, without due process of law; nor deny to any person within its jurisdiction the equal protection of the laws.

Section 2.

Representatives shall be apportioned among the several States according to their respective numbers, counting the whole number of persons in each State, excluding Indians not taxed. But when the right to vote at any election for the choice of electors for President and Vice-President of the United States, Representatives in Congress, the Executive and Judicial officers of a State, or the members of the Legislature thereof, is denied to any of the male inhabitants of such State, being twenty-one years of age, and citizens of the United States, or in any way abridged, except for participation in rebellion, or other crime, the basis of representation therein shall be reduced in the proportion which the number of such male citizens shall bear to the whole number of male citizens twenty-one years of age in such State.

Section 3.

No person shall be a Senator or Representative in Congress, or elector of President and Vice-President, or hold any office, civil or military, under the United States, or under any State, who, having previously taken an oath, as a member of Congress, or as an officer of the United States, or as a member of any State legislature, or as an executive or judicial officer of any State, to support the Constitution of the United States, shall have engaged in insurrection or rebellion against the same, or given aid or comfort to the enemies thereof. But Congress may by a vote of two-thirds of each House, remove such disability.

Section 4.

The validity of the public debt of the United States, authorized by law, including debts incurred for payment of pensions and bounties for services in suppressing insurrection or rebellion, shall not be questioned. But neither the United States nor any State shall assume or pay any debt or obligation incurred in aid of insurrection or rebellion against the United States, or any claim for the loss or emancipation of any slave; but all such debts, obligations and claims shall be held illegal and void.

Section 5.

The Congress shall have the power to enforce, by appropriate legislation, the provisions of this article.

The "Red Ruby"

Address to the Jury
by
Benjamin Gitlow

ALSO

Darrow
The Judge
Giovanitti

"He would make America a Red Ruby in the
Red Treasure Chest of the Red Terror."
Prosecutor Rorke's Compliment to Gitlow.

Published by
THE COMUNIST LABOR PARTY
United States of America

First page of reporting of speeches including Benjamin Gitlow's address to the jury at his trial.

A Red Ruby in the Red Treasure Chest

FOREWORD: Benjamin Gitlow, member of the Labor Committee of the Communist Labor Party and of the staff of the "Voice of Labor", is the first communist in the United States to be convicted for espousing the principles of the Third International as proclaimed in the Left Wing Manifesto. He was found guilty by the jury and sentenced by Judge Weeks to serve from five to ten years at hard labor in Sing-Sing.

The address to the jury by Gitlow is indeed a "red ruby in the red treasure chest" of red literature. Facing capitalism's judicial machinery with a courage which only comes to those who understand and idealize communism, he told in language understandable by all, just where world capitalism is at and what world communism is driving at. But the judge interrupted many times. Gitlow was telling too much.

This spamphlet also contains the court's "thank you" to the jury, which is rich in Americanism, as well as extracts from the address by Clarence Darrow and paragraphs from Giovanitti's article in "The Liberator".

Foreword to The Red Ruby, *published by The Communist Labor Party of America, 1920.*

Lenin on Capitalism and Proletarian Dictatorship

"That which definitely distinguishes a dictatorship of the proletariat from a dictatorship of the other classes, from a dictatorship of the bourgeoisie in all the civilized capitalist countries, is that the dictatorship of the landlords and of the bourgeoisie was the forcible suppression of the resistance of the **overwhelming majority of the population,** namely, the toilers. On the other hand, the dictatorship of the proletariat is the forcible suppression of the resistance of the exploiters, that is, of **an insignificant minority of the population** — of landlords and capitalists.

"It therefore follows that a dictatorship of the proletariat must necessarily carry with it not only changes in the form and institutions of democracy, speaking in general terms, but specifically such a change as would secure an extension such as has never been seen in the history of the world of the **actual use of democratism** by the toiling classes.

"And in actual fact the form of dictatorship of the proletariat which has already been worked out in practice, that is, the Soviet authority in Russia, the Rate system in Germany, the Shop Stewards' Committees, and other similar Soviet institutions in other countries, all represent and realize for the toiling classes, that is, for the **overwhelming majority of the population,** this actual possibility to use democratic rights and freedom, which possibility never existed, even approximately, in the very best and most democratic bourgeois republics."

The Gitlow Case Must Be Appealed Defense Funds Are Needed

> # Help—Lend a Hand
> ### Dollars   Talk   Loudest
> #### *RIGHT NOW—*
> ### Therefore---Speak Up--- Quick !

Send all the Dollars you can to
GERTRUDE NAFE
Treasurer Defense Committee

164 Waverly Place   :-:   :-:   **New York City**

Back cover of The Red Ruby, *published by The Communist Labor Party of America, 1920*

Document Analysis and Impact

The application of the free speech clause to the states seen in *Gitlow v. New York* was a watershed decision in civil liberties cases: Today, most provisions of the Bill of Rights have been found to be binding upon the states. The *Gitlow* case also redefined the scope of the "clear and present danger" test, by applying a wartime doctrine during a time of peace and by accepting the legislative judgment of the harmful potential of the speech instead of scrutinizing the facts independently to see whether a danger existed. The line of cases that permitted government to suppress subversive speech that might have harmful effects—of which *Gitlow v. New York* is illustrative—came to an end in 1969, when the justices held in *Brandenburg v. Ohio*

that the free speech clause protected the advocacy of illegal action unless such advocacy was intended and likely to produce "imminent lawless action."

—Thomas Tandy Lewis and Richard A. Glenn

Bibliography and Additional Reading

Kersch, Kenneth I. *Freedom of Speech: Rights and Liberties Under the Law*. Santa Barbara, Calif.: ABC-CLIO, 2003.

Lendler, Marc. *Gitlow v. New York: Every Idea an Incitement*. Lawrence: University Press of Kansas, 2012.

Stone, Geoffrey R. *Perilous Times: Free Speech in Wartime from the Sedition Act of 1798 to the War on Terrorism*. New York: Norton, 2005.

■ The Press Under a Free Government

Date: July 17, 1925
Author: Calvin Coolidge
Genre: Speech

Summary Overview

In a speech before the American Society of Newspaper Editors, President Calvin Coolidge offered his opinions on the role the media should play in the modern United States. He encouraged the press to avoid engaging in propaganda and to be mindful of the motivations of sources. The press, Coolidge said, has a dual purpose—to inform the public of important news and to generate profits as a business. There is no reason to believe that American journalism as a whole would betray the public, he said, but he advised that there would be those who sought to corrupt the press. The concept that would best protect the integrity of the press, he concluded, was the idealism prevalent in every part of American society.

Defining Moment

By the 1920s, America's collective attention had turned away from the activist ideals of the Progressive Era to what President Warren Harding referred to as a period of "normalcy." Politically, Americans looked for more conservative initiatives from their leaders, electing the more conservative Republican Warren G. Harding to succeed the liberalism of Democrat Woodrow Wilson. The more popular themes of this era included the desire for government to be minimally intrusive—to help Americans who could not help themselves, but to avoid unnecessary regulation and excessive taxation.

At the same time, however, America was continuing to change economically and socially. There were a number of race riots, for example, as well as a resurgent Ku Klux Klan in the South. Additionally, while most major industries were seeing great strength, their success was challenged by organized labor, which was attempting to find new, national support by engaging in strikes and other campaigns. With the start of Prohibition in 1920, crime—from violation of the Volstead Act to alcohol smuggling and gangland violence—was on the upswing during this period. Indeed, the 1920s was a period replete with newsworthy developments.

On an international scale, the rise of Bolshevism and Communism in Eastern Europe and Russia was seen as a threat to the American way of life. Americans accused organized labor of demonstrating Communist tendencies (some even believed that Bolsheviks were behind a number of strikes and union organization campaigns). Accused European Communists were also arrested and deported under the auspices of outdated sedition laws. Even the press was accused of having ties to left-leaning activities and, in light of this fact, many news outlets felt compelled to report the news in a manner that would not invite such accusations.

In Washington, President Warren Harding's death in 1923 brought to office his vice president, Calvin Coolidge. Coolidge developed a positive reputation in the media for his unprecedented accessibility. Of the seventeen presidents who have held press conferences in the twentieth and twenty-first centuries, Coolidge has held the second-largest number—521—during his tenure. Only three-term president Franklin D. Roosevelt held more, with 1,020. Although he was careful not to insert himself into controversies, Coolidge was one of the most visible presidents of the twentieth century. He was also the first president to use the radio to address the American people.

In light of his apparent willingness to appear before, and even build relationships with, the press, Coolidge was invited to speak before a 1925 conference of newspaper editors in Washington. Coolidge took advantage of this venue to provide his thoughts on the role of the media during this tumultuous period in American history.

Author Biography

Calvin Coolidge was born in Plymouth Notch, Vermont, on July 4, 1872. His father was a storekeeper. Coolidge graduated from Amherst College in Amherst, Massachusetts. Thereafter, he pursued a career in law and government. Coolidge won a seat on the Northampton City Council in 1900 and, from there, became chairman of the Northampton's local Republican organization in 1904, mayor of Northampton in 1910, Massachusetts senator in 1912, and eventually governor of Massachusetts in 1919. He left that office to serve as Republican president Warren Harding's vice president. In 1923, Harding died, leaving Coolidge president. In 1924, Coolidge won a full term, holding office until 1929. Coolidge retired to Northampton and died on January 5, 1933.

President Calvin Coolidge with reporters and cameramen, 1923.

HISTORICAL DOCUMENT

The relationship between governments and the press has always been recognized as a matter of large importance. Wherever despotism abounds, the sources of public information are the first to be brought under its control. Wherever the cause of liberty is making its way, one of its highest accomplishments is the guarantee of the freedom of the press. It has always been realized, sometimes instinctively, oftentimes expressly, that truth and freedom are inseparable. An absolutism could never rest upon anything save a perverted and distorted view of human relationships and upon false standards set up and maintained by force. It has always found it necessary to attempt to dominate the entire field of education and instruction. It has thrived on ignorance. While it has sought to train the minds of a few, it has been largely with the purpose of attempting to give them a superior facility for misleading the many. Men have been educated under absolutism, not that they might bear witness to the truth, but that they might be the more ingenious advocates and defenders of false standards and hollow pretenses. This has always been the method of privilege, the method of class and caste, the method of master and slave.

When a community has sufficiently advanced so that its government begins to take on that of the nature of a republic, the processes of education become even more important, but the method is necessarily reversed. It is all the more necessary under a system of free government that the people should be enlightened, that they should be correctly informed, than it is under an absolute government that they should be ignorant. Under a republic the institutions of learning, while bound by the constitution and laws, are in no way subservient to the government. The principles which they enunciate do not depend for their authority upon whether they square with the wish of the ruling dynasty, but whether they square with the everlasting truth. Under these conditions the press, which had before been made an instrument for concealing or perverting the facts, must be made an instrument

for their true representation and their sound and logical interpretation. From the position of a mere organ, constantly bound to servitude, public prints [i.e., newsprint; the press] rise to a dignity, not only of independence, but of a great educational and enlightening factor. They attain new powers, which it is almost impossible to measure, and become charged with commensurate responsibilities.

The public press under an autocracy is necessarily a true agency of propaganda. Under a free government it must be the very reverse. Propaganda seeks to present a part of the facts, to distort their relations, and to force conclusions which could not be drawn from a complete and candid survey of all the facts. It has been observed that propaganda seeks to close the mind, while education seeks to open it. This has become one of the dangers of the present day.

The great difficulty in combating unfair propaganda, or even in recognizing it, arises from the fact that at the present time we confront so many new and technical problems that it is an enormous task to keep ourselves accurately informed concerning them. In this respect, you gentlemen of the press face the same perplexities that are encountered by legislators and government administrators. Whoever deals with current public questions is compelled to rely greatly upon the information and judgments of experts and specialists. Unfortunately, not all experts are to be trusted as entirely disinterested. Not all specialists are completely without guile. In our increasing dependence on specialized authority, we tend to become easier victims for the propagandists, and need to cultivate sedulously the habit of the open mind. No doubt every generation feels that its problems are the most intricate and baffling that have ever been presented for solution. But with all recognition of the disposition to exaggerate in this respect, I think we can fairly say that our times in all their social and economic aspects are more complex than any past period. We need to keep our minds free from prejudice and bias. Of education, and of real information we cannot get too much. But of propaganda, which is tainted or perverted information, we cannot have too little.

Newspaper men, therefore, endlessly discuss the question of what is news. I judge that they will go on discussing it as long as there are newspapers. It has seemed to me that quite obviously the news-giving function of a newspaper cannot possibly require that it give a photographic presentation of everything that happens in the community. That is an obvious impossibility. It seems fair to say that the proper presentation of the news bears about the same relation to the whole field of happenings that a painting does to a photograph. The photograph might give the more accurate presentation of details, but in doing so it might sacrifice the opportunity the more clearly to delineate character. My college professor was wont to tell us a good many years ago that if a painting of a tree was only the exact representation of the original, so that it looked just like the tree, there would be no reason for making it; we might as well look at the tree itself. But the painting, if it is of the right sort, gives something that neither a photograph nor a view of the tree conveys. It emphasizes something of character, quality, individuality. We are not lost in looking at thorns and effects; we catch a vision of the grandeur and beauty of a king of the forest.

And so I have conceived that the news, properly presented, should be a sort of cross-section of the character of current human experience. It should delineate character, quality, tendencies and implications. In this way the reporter exercises his genius. Out of the current events he does not make a drab and sordid story, but rather an informing and enlightened epic. His work becomes no longer imitative, but rises to an original art.

Our American newspapers serve a double purpose. They bring knowledge and information to their readers, and at the same time they play a most important part in connection with the business interests of the community, both through their news and advertising departments. Probably there is no rule of your profession to which you gentlemen are more devoted than that which prescribes that the editorial and the business policies of the paper are to be conducted by strictly separate departments.

Editorial policy and news policy must not be influenced by business consideration; business policies must not be affected by editorial programs. Such a dictum strikes the outsider as involving a good deal of difficulty in the practical adjustments of every-day management. Yet, in fact, I doubt if those adjustments are any more difficult than have to be made in every other department of human effort. Life is a long succession of compromises and adjustments, and it may be doubted whether the press is compelled to make them more frequently than others do.

When I have contemplated these adjustments of business and editorial policy, it has always seemed to me that American newspapers are peculiarly representative of the practical idealism of our country. Quite recently the construction of a revenue statute resulted in giving publicity to some highly interesting facts about incomes. It must have been observed that nearly all the newspapers published these interesting facts in their news columns, while very many of them protested in their editorial columns that such publicity was a bad policy. Yet this was not inconsistent. I am referring to the incident by way of illustrating what I just said about the newspapers representing the practical idealism of America. As practical newsmen they printed the facts. As editorial idealists they protested that there ought to be no such facts available.

Some people feel concerned about the commercialism of the press. They note that great newspapers are great business enterprises earning large profits and controlled by men of wealth. So they fear that in such control the press may tend to support the private interests of those who own the papers, rather than the general interest of the whole people. It seems to me, however, that the real test is not whether the newspapers are controlled by men of wealth, but whether they are sincerely trying to serve the public interests. There will be little occasion for worry about who owns a newspaper, so long as its attitudes on public questions are such as to promote the general welfare. A press which is actuated by the purpose of genuine usefulness to the public interest can never be too strong financially, so long as its strength is used for the support of popular government.

There does not seem to be cause for alarm in the dual relationship of the press to the public, whereby it is on one side a purveyor of information and opinion and on the other side a purely business enterprise. Rather, it is probably that a press which maintains an intimate touch with the business currents of the nation, is likely to be more reliable than it would be if it were a stranger to these influences. After all, the chief business of the American people is business. They are profoundly concerned with producing, buying, selling, investing and prospering in the world. I am strongly of opinion that the great majority of people will always find these are moving impulses of our life. The opposite view was oracularly and poetically set forth in those lines of Goldsmith which everybody repeats, but few really believe: "Ill fares the land, to hastening ills a prey, Where wealth accumulates, and men decay." Excellent poetry, but not a good working philosophy. Goldsmith would have been right, if, in fact, the accumulation of wealth meant the decay of men. It is rare indeed that the men who are accumulating wealth decay. It is only when they cease production, when accumulation stops, that an irreparable decay begins. Wealth is the product of industry, ambition, character and untiring effort. In all experience, the accumulation of wealth means the multiplication of schools, the increase of knowledge, the dissemination of intelligence, the encouragement of science, the broadening of outlook, the expansion of liberties, the widening of culture. Of course, the accumulation of wealth cannot be justified as the chief end of existence. But we are compelled to recognize it as a means to well-nigh every desirable achievement. So long as wealth is made the means and not the end, we need not greatly fear it. An there never was time when wealth was so generally regarded as a means, or so little regarded as an end, as today.

Just a little time ago we read in your newspapers that two leaders of American business, whose efforts at accumulation had been most astonishingly successful, had given fifty or sixty million dollars as endowments to educational works. That was real

news. It was characteristic of our American experience with men of large resources. They use their power to serve, not themselves and their own families, but the public. I feel sure that the coming generations, which will benefit by those endowments, will not be easily convinced that they have suffered greatly because of these particular accumulations of wealth.

So there is little cause for the fear that our journalism, merely because it is prosperous, is likely to betray us. But it calls for additional effort to avoid even the appearance of the evil of selfishness. In every worthy profession, of course, there will always be a minority who will appeal to the baser instinct. There always have been, and probably always will be some who will feel that their own temporary interest may be furthered by betraying the interest of others. But these are becoming constantly a less numerous and less potential element in the community. Their influence, whatever it may seem at a particular moment, is always ephemeral. They will not long interfere with the progress of the race which is determined to go its own forward and upward way. They may at times somewhat retard and delay its progress, but in the end their opposition will be overcome. They have no permanent effect. They accomplish no permanent result. The race is not traveling in that direction. The power of the spirit always prevails over the power of the flesh. These furnish us no justification for interfering with the freedom of the press, because all freedom, though it may sometime tend toward excesses, bears within it those remedies which will finally effect a cure for its own disorders.

American newspapers have seemed to me to be particularly representative of this practical idealism of our people. Therefore, I feel secure in saying that they are the best newspapers in the world. I believe that they print more real news and more reliable and characteristic news than any other newspaper. I believe their editorial opinions are less colored in influence by mere partisanship or selfish interest, than are those of any other country. Moreover, I believe that our American press is more independent, more reliable and less partisan today than at any other time in its history. I believe this of our press, precisely as I believe it of those who manage our public affairs. Both are cleaner, finer, less influenced by improper considerations, than ever before. Whoever disagrees with this judgment must take the chance of marking himself as ignorant of conditions which notoriously affected our public life, thoughts and methods, even within the memory of many men who are still among us.

It can safely be assumed that self-interest will always place sufficient emphasis on the business side of newspapers, so that they do not need any outside encouragement for that part of their activities. Important, however, as this factor is, it is not the main element which appeals to the American people. It is only those who do not understand our people, who believe that our national life is entirely absorbed by material motives. We make no concealment of the fact that we want wealth, but here are many other things that we want very much more. We want peace and honor, and that charity which is so strong an element of all civilization. The chief ideal of the American people is idealism. I cannot repeat too often that America is a nation of idealists. That is the only motive to which they every give any strong and lasting reaction. No newspaper can be a success which fails to appeal to that element of our national life. It is in this direction that the public press can lend its strongest support to our Government. I could not truly criticize the vast importance of the counting room, but my ultimate faith I would place in the high idealism of the editorial room of the American newspaper.

GLOSSARY

absolutism: rule by a single person or group

actuate: to put into motion; activate

despotism: absolute, autocratic rule; tyranny

oracular: of or relating to an oracle; prophetic or mysterious

republic: government by elected representatives of the people

sedulously: constantly and persistently; diligently

sordid: dirty or foul; morally degraded

Document Analysis

Speaking to an audience of newspaper editors, Coolidge highlights the value of the press in a democratic society. According to Coolidge, the media is responsible for providing full, unbiased information about issues of import to the people of the United States. However, he cautions, the press should be mindful not to become agents of propaganda. He states that the editorial nature of the press can capture not only the facts, but the character of a particular issue. Although he believes that the business responsibilities of a given newspaper serve as a check on corruption, Coolidge says that the risks of corruption are still present.

Coolidge begins his speech by addressing the differences between the press in a free, democratic society and the press in an autocratic nation. The latter form of government, he says, could never survive without using the press to disseminate skewed and manipulated information. The press, therefore, becomes an agent of government propaganda, perpetuating the power of the despot. In a democratic republic, however, the press becomes an agent of information itself, not the government. The press, in this setting, is responsible for educating and enlightening the people, giving to the information it disseminates what Coolidge calls "dignity."

Coolidge continues by encouraging the press to take notice of the difference between information and propaganda. It is not an easy task to combat the latter, he says—there are sources who claim to be "specialists," for example, but are instead untrustworthy, being driven by self-interest and capable of beguiling even the most careful of reporters. The newspapers stand in the difficult position, he says, of ensuring that the information they print is factual and free of prejudice.

Adding to the challenge of being a newspaperman, Coolidge says, is the fact that the press needs to capture the attention of the reader. Mere facts are often not sufficient to sell papers, he says—there is a need for a story to capture the character, human experience, and the spirit of American idealism. The editorial provides a vehicle for combining idealism with unadulterated information. In this regard, Coolidge says, newspapers elevate their storytelling to the level of art.

The very fact that American newspapers are businesses that rely on sales profits, Coolidge states, makes it unlikely that a mainstream newspaper would deal in overt misinformation and propaganda. The press uses a news story to report on the facts, and its editorial pages to comment on and analyze those facts. The focus of either approach, Coolidge adds, should be on the public interest and not any motivating factors driven by the business entities behind the media.

Because of the positive characteristics Coolidge ascribes to the American press—its relative immunity to propaganda and corruption, its motivation to serve the public interest, and its ability to capture American idealism—he calls America's newspapers the "best newspapers in the world." This distinction is important, he adds, as it means that despite the negative and corrupting influences that exist, the American press is more suited to reporting on the ever-changing world than ever before.

Essential Themes

Dubbed "Silent Cal," Calvin Coolidge was, to many, surprisingly accessible to the press. In his speech to the American Society of Newspaper Editors, Coolidge is highly complimentary of the American media, particularly in an era when the press was susceptible to the corruptive elements of 1920s society.

He comments on the fact that in other political systems—those ruled by dictators and despots—the media is a tool of the leadership. Such leadership uses the press to provide only the type of information that will keep the people loyal to the government. In the case of the American democratic landscape, he says, the press is a resource of the people. It is willing to seek objective fact, regardless of whether it proves critical of the government.

The American press, Coolidge says, is the best in the world for a number of reasons. First, the press is dedicated to the facts, even if they are contrary to the preferences of the government. Second, the American press is far less susceptible to propaganda than the media in other nations. Third, the American media, through its editorials, is able to capture not only the facts of the news, but the character of the people and society behind that the news as well.

To be sure, Coolidge says, there remains a risk that the media could be corrupted by propagandists. He advises his audience to remain vigilant against false and misleading information. But the free press is a definitively American industry, Coolidge says, focused not on serving the government or private business interests, but on serving its readers and the general public.

—*Michael P. Auerbach*

Bibliography and Additional Reading

Allen, Frederick Lewis. *Only Yesterday: An Informal History of the 1920's*. Marblehead, MA: Wiley, 1931.

Ferrell, Robert H. *The Presidency of Calvin Coolidge*. Lawrence: University Press of Kansas, 1998.

Goldberg, David J. *Discontented America: The United States of the 1920s*. Baltimore: Johns Hopkins University Press, 1999.

■ *Near v. Minnesota*

Date: June 1, 1931
Author: U.S. Supreme Court
Genre: Court opinion

Summary

In this case the U.S. Supreme Court ruled that a state law violated freedom of the press and held, for the first time, that injunctions on the press to prevent publication are presumptively unconstitutional "prior restraints" and that the parties seeking them have a heavy burden to overcome; however, it also suggested that prior restraints could be acceptable under certain circumstances.

The case of *Near v. Minnesota* originated when a Minnesota man, Jay Near, publisher of *The Saturday Press*, was charged with violating a state law prohibiting publication of "malicious, scandalous and defamatory" articles. From 1919 through 1933, the manufacture, sale, or importation of intoxicating liquor was prohibited in the United States. Bootlegging and associated illegal activities attempted to circumvent such prohibitions. In 1927, Near's newspaper published articles claiming that a Jewish gangster controlled gambling and bootlegging in Minneapolis and that local officials—including the city's chief of police, the county attorney, and the mayor—failed to perform their duties and were complicit with the criminals. The articles leveled serious allegations against these public officials. Minnesota officials obtained a gag order enjoining continued publication of the newspaper. The injunction could be lifted only by the judge who issued it, and that judge would have to be convinced that Near's publication would not be objectionable in the future.

When Near's challenge to the Minnesota law reached the U.S. Supreme Court in 1931, the Court voted five to four to invalidate the law. Writing for the majority, Chief Justice Charles Evans Hughes observed that there was no doubt that freedom of the press was a liberty protected by the Fourteenth Amendment's due process clause. The law allowed public authorities to bring a publisher before a judge and to obtain an order suppressing further publication. This, Hughes said, constituted censorship. Reviewing the historical record, Hughes concluded that a chief purpose of liberty of the press is to prevent previous restraints on publication. He also wrote that public officers objecting to press characterizations of their conduct could take action under libel laws, but not by restraining publication before the fact. Subsequent punishment for false accusations was the appropriate remedy. The fact that press liberty may be abused by "miscreant purveyors of scandal" did not justify prior restraint upon publication.

The October 15, 1927 edition of The Saturday Press *is part of the background of the case.*

Chief Justice Charles Evans Hughes observed that there was no doubt that freedom of the press was a liberty protected by the Fourteenth Amendment's due process clause. Hughes is shown here in Winona, Minnesota, during the 1916 presidential campaign.

HISTORICAL DOCUMENT

U.S. Supreme Court

Near v. Minnesota, 283 U.S. 697 (1931)

Near v. Minnesota

No. 91

Argued January 30, 1931

Decided June 1, 1931

283 U.S. 697

MR. CHIEF JUSTICE HUGHES delivered the opinion of the Court.

[Background Facts]

Chapter 285 of the Session Laws of Minnesota for the year 1925 provides for the abatement, as a public nuisance, of a "malicious, scandalous and defamatory newspaper, magazine or other periodical." Section one of the Act is as follows:

"Section 1. Any person who, as an individual, or as a member or employee of a firm, or association or organization, or as an officer, director, member or employee of a corporation, shall be engaged in the business of regularly or customarily producing, publishing or circulating, having in possession, selling or giving away"

"(a) an obscene, lewd and lascivious newspaper, magazine, or other periodical, or"

"(b) a malicious, scandalous and defamatory newspaper, magazine or other periodical,"

is guilty of a nuisance, and all persons guilty of such nuisance may be enjoined, as hereinafter provided. "Participation in such business shall constitute a commission of such nuisance and render the participant liable and subject to the proceedings, orders and judgments provided for in this Act. Ownership, in whole or in part, directly or indirectly, of any such periodical, or of any stock or interest in any corporation or organization which owns the same in whole or in part, or which publishes the same, shall constitute such participation."

"In actions brought under (b) above, there shall be available the defense that the truth was published with good motives and for justifiable ends and in such actions the plaintiff shall not have the right to report (*sic*) to issues or editions of periodicals taking place more than three months before the commencement of the action."

Section two provides that, whenever any such nuisance is committed or exists, the County Attorney of any county where any such periodical is published or circulated, or, in case of his failure or refusal to proceed upon written request in good faith of a reputable citizen, the Attorney General, or, upon like failure or refusal of the latter, any citizen of the county may maintain an action in the district court of the county in the name of the State to enjoin perpetually the persons committing or maintaining any such nuisance from further committing or maintaining it. Upon such evidence as the court shall deem sufficient, a temporary injunction may be granted. The defendants have the right to plead by demurrer or answer, and the plaintiff may demur or reply as in other cases.

The action, by section three, is to be "governed by the practice and procedure applicable to civil actions for injunctions," and, after trial, the court may enter judgment permanently enjoining the defendants found guilty of violating the Act from continuing the violation, and, "in and by such judgment, such nuisance may be wholly abated." The court is empowered, as in other cases of contempt, to punish disobedience to a temporary or permanent injunction by fine of not more than $1,000 or by imprisonment in the county jail for not more than twelve months.

Under this statute, clause (b), the County Attorney of Hennepin County brought this action to enjoin the publication of what was described as a "malicious, scandalous and defamatory newspaper, magazine and periodical" known as "The Saturday

Press," published by the defendants in the city of Minneapolis. The complaint alleged that the defendants, on September 24, 1927, and on eight subsequent dates in October and November, 1927, published and circulated editions of that periodical which were "largely devoted to malicious, scandalous and defamatory articles" concerning Charles G. Davis, Frank W. Brunskill, the Minneapolis Tribune, the Minneapolis Journal, Melvin C. Passolt, George E. Leach, the Jewish Race, the members of the Grand Jury of Hennepin County impaneled in November, 1927, and then holding office, and other persons, as more fully appeared in exhibits annexed to the complaint, consisting of copies of the articles described and constituting 327 pages of the record. While the complaint did not so allege, it appears from the briefs of both parties that Charles G. Davis was a special law enforcement officer employed by a civic organization, that George E. Leach was Mayor of Minneapolis, that Frank W. Brunskill was its Chief of Police, and that Floyd B. Olson (the relator in this action) was County Attorney.

Without attempting to summarize the contents of the voluminous exhibits attached to the complaint, we deem it sufficient to say that the articles charged in substance that a Jewish gangster was in control of gambling, bootlegging and racketeering in Minneapolis, and that law enforcing officers and agencies were not energetically performing their duties. Most of the charges were directed against the Chief of Police; he was charged with gross neglect of duty, illicit relations with gangsters, and with participation in graft. The County Attorney was charged with knowing the existing conditions and with failure to take adequate measures to remedy them. The Mayor was accused of inefficiency and dereliction. One member of the grand jury was stated to be in sympathy with the gangsters. A special grand jury and a special prosecutor were demanded to deal with the situation in general, and, in particular, to investigate an attempt to assassinate one Guilford, one of the original defendants, who, it appears from the articles, was shot by gangsters after the first issue of the periodical had been published. There is no question but that the articles made serious accusations against the public officers named and others

in connection with the prevalence of crimes and the failure to expose and punish them.

At the beginning of the action, on November 22, 1927, and upon the verified complaint, an order was made directing the defendants to show cause why a temporary injunction should not issue and meanwhile forbidding the defendants to publish, circulate or have in their possession any editions of the periodical from September 24, 1927, to November 19, 1927, inclusive, and from publishing, circulating, or having in their possession, "any future editions of said *The Saturday Press*" and "any publication, known by any other name whatsoever containing malicious, scandalous and defamatory matter of the kind alleged in plaintiff's complaint herein or otherwise."

The defendants demurred to the complaint upon the ground that it did not state facts sufficient to constitute a cause of action, and on this demurrer challenged the constitutionality of the statute. The District Court overruled the demurrer and certified the question of constitutionality to the Supreme Court of the State. The Supreme Court sustained the statute (174 Minn. 457, 219 N.W. 770), and it is conceded by the appellee that the Act was thus held to be valid over the objection that it violated not only the state constitution, but also the Fourteenth Amendment of the Constitution of the United States.

Thereupon, the defendant Near, the present appellant, answered the complaint. He averred that he was the sole owner and proprietor of the publication in question. He admitted the publication of the articles in the issues described in the complaint, but denied that they were malicious, scandalous or defamatory as alleged. He expressly invoked the protection of the due process clause of the Fourteenth Amendment. The case then came on for trial. The plaintiff offered in evidence the verified complaint, together with the issues of the publication in question, which were attached to the complaint as exhibits. The defendant objected to the introduction of the evidence, invoking the constitutional provisions to which his answer referred. The objection was overruled, no further evidence was presented, and the plaintiff rested. The defendant then rested without offering evidence. The plaintiff moved that the court direct the issue of a permanent injunction, and this was done.

The District Court made findings of fact which followed the allegations of the complaint and found in general terms that the editions in question were "chiefly devoted to malicious, scandalous and defamatory articles" concerning the individuals named. The court further found that the defendants, through these publications, "did engage in the business of regularly and customarily producing, publishing and circulating a malicious, scandalous and defamatory newspaper," and that "the said publication" "under said name of *The Saturday Press*, or any other name, constitutes a public nuisance under the laws of the State." Judgment was thereupon entered adjudging that "the newspaper, magazine and periodical known as The Saturday Press," as a public nuisance, "be and is hereby abated." The Judgment perpetually enjoined the defendants "from producing, editing, publishing, circulating, having in their possession, selling or giving away any publication whatsoever which is a malicious, scandalous or defamatory newspaper, as defined by law," and also "from further conducting said nuisance under the name and title of said The Saturday Press or any other name or title."

The defendant Near appealed from this judgment to the Supreme Court of the State, again asserting his right under the Federal Constitution, and the judgment was affirmed upon the authority of the former decision…

From the judgment as thus affirmed, the defendant Near appeals to this Court.

[Opinion]

This statute, for the suppression as a public nuisance of a newspaper or periodical, is unusual, if not unique, and raises questions of grave importance transcending the local interests involved in the particular action. It is no longer open to doubt that the liberty of the press, and of speech, is within the liberty safeguarded by the due process clause of the Fourteenth Amendment from invasion by state action. It was found impossible to conclude that this essential personal liberty of the citizen was left unprotected by the general guaranty of fundamental rights of person and property. *Gitlow v. New York*,;

Whitney v. California,; *Fiske v. Kansas*,; *Stromberg v. California, ante*. In maintaining this guaranty, the authority of the State to enact laws to promote the health, safety, morals and general welfare of its people is necessarily admitted. The limits of this sovereign power must always be determined with appropriate regard to the particular subject of its exercise. Thus, while recognizing the broad discretion of the legislature in fixing rates to be charged by those undertaking a public service, this Court has decided that the owner cannot constitutionally be deprived of his right to a fair return, because that is deemed to be of the essence of ownership. *Railroad Commission Cases*; *Northern Pacific Ry. Co. v. North Dakota*. So, while liberty of contract is not an absolute right, and the wide field of activity in the making of contracts is subject to legislative supervision (*Frisbie v. United States*), this Court has held that the power of the State stops short of interference with what are deemed to be certain indispensable requirements of the liberty assured, notably with respect to the fixing of prices and wages. *Tyson Bros. v. Banton*; *Ribnik v. McBride*; *Adkins v. Children's Hospital*, 261 U. S. 561. Liberty of speech, and of the press, is also not an absolute right, and the State may punish its abuse. *Whitney v. California, supra*; *Stromberg v. California, supra*. Liberty, in each of its phases, has its history and connotation, and, in the present instance, the inquiry is as to the historic conception of the liberty of the press and whether the statute under review violates the essential attributes of that liberty.

…It is thus important to note precisely the purpose and effect of the statute as the state court has construed it.

First. The statute is not aimed at the redress of individual or private wrongs. Remedies for libel remain available and unaffected. The statute, said the state court, "is not directed at threatened libel, but at an existing business which, generally speaking, involves more than libel." It is aimed at the distribution of scandalous matter as "detrimental to public morals and to the general welfare," tending "to disturb the peace of the community" and "to provoke assaults and the commission of crime." In order to obtain an injunction to suppress the future publication of the newspaper or periodical, it is not necessary to prove the falsity of the charges that have been made in the publication condemned. In the present action, there was no allegation that the matter published was not true. It is alleged, and the statute requires the allegation, that the publication was "malicious." But, as in prosecutions for libel, there is no requirement of proof by the State of malice in fact, as distinguished from malice inferred from the mere publication of the defamatory matter. The judgment in this case proceeded upon the mere proof of publication. The statute permits the defense not of the truth alone, but only that the truth was published with good motives and for justifiable ends. It is apparent that, under the statute, the publication is to be regarded as defamatory if it injures reputation, and that it is scandalous if it circulates charges of reprehensible conduct, whether criminal or otherwise, and the publication is thus deemed to invite public reprobation and to constitute a public scandal. The court sharply defined the purpose of the statute, bringing out the precise point, in these words:

"There is no constitutional right to publish a fact merely because it is true. It is a matter of common knowledge that prosecutions under the criminal libel statutes do not result in efficient repression or suppression of the evils of scandal. Men who are the victims of such assaults seldom resort to the courts. This is especially true if their sins are exposed and the only question relates to whether it was done with good motives and for justifiable ends. This law is not for the protection of the person attacked, nor to punish the wrongdoer. It is for the protection of the public welfare."

Second. The statute is directed not simply at the circulation of scandalous and defamatory statements with regard to private citizens, but at the continued publication by newspapers and periodicals of charges against public officers of corruption, malfeasance in office, or serious neglect of duty. Such charges, by their very nature, create a public scandal. They are scandalous and defamatory within the meaning of the statute, which has its normal operation in relation to publications dealing prominently and chiefly with the alleged derelictions of public officers.

Third. The object of the statute is not punishment, in the ordinary sense, but suppression of the offending newspaper or periodical. The reason for the enactment, as the state court has said, is that prosecutions to enforce penal statutes for libel do not result in "efficient repression or suppression of the evils of scandal." Describing the business of publication as a public nuisance does not obscure the substance of the proceeding which the statute authorizes. It is the continued publication of scandalous and defamatory matter that constitutes the business and the declared nuisance. In the case of public officers, it is the reiteration of charges of official misconduct, and the fact that the newspaper or periodical is principally devoted to that purpose, that exposes it to suppression. In the present instance, the proof was that nine editions of the newspaper or periodical in question were published on successive dates, and that they were chiefly devoted to charges against public officers and in relation to the prevalence and protection of crime. In such a case, these officers are not left to their ordinary remedy in a suit for libel, or the authorities to a prosecution for criminal libel. Under this statute, a publisher of a newspaper or periodical, undertaking to conduct a campaign to expose and to censure official derelictions, and devoting his publication principally to that purpose, must face not simply the possibility of a verdict against him in a suit or prosecution for libel, but a determination that his newspaper or periodical is a public nuisance to be abated, and that this abatement and suppression will follow unless he is prepared with legal evidence to prove the truth of the charges and also to satisfy the court that, in addition to being true, the matter was published with good motives and for justifiable ends.

This suppression is accomplished by enjoining publication, and that restraint is the object and effect of the statute.

Fourth. The statute not only operates to suppress the offending newspaper or periodical, but to put the publisher under an effective censorship. When a newspaper or periodical is found to be "malicious, scandalous, and defamatory," and is suppressed as such, resumption of publication is punishable as a contempt of court by fine or imprisonment. Thus, where a newspaper or periodical has been suppressed because of the circulation of charges against public officers of official misconduct, it would seem to be clear that the renewal of the publication of such charges would constitute a contempt, and that the judgment would lay a permanent restraint upon the publisher, to escape which he must satisfy the court as to the character of a new publication. Whether he would be permitted again to publish matter deemed to be derogatory to the same or other public officers would depend upon the court's ruling. In the present instance, the judgment restrained the defendants from "publishing, circulating, having in their possession, selling or giving away any publication whatsoever which is a malicious, scandalous or defamatory newspaper, as defined by law."

The law gives no definition except that covered by the words "scandalous and defamatory," and publications charging official misconduct are of that class....

If we cut through mere details of procedure, the operation and effect of the statute, in substance, is that public authorities may bring the owner or publisher of a newspaper or periodical before a judge upon a charge of conducting a business of publishing scandalous and defamatory matter – in particular, that the matter consists of charges against public officers of official dereliction – and, unless the owner or publisher is able and disposed to bring competent evidence to satisfy the judge that the charges are true and are published with good motives and for justifiable ends, his newspaper or periodical is suppressed and further publication is made punishable as a contempt. This is of the essence of censorship.

The question is whether a statute authorizing such proceedings in restraint of publication is consistent with the conception of the liberty of the press as historically conceived and guaranteed. In determining the extent of the constitutional protection, it has been generally, if not universally, considered that it is the chief purpose of the guaranty to prevent previous restraints upon publication. The struggle in England, directed against the legislative power of the licenser, resulted in renunciation of the censorship of the press. The liberty deemed to be established was thus described by Blackstone:

"The liberty of the press is indeed essential to the nature of a free state; but this consists in laying no *previous* restraints upon publications, and not in freedom from censure for criminal matter when published. Every freeman has an undoubted right to lay what sentiments he pleases before the public; to forbid this is to destroy the freedom of the press; but if he publishes what is improper, mischievous or illegal, he must take the consequence of his own temerity."

The distinction was early pointed out between the extent of the freedom with respect to censorship under our constitutional system and that enjoyed in England. Here, as Madison said, "the great and essential rights of the people are secured against legislative as well as against executive ambition. They are secured not by laws paramount to prerogative, but by constitutions paramount to laws. This security of the freedom of the press requires that it should be exempt not only from previous restraint by the Executive, a in Great Britain, but from legislative restraint also."

This Court said, in *Patterson v. Colorado*:

"In the first place, the main purpose of such constitutional provisions is 'to prevent all such previous restraints upon publications as had been practiced by other governments,' and they do not prevent the subsequent punishment of such as may be deemed contrary to the public welfare. *Commonwealth v. Blanding*; *Respublica v. Oswald*. The preliminary freedom extends as well to the false as to the true; the subsequent punishment may extend as well to the true as to the false. This was the law of criminal libel apart from statute in most cases, if not in all. *Commonwealth v. Blanding, ubi sup*"

The criticism upon Blackstone's statement has not been because immunity from previous restraint upon publication has not been regarded as deserving of special emphasis, but chiefly because that immunity cannot be deemed to exhaust the conception of the liberty guaranteed by state and federal constitutions. The point of criticism has been "that the mere exemption from previous restraints cannot be all that is secured by the constitutional provisions", and that "the liberty of the press might be rendered a mockery and a delusion, and the phrase itself a byword, if, while every man was at liberty to publish what he pleased, the public authorities might nevertheless punish him for harmless publications."

…But it is recognized that punishment for the abuse of the liberty accorded to the press is essential to the protection of the public, and that the common law rules that subject the libeler to responsibility for the public offense, as well as for the private injury, are not abolished by the protection extended in our constitutions. *Id.,* pp. 883, 884. The law of criminal libel rests upon that secure foundation. There is also the conceded authority of courts to punish for contempt when publications directly tend to prevent the proper discharge of judicial functions. *Patterson v. Colorado, supra; Toledo Newspaper Co. v. United States.* In the present case, we have no occasion to inquire as to the permissible scope of subsequent punishment. For whatever wrong the appellant has committed or may commit by his publications the State appropriately affords both public and private redress by its libel laws. As has been noted, the statute in question does not deal with punishments; it provides for no punishment, except in case of contempt for violation of the court's order, but for suppression and injunction, that is, for restraint upon publication.

The objection has also been made that the principle as to immunity from previous restraint is stated too broadly, if every such restraint is deemed to be prohibited. That is undoubtedly true; the protection even as to previous restraint is not absolutely unlimited. But the limitation has been recognized only in exceptional cases: "When a nation is at war, many things that might be said in time of peace are such a hindrance to its effort that their utterance will not be endured so long as men fight, and that no Court could regard them as protected by any constitutional right."

…No one would question but that a government might prevent actual obstruction to its recruiting service or the publication of the sailing dates of transports or the number and location of troops. On similar grounds, the primary requirements of decency may be enforced against obscene publications. The security of the community life may be protected against incitements to acts of violence and the overthrow by force of orderly government. The constitutional guaranty of free speech does not "protect a man from an injunction against uttering words that may have all the effect of force. *Gompers v. Buck Stove & Range Co.".*…These limitations are not applicable here. Nor are we now concerned with questions as to the extent of authority to prevent publications in order to protect private rights according to the principles governing the exercise of the jurisdiction of courts of equity.

The exceptional nature of its limitations places in a strong light the general conception that liberty of the press, historically considered and taken up by the Federal Constitution, has meant, principally, although not exclusively, immunity from previous restraints or censorship. The conception of the liberty of the press in this country had broadened with the exigencies of the colonial period and with the efforts to secure freedom from oppressive administration. That liberty was especially cherished for the immunity it afforded from previous restraint of the publication of censure of public officers and charges of official misconduct. As was said by Chief Justice Parker, in *Commonwealth v. Blanding,* with respect to the constitution of Massachusetts:

"Besides, it is well understood, and received as a commentary on this provision for the liberty of the press, that it was intended to prevent all such *previous restraints* upon publications as had been practiced by other governments, and in early times here, to stifle the efforts of patriots towards enlightening their fellow subjects upon their rights and the duties of rulers. The liberty of the press was to be unrestrained, but he who used it was to be responsible in case of its abuse."

In the letter sent by the Continental Congress (October 26, 1774) to the Inhabitants of Quebec, referring to the "five great rights," it was said:

"The last right we shall mention regards the freedom of the press. The importance of this consists, besides the advancement of truth, science, morality, and arts in general, in its diffusion of liberal sentiments on the administration of Government, its ready communication of thoughts between subjects, and its consequential promotion of union among them whereby oppressive officers are shamed or intimidated into more honourable and just modes of conducting affairs."

Madison, who was the leading spirit in the preparation of the First Amendment of the Federal Constitution, thus described the practice and sentiment which led to the guaranties of liberty of the press in state constitutions:

"In every State, probably, in the Union, the press has exerted a freedom in canvassing the merits and measures of public men of every description which has not been confined to the strict limits of the common law. On this footing the freedom of the press has stood; on this footing it yet stands … Some degree of abuse is inseparable from the proper use of everything, and in no instance is this more true than in that of the press. It has accordingly been decided by the practice of the States that it is better to leave a few of its noxious branches to their luxuriant growth than, by pruning them away, to injure the vigour of those yielding the proper fruits. And can the wisdom of this policy be doubted by any who reflect that to the press alone, chequered as it is with abuses, the world is indebted for all the triumphs which have been gained by reason and humanity over error and oppression; who reflect that to the same beneficent source the United States owe much of the lights which conducted them to the ranks of a free and independent nation, and which have improved their political system into a shape so auspicious to their happiness? Had 'Sedition Acts,' forbidding every publication that might bring the constituted agents into contempt or disrepute, or that might excite the hatred of the people against the authors of unjust or pernicious measures, been uniformly enforced against the press, might not the United States have been languishing at this day under the infirmities of a sickly Confederation? Might they not, possibly, be miserable colonies, groaning under a foreign yoke?"

The fact that, for approximately one hundred and fifty years, there has been almost an entire absence of attempts to impose previous restraints upon publications relating to the malfeasance of public officers is significant of the deep-seated conviction that such restraints would violate constitutional right. Public officers, whose character and conduct remain open to debate and free discussion in the press, find their remedies for false accusations in actions under libel laws providing for redress and punishment, and not in proceedings to restrain the publication of newspapers and periodicals. The general principle that the constitutional guaranty of the liberty of the press gives immunity from previous restraints has been approved in many decisions under the provisions of state constitutions.

The importance of this immunity has not lessened. While reckless assaults upon public men, and efforts to bring obloquy upon those who are endeavoring faithfully to discharge official duties, exert a baleful influence and deserve the severest condemnation in public opinion, it cannot be said that this abuse is greater, and it is believed to be less, than that which characterized the period in which our institutions took shape. Meanwhile, the administration of government has become more complex, the opportunities for malfeasance and corruption have multiplied, crime has grown to most serious proportions, and the danger of its protection by unfaithful officials and of the impairment of the fundamental security of life and property by criminal alliances and official neglect, emphasizes the primary need of a vigilant and courageous press, especially in great cities. The fact that the liberty of the press may be abused by miscreant purveyors of scandal does not make any the less necessary the immunity of the press from previous restraint in dealing with official misconduct. Subsequent punishment for such abuses as may exist is the appropriate remedy consistent with constitutional privilege.

In attempted justification of the statute, it is said that it deals not with publication *per se,* but with the "business" of publishing defamation. If, however, the publisher has a constitutional right to publish, without previous restraint, an edition of his newspaper charging official derelictions, it cannot be denied that he may publish subsequent editions for the same purpose. He does not lose his right by exercising it. If his right exists, it may be exercised in publishing nine editions, as in this case, as well as in one edition. If previous restraint is permissible, it may be imposed at once; indeed, the wrong may be as serious in one publication as in several. Characterizing the publication as a business, and the business as a nuisance, does not permit an invasion of the constitutional immunity against restraint. Similarly, it does not matter that the newspaper or periodical is found to be "largely" or "chiefly" devoted to the publication of such derelictions. If the publisher has a right, without previous restraint, to publish them, his right cannot be deemed to be dependent upon his publishing something else, more or less, with the matter to which objection is made....

The statute in question cannot be justified by reason of the fact that the publisher is permitted to show, before injunction issues, that the matter published is true and is published with good motives and for justifiable ends. If such a statute, authorizing suppression and injunction on such a basis, is constitutionally valid, it would be equally permissible for the legislature to provide that at any time the publisher of any newspaper could be brought before a court, or even an administrative officer (as the constitutional protection may not be regarded as resting on mere procedural details) and required to produce proof of the truth of his publication, or of what he intended to publish, and of his motives, or stand enjoined. If this can be done, the legislature may provide machinery for determining in the complete exercise of its discretion what are justifiable ends, and restrain publication accordingly. And it would be but a step to a complete system of censorship. The recognition of authority to impose previous restraint upon publication in order to protect the community against the circulation of charges of misconduct, and especially of official misconduct, necessarily would carry with it the admission of the authority of the censor against which the constitutional barrier was erected. The preliminary freedom, by virtue of the very reason for its existence, does not depend, as this Court has said, on proof of truth.

Equally unavailing is the insistence that the statute is designed to prevent the circulation of scandal which tends to disturb the public peace and to provoke assaults and the commission of crime. Charges of reprehensible conduct, and in particular of official malfeasance, unquestionably create a public scandal, but the theory of the constitutional guaranty is that even a more serious public evil would be caused by authority to prevent publication.

"To prohibit the intent to excite those unfavorable sentiments against those who administer the Government is equivalent to a prohibition of the actual excitement of them, and to prohibit the actual excitement of them is equivalent to a prohibition of discussions having that tendency and effect, which, again, is equivalent to a protection of those who administer the Government, if they should at any time deserve the contempt or hatred of the people, against being exposed to it by free animadversions on their characters and conduct."

There is nothing new in the fact that charges of reprehensible conduct may create resentment and the disposition to resort to violent means of redress, but this well understood tendency did not alter the determination to protect the press against censorship and restraint upon publication. As was said in *New Yorker Staats-Zeitung v. Nolan*:

"If the township may prevent the circulation of a newspaper for no reason other than that some of its inhabitants may violently disagree with it, and resent its circulation by resorting to physical violence, there is no limit to what may be prohibited."

The danger of violent reactions becomes greater with effective organization of defiant groups resenting exposure, and if this consideration warranted legislative interference with the initial freedom of publication, the constitutional protection would be reduced to a mere form of words.

For these reasons we hold the statute, so far as it authorized the proceedings in this action under clause (b) of section one, to be an infringement of the liberty of the press guaranteed by the Fourteenth Amendment. We should add that this decision rests upon the operation and effect of the statute, without regard to the question of the truth of the charges contained in the particular periodical. The fact that the public officers named in this case, and those associated with the charges of official dereliction, may be deemed to be impeccable cannot affect the conclusion that the statute imposes an unconstitutional restraint upon publication.

Judgment reversed.

MR. JUSTICE BUTLER, dissenting.

The decision of the Court in this case declares Minnesota and every other State powerless to restrain by injunction the business of publishing and circulating among the people malicious, scandalous and defamatory periodicals that in due course of judicial procedure has been adjudged to be a public nuisance. It gives to freedom of the press a meaning and a scope not heretofore recognized, and construes "liberty" in the due process clause of the Fourteenth Amendment to put upon the States a federal restriction that is without precedent....

The Court quotes Blackstone in support of its condemnation of the statute as imposing a previous restraint upon publication. But the previous restraints referred to by him subjected the press to the arbitrary will of an administrative officer. He describes the practice (Book IV, p. 152):

"To subject the press to the restrictive power of a licenser, as was formerly done both before and since the revolution [of 1688], is to subject all freedom of sentiment to the prejudices of one man and make him the arbitrary and infallible judge of all controverted points in learning, religion, and government."

Story gives the history alluded to by Blackstone (§ 1882):

"The art of printing, soon after its introduction, we are told, was looked upon, as well in England as in other countries, as merely a matter of state, and subject to the coercion of the crown. It was, therefore, regulated in England by the king's proclamations, prohibitions, charters of privilege, and licenses, and finally by the decrees of the Court of Star-Chamber, which limited the number of printers and of presses which each should employ, and prohibited new publications unless previously approved by proper licensers. On the demolition of this odious jurisdiction, in 1641, the Long Parliament of Charles the First, after their rupture with that prince, assumed the same powers which the Star-Chamber exercised with respect to licensing books, and during the Commonwealth (such is human frailty and the love of power even in republics), they issued their ordinances for that purpose, founded principally upon a Star-Chamber decree of 1637. After the restoration of Charles the Second, a statute on the same subject was passed, copied, with some few alterations, from the parliamentary ordinances. The act expired in 1679, and was revived and continued for a few years after the revolution of 1688. Many attempts were made by the government to keep it in force, but it was so strongly resisted by Parliament that it expired in 1694, and has never since been revived."

It is plain that Blackstone taught that, under the common law liberty of the press means simply the absence of restraint upon publication in advance as distinguished from liability, civil or criminal, for libelous or improper matter so published....

The Minnesota statute does not operate as a *previous* restraint on publication within the proper meaning of that phrase. It does not authorize administrative control in advance such as was formerly exercised by the licensers and censors but prescribes a remedy to be enforced by a suit in equity. In this case, there was previous publication made in the course of the business of regularly producing malicious, scandalous and defamatory periodicals. The business and publications unquestionably constitute an abuse of the right of free press. The statute denounces the things done as a nuisance on the ground, as stated by the state supreme court, that they threaten morals, peace and good order. There is no question of the power of the State to denounce such transgressions. The restraint authorized is only in respect of continuing to do what has been duly adjudged to constitute a nuisance. The controlling words are

"All persons guilty of such nuisance may be enjoined, as hereinafter provided ... Whenever any such nuisance is committed..., an action in the name of the State" may be brought "to perpetually enjoin the person or persons committing, conducting or maintaining any such nuisance, *from further committing, conducting or maintaining any such nuisance* ... The court may make its order and judgment permanently enjoining ... defendants found guilty ... from committing or continuing the acts prohibited hereby, and in and by such judgment, such nuisance may be wholly abated..."

MR. JUSTICE VAN DEVANTER, MR. JUSTICE McREYNOLDS, and MR. JUSTICE SUTHERLAND concur in this opinion.

Document Themes and Impact

Since the *Near v. Minnesota* ruling, the Supreme Court has upheld the doctrine against prior restraints on the media. With only narrow exceptions, governmental restraints on publication before the fact have been regarded as constitutionally impermissible.

—Joseph A. Melusky

Bibliography and Reading

Edelman, Rob, ed. *Freedom of the Press*. San Diego: Greenhaven Press, 2007.

Kersch, Ken I. *Freedom of Speech: Rights and Liberties Under the Law*. Santa Barbara, Calif.: ABC-Clio, 2003.

■ A Free and Responsible Press

Date: March 1947
Author: The Commission on Freedom of the Press
Genre: Report

Summary Overview

Although freedom of the press was one of the founding ideals of the United States, up until the 1940s it was assumed that the protection offered by the Bill of Rights assured its continuation. After witnessing the dramatic transformation of German society by fascist ideology in the 1930s and '40s, however, some observers began to wonder about the security of the press in the United States. The Commission on Freedom of the Press (also known as the Hutchins Commission, after its chairman) undertook a three-year, independent study of the press in American society. The conclusion of this study, whose findings were published in book form, was that press freedom in the United States was under pressure. The Commission believed that it was imperative that a strong and free press should exist in the nation. The authors called on the government to protect that freedom, urged the press to act vigorously yet responsibly, and asked the general public to support such action.

Defining Moment

In December 1942, the publisher of *Time*, and several other magazines, Henry R. Luce visited with Robert M. Hutchins, president of the University of Chicago, regarding the establishment of a commission to answer the question, "Is the freedom of the press in danger?" It took a few years to organize this commission, and with Hutchins moving from president of the university to chancellor, he had more time to devote to the project. Luce donated $200,000 to fund the endeavor (equivalent of over $3.2 million 2019) with the Encyclopedia Britannica later funding an additional $15,000 of the expenses. Internationally, freedom of the press had begun to disappear with the fascists taking over much of Western Europe and the Communist Party taking control in Eastern Europe. Therefore, for concern to be aired about what was happening in the United States seemed to be a legitimate response.

Excluding working members of the press, Hutchins drew together members of the academic community who could use their expertise in innovative ways to study whether or not the press was truly free. Exactly why Luce, a staunch opponent of President Franklin D. Roosevelt, had requested this study has been discussed by scholars. Some believe that since the request was made in 1942, during wartime restrictions on the press, Luce wanted the study completed in order to reduce the possibility of future restrictions on the press. (And, indeed, in the following year Roosevelt forbade U.S. publishers from visiting war zones.) Others have taken Luce's funding at face value, believing that as the most influential American publisher at the time Luce really did want a philosophical answer to what constituted a free press in a democratic society. In any event, he, and the rest of the nation, received an extensive, albeit not totally complete, study of this issue.

Changing technologies were affecting the press in the late 1940s. In the decade prior to the request for the report, people's preferences had moved away from the traditional daily newspapers, to newsreels, radio, or weekly news magazines. By the time this report was issued, further changes were taking shape, with newsreels fading in importance and the new broadcast medium, television, starting to emerge as an important source of news. Whatever form the "press" took, however, the question of whether it was fully free or not was a valid one.

Author Biography

The Commission on Freedom of the Press was composed of thirteen members: Robert M. Hutchins, Chancellor of the University of Chicago, chair; Zechariah Chafee Jr, professor at Harvard University, vice-chair; John M. Clark, professor at Columbia University; John Dickinson, professor at the University of Pennsylvania; William K. Hocking, professor emeritus at Harvard University; Harold D. Lasswell, professor at Yale University; Archibald MacLeish, former Assistant Secretary of State; Charles E. Merriam, professor emeritus at the University of Chicago; Reinhold Niebuhr, professor at Union Theological Seminary; Robert Redfield, professor at the University of Chicago; Beardsley Ruml, chairman of the Federal Reserve Bank of New York; Arthur M. Schlesinger, professor at Harvard University; and George N. Shuster, president

Illustration shows a male newspaper owner and editor dressed as a female prostitute called "The Madam," taking money from a man labeled "Big Advertisers" as staff sit under a sign with the message "Obey the Madam."

of Hunter College; with John Grierson, Canada; Hu Shih, China; Jacques Maritain, France; and Kurt Riezler, Germany. Only Hutchins, with his previous responsibilities at the University of Chicago Press, had any publishing experience. The committee members were white males virtually all with terminal degrees and related to universities or institutions in Chicago or the Northeastern region of the United States.

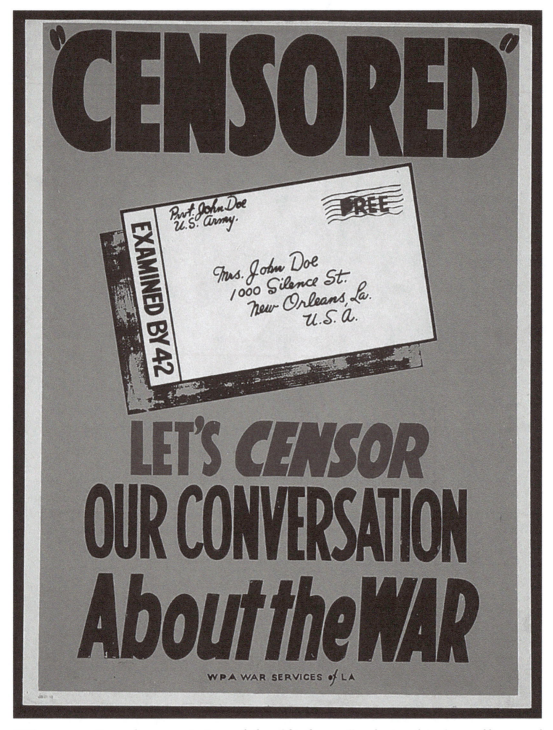

WPA poster suggesting careless communication may be harmful to the war effort, showing a letter from a soldier stamped "examined by 42." (WPA Federal Art Project—Work Projects Administration Poster Collection, Library of Congress)

HISTORICAL DOCUMENT

A FREE AND RESPONSIBLE PRESS

A General Report on Mass Communication: Newspapers, Radio, Motion Pictures, Magazines, and Books

THE PROBLEM AND THE PRINCIPLES

The Problem

THE Commission set out to answer the question: Is the freedom of the press in danger? Its answer to that question is: Yes. It concludes that the freedom of the press is in danger for three reasons:

First, the importance of the press to the people has greatly increased with the development of the press as an instrument of mass communication. At the same time the development of the press as an instrument of mass communication has greatly decreased the proportion of the people who can express their opinions and ideas through the press.

Second, the few who are able to use the machinery of the press as an instrument of mass communication have not provided a service adequate to the needs of the society.

Third, those who direct the machinery of the press have engaged from time to time in practices which the society condemns and which, if continued, it will inevitably undertake to regulate or control.

When an instrument of prime importance to all the people is available to a small minority of the people only, and when it is employed by that small minority in such a way as not to supply the people with the service they require, the freedom of the minority in the employment of that instrument is in danger.

This danger, in the case of the freedom of the press, is in part the consequence of the economic structure of the press, in part the consequence of the industrial organization of modern society, and in part the result of the failure of the directors of the press to recognize the press needs of a modern nation and to estimate and accept the responsibilities which those needs impose upon them.

We do not believe that the danger to the freedom of the press is so great that that freedom will be swept away overnight. In our view the present crisis is simply a stage in the long struggle for free expression. Freedom of expression, of which freedom of the press is a part, has always been in danger. Indeed, the Commission can conceive no state of society in which it will not be in danger. The desire to suppress opinion different from one's own is inveterate and probably ineradicable.

Neither do we believe that the problem is one to which a simple solution can be found. Government ownership, government control, or government action to break up the greater agencies of mass communication might cure the ills of freedom of the press, but only at the risk of killing the freedom in the process. Although, as we shall see later, government has an important part to play in communications, we look principally to the press and the people to remedy the ills which have chiefly concerned us.

But though the crisis is not unprecedented and though the cures may not be dramatic, the problem is nevertheless a problem of peculiar importance to this generation. And not in the United States alone but in England and Japan and Australia and Austria and France and Germany as well; and in Russia and in the Russian pale. The reasons are obvious. The relation of the modern press to modern society is a new and unfamiliar relation.

The modern press itself is a new phenomenon. Its typical unit is the great agency of mass communication. These agencies can facilitate thought and discussion. They can stifle it. They can advance the progress of civilization or they can thwart it. They can debase and vulgarize mankind. They can endanger the peace of the world; they can do so accidentally, in a fit of absence of mind. They can play up or down the news and its significance, foster and feed emotions, create complacent fictions and blind spots, misuse the great words, and uphold empty slogans. Their scope and power are increasing every day as new instruments become available to them.

These instruments can spread lies faster and farther than our forefathers dreamed when they enshrined the freedom of the press in the First Amendment to our Constitution.

With the means of self-destruction that are now at their disposal, men must live, if they are to live at all, by self-restraint, moderation, and mutual understanding. They get their picture of one another through the press. The press can be inflammatory, sensational, and irresponsible. If it is, it and its freedom will go down in the universal catastrophe. On the other hand, the press can do its duty by the new world that is struggling to be born. It can help create a world community by giving men everywhere knowledge of the world and of one another, by promoting comprehension and appreciation of the goals of a free society that shall embrace all men.

We have seen in our time a revival of the doctrine that the state is all and that the person is merely an instrument of its purposes. We cannot suppose that the military defeat of totalitarianism in its German and Italian manifestations has put an end to the influence and attractiveness of the doctrine. The necessity of finding some way through the complexities of modern life and of controlling the concentrations of power associated with modern industry will always make it look as though turning over all problems to the government would easily solve them.

This notion is a great potential danger to the freedom of the press. That freedom is the first which totalitarianism strikes down. But steps toward totalitarianism may be taken, perhaps unconsciously, because of conditions within the press itself. A technical society requires concentration of economic power. Since such concentration is a threat to democracy, democracy replies by breaking up some centers of power that are too large and too strong and by controlling, or even owning, others. Modern society requires great agencies of mass communication. They, too, are concentrations of power. But breaking up a vast network of communication is a different thing from breaking up an oil monopoly or a tobacco monopoly. If the people set out to break up a unit of communication on the theory that it is too large and strong, they may destroy a service which they require. Moreover, since action to break up an agency

of communication must be taken at the instance of a department of the government, the risk is considerable that the freedom of the press will be imperiled through the application of political pressure by that department.

If modern society requires great agencies of mass communication, if these concentrations become so powerful that they are a threat to democracy, if democracy cannot solve the problem simply by breaking them up then those agencies must control themselves or be controlled by government. If they are controlled by government, we lose our chief safeguard against totalitarianism and at the same time take a long step toward it.

The Principles

Freedom of the press is essential to political liberty. Where men cannot freely convey their thoughts to one another, no freedom is secure. Where freedom of expression exists, the beginnings of a free society and a means for every extension of liberty are already present. Free expression is therefore unique among liberties: it promotes and protects all the rest.\ It is appropriate that freedom of speech and freedom of the press are contained in the first of those constitutional enactments which are the American Bill of Rights.

Civilized society is a working system of ideas. It lives and changes by the consumption of ideas. Therefore it must make sure that as many as possible of the ideas which its members have are available for its examination. It must guarantee freedom of expression, to the end that all adventitious hindrances to the flow of ideas shall be removed. Moreover, a significant innovation in the realm of ideas is likely to arouse resistance. Valuable ideas may be put forth first in forms that are crude, indefensible, or even dangerous. They need the chance to develop thoroughly free criticism as well as the chance to survive on the basis of their ultimate worth. Hence the man who publishes ideas requires special protection.

The reason for the hostility which the critic or innovator may expect is not merely that it is easier and more natural to suppress or discourage him than to meet his arguments. Irrational elements are always present in the critic, the innovator, and their audience. The utterance of critical or new ideas is seldom an appeal to pure reason, devoid of emotion, and the response is not necessarily a debate; it is always a function of the intelligence, the prejudice, the emotional biases of the audience. Freedom of the press to appeal to reason may always be construed as freedom of the press to appeal to public passion and ignorance, vulgarity and cynicism. As freedom of the press is always in danger, so is it always dangerous. The freedom of the press illustrates the commonplace that if we are to live progressively we must live dangerously.

Across the path of the flow of ideas lie the existing centers of social power. The primary protector of freedom of expression against their obstructive influence is government. Government acts by maintaining order and by exercising on behalf of free speech and a free press the elementary sanctions against the expressions of private interest or resentment: sabotage, blackmail, and corruption.

But any power capable of protecting freedom is also capable of endangering it. Every modern government, liberal or otherwise, has a specific position in the field of ideas; its stability is vulnerable to critics in proportion to their ability and persuasiveness. A government resting on popular suffrage is no exception to this rule. It also may be tempted—just because public opinion is a factor in official livelihood—to manage the ideas and images entering public debate.

If the freedom of the press is to achieve reality, government must set limits on its capacity to interfere with, regulate, or suppress the voices of the press or to manipulate the data on which public judgment is formed.

Government must set these limits on itself, not merely because freedom of expression is a reflection of important interests of the community, but also because it is a moral right. It is a moral right because it has an aspect of duty about it.

It is true that the motives for expression are not all dutiful. They are and should be as multiform as human emotion itself, grave and gay, casual and purposeful, artful and idle. But there is a vein of expression which has the added impulsion of duty, and that is the expression of thought. If a man is burdened with an idea, he not only desires to express it; he ought to express it. He owes it to his conscience and the common good. The indispensable function of expressing ideas is one of obligation—to the community and also to something beyond the community—let us say to truth. It is the duty of the scientist to his result and of Socrates to his oracle; it is the duty of every man to his own belief. Because of this duty to what is beyond the state, freedom of speech and freedom of the press are moral rights which the state must not infringe.

The moral right of free expression achieves a legal status because the conscience of the citizen is the source of the continued vitality of the state. Wholly apart from the traditional ground for a free press— that it promotes the "victory of truth over falsehood" in the public arena—we see that public discussion is a necessary condition of a free society and that freedom of expression is a necessary condition of adequate public discussion. Public discussion elicits mental power and breadth; it is essential to the building of a mentally robust public; and, without something of the kind, a self-governing society could not operate. The original source of supply for this process is the duty of the individual thinker to his thought; here is the primary ground of his right.

This does not mean that every citizen has a moral or legal right to own a press or be an editor or have access, as of right, to the audience of any given medium of communication. But it does belong to the intention of the freedom of the press that an idea shall have its chance even if it is not shared by those who own or manage the press. The press is not free if those who operate it behave as though their position conferred on them the privilege of being deaf to ideas which the processes of free speech have brought to public attention.

But the moral right of free public expression is not unconditional. Since the claim of the right is based on the duty of a man to the common good and to his thought, the ground of the claim disappears when this duty is ignored or rejected. In the absence of accepted moral duties there are no moral rights. Hence, when the man who claims the moral right of free expression is a liar, a prostitute whose political judgments can be bought, a dishonest inflamer of hatred and suspicion, his claim is unwarranted and groundless. From the moral point of view, at least, freedom of expression does not include the right to lie as a deliberate instrument of policy.

The right of free public expression does include the right to be in error. Liberty is experimental. Debate itself could not exist unless wrong opinions could be rightfully offered by those who suppose them to be right. But the assumption that the man in error is actually trying for truth is of the essence of his claim for freedom. What the moral right does not cover is the right to be deliberately or irresponsibly in error.

But a moral right can be forfeited and a legal right retained. Legal protection cannot vary with the fluctuations of inner moral direction in individual wills; it does not cease whenever a person has abandoned the moral ground of his right. It is not even desirable that the whole area of the responsible use of freedom should be made legally compulsory, even if it were possible; for in that case free self-control, a necessary ingredient of any free state, would be superseded by mechanism.

Many a lying, venal, and scoundrelly public expression must continue to find shelter under a "freedom of the press" built for widely different purposes, for to impair the legal right even when the moral right is gone may easily be a cure worse than the disease. Each definition of an abuse invites abuse of the definition. If the courts had to determine the inner corruptions of personal intention, honest and necessary criticisms would proceed under an added peril.

Though the presumption is against resort to legal action to curb abuses of the press, there are limits to legal toleration. The already recognized areas of legal correction of misused liberty of expression—libel, misbranding, obscenity, incitement to riot, sedition—in case of clear and present danger have a common principle; namely, that an utterance or publication invades in a serious, overt, and demonstrable manner personal rights or vital social interests. As new categories of abuse come within this definition, the extension of legal sanctions is justified. The burden of proof will rest on those who would extend these categories, but the presumption is not intended to render society supine before possible new developments of misuse of the immense powers of the contemporary press.

GLOSSARY

adventitious: occurring by chance, not planned

inveterate and … ineradicable: firmly established and incapable of being removed

totalitarianism: absolute control by the governing regime

venal: open to taking bribes

Document Analysis

Although Luce requested that Hutchins establish a Freedom of the Press Commission in 1942, it was not until 1945 that the work really began. As a nongovernmental body, the Commission was free to investigate the issue from any angle. The result was an affirmation that freedom of the press was at risk, but not necessarily from governmental intervention. It may have been surprising to some that the Commission did not focus on the influence of government regarding press freedom but instead looked at the threats posed by technology and economics. Indeed, some sections of the report were poorly received, yet the philosophy presented in the opening section of it (making up this excerpt) was very much in line with American belief about a free press being needed for the smooth functioning of democracy and the realization of progress.

After opening the report with a forthright "Yes" to the question, the Commission succinctly states the basis for its answer. The press has become "mass communication" which allows fewer people to reach a larger number of readers/listeners/observers than ever before. At the same time, the authors assert that communicators fail to meet the social goals established for a free press and in fact often undertake actions that are antithetical to society. Unlike the case of Fascist- or Communist-controlled nations, the problem in the United States had little to do with government intervention. True, any move to "regulate or control" the press would amount to a restraint, but the Commission members saw the impetus for such a move coming, if from any single source, from the people themselves in their desire to quell unfavorable information. This is why the Commission did not believe that "freedom will be swept away overnight." Nonetheless, pressure for control of the press could build slowly among the populace and eventuate in unjustifiable restrictions.

At the same time, the cost of creating any new mass communications entity severely limited competition. Thus, if some publisher was intentionally lax about facts or intentionally published falsehoods, the "moral right" to participate in a free press should be forfeited by that individual, according to the Commission. While the report almost continually warns against governmental intervention to establish/keep a free press, the Commission does understand that a government might have to intervene on a very limited basis in the case of persons publishing deliberate falsehoods or malignant

lies. (This is before the rise of modern tabloid newspapers with their stories of space aliens and celebrity affairs—publications marketed nowadays not as news media but as "entertainment" venues.) In all cases, according to the Commission, a democratic government must balance the value of free expression with the danger posed by the misuse of press freedoms by unscrupulous actors.

Thus, the limitation on governmental action against the free press was one aspect of the basic philosophy adopted by the Commission. The fact that the Commission was willing to entertain the idea that at certain times the government should limit press freedom was one aspect of the report that was questioned by members of the press. The Commission agreed that a free press was essential for the intellectual development of society and the maintenance of a true democracy. They came out strongly against those who intentionally lied even while admitting that that intellectual undertakings sometimes produced erroneous conclusions or communications that are partly wrong. Although not desirable, such outcomes were deemed acceptable if they were the result of the free exercise of the spirit of inquiry. In addition, even though they recognized the innate desire to suppress opinions contrary to one's own, the Commission believed that a "responsible" press would be able to survive such temptations, even as the number of corporations that controlled the various press media had diminished—fewer corporations owned more media.

Essential Themes

In its seventeen meetings, the Hutchins Commission met with 58 witnesses, while the staff interviewed 225 others. Working through multiple revisions of the report, the Commission eventually reached a strong consensus on the topic of the status of press freedoms in the United States, and to a lesser extent in other nations. The Commission's understanding of what were the current risks to a free press was different from many discussed within the press itself. As a result, many readers, including Henry Luce, found fault with the report. Members of the press recognized the need for some restrictions, such as the application of libel laws, but they generally wanted as little government intervention as possible. The liberties undergirded by a free press overrode the value of such interference as far as most members of the press were concerned. For the Commission, on the other hand, political and social liberties would not be threatened by a small amount of governmental regulation for the sake of truth and progress.

The main threat to a free press, according to the Commission, was changing economics. The Commission members believed that the drive for profits had replaced social betterment as the central goal of the press. This being the case, for the Commission the press was not fulfilling its duties. The seeming disregard which some publishers had for the role of the press as a foundation of liberty was the real threat to a free press. This was exacerbated by the concentration of economic resources, causing fewer people to have control over larger shares of the publishing industry. Thus, the Commission put forward the idea that society should "look principally to the press and the people to remedy the ills" faced by the press.

—Donald A. Watt

Bibliography and Additional Reading

Blevins, Fred. "The Hutchins Commission Turns 50: Recurring Themes in Today's Public and Civic Journalism." *The Montana Professor.* Bozeman: Montana State University, 1997.

Brown, Ralph S., Jr. "Book Review: The Commission on Freedom of the Press, A Free and Responsible Press: A General Report on Mass Communications, Newspapers, Radio, Motion Pictures, Magazines and Books." *Yale Law School Legal Scholarship Repository.* New Haven, CT: Yale Law School, 1948.

Commission on Freedom of the Press. "A Free and Responsible Press." *Internet Archives.* Chicago: University of Chicago Press, 1947.

Lowrey, Wilson, ed. *Changing the News.* (Routledge Communication Series.) New York: Routledge, 2011.

Pease, Edward C. "The Hutchins Commission: An Historical Perspective." *Intro to Mass Comm.* Logan: Utah State University, 2010.

■ Smith-Mundt Act

Date: January 27, 1948
Authors: H. Alexander Smith and Karl E. Mundt
Genre: Legislation

Summary Overview

The Smith-Mundt Act, or, to give it its formal name, the United States Information and Educational Exchange Act of 1948, would be a key element of American foreign policy and public diplomacy during the Cold War. The Smith-Mundt Act authorized the U.S. Department of State (the cabinet-level department responsible for American diplomacy and foreign relations) to use a variety of means (including broadcasting, personal visits, and educational exchange programs) to promote American interests to an international audience. To cynical observers, the Smith-Mundt Act represented an open, governmental sanction of propaganda efforts. Media and programing created under the Smith-Mundt Act would provide an officially sanctioned American point-of-view to persuade people around the world of the rightness of American policies and practices. The Smith-Mundt Act is only fully understandable within the context of the Cold War. As noted below (in the Defining Moment section), the creation of a State Department propaganda and international public relations effort was mired in Cold War anti-Communism and political paranoia. Entities developed, managed, or supported by the State Department under the Smith-Mundt Act would include Radio Free Europe and *Radio y Televisíon Martí*, which broadcasts to Cuba.

Defining Moment

The U.S. Information and Educational Exchange Act had a long road to passage into law and its legislative journey is best understood within the broader contexts of both the developing Cold War between the United States and the Soviet Union as well as the rising fees of Communist subversion within the U.S. government.

In 1945, Representative Karl E. Mundt, Republican from South Dakota, introduced the earliest form of the law, known at the time as the Bloom Bill. This was partially in response to the closure of the Office of War Information—which the Roosevelt administration had created in 1942 as a conduit for radio broadcasts and publications to support the US efforts in the Second World War. There were also other existing programs that authorized the State Department to engage in information programs in the Western Hemisphere. Despite numerous revisions, the bill failed to gain traction in 1946 and met further resistance in 1946.

One of the key objections coming from both Republicans and Democrats was concern about the State Department's policy stances, citing concerns about possible "communist infiltration" in the State Department. The bill contained no provision for Congressional oversight of the content of the material that the State Department would be distributing around the world. At the same time that there were concerns about the State Department as an institution, there was also suspicion of individuals the Department might recruit to take part in the proposed international exchange and education programs.

Mundt reintroduced the bill in March 1947 and throughout the year Congress saw debate and testimony over the bill take place featuring Secretary of State George Marshall and other officials. By this point, tensions between the United States and the Soviet Union had begun to intensify, and concerns began to emerge about Soviet propaganda having an effect in Europe. In the same year, George Kennan's anonymous article "The Sources of Soviet Conduct" appeared in *Foreign Affairs*, recommending a policy of "containment" of Soviet expansion and influence. The types of broadcasts and educational efforts proposed by the State Department and encompassed by Mundt's bill could serve as a tool of containment and serve to promote American interests on the ideological battlefields of the Cold War.

Author Biographies

Howard Alexander Smith (1880–1966) was the Senate coauthor of the Smith-Mundt Act. Smith was a lawyer and political operative who served as the chair of the Republican State Committee of New Jersey and a member of the Republican national committee. In 1944, Smith won a special election to fill a vacant seat in the U.S. Senate. He was reelected in 1946, and again in 1959. While in the Senate, in addition to cosponsoring the Smith-Mundt Act, he chaired the Committee on Labor and Public Welfare. After leaving the Senate, he worked as a foreign policy consultant.

Karl E. Mundt (1900–1974) was an educator who represented South Dakota in the House of Representatives from 1939 to 1948 and in the Senate from 1948–1973. While in the House, in addition to shepherding the Smith-Mundt Act to passage for a number of years (see Defining Moment, above), Mundt served on the House Un-American Activities Committee where he tried—but failed—to persuade the committee to more thoroughly monitor and investigate the Ku Klux Klan. In the Senate, he chaired the Senate Subcommittee on Investigations, overseeing the Army-McCarthy Hearings. Outside of politics, Mundt served as the president of the National Forensic League, which promotes speech and debate in American high schools, from 1932 to 1971.

The Smith-Mundt Act encouraged communications efforts outside the United States such as this anti-Japanese leaflet from Office of War Information (OWI), aimed at assuring that the Filipino people threw their entire resources and manpower into the struggle on the side of the United States.

HISTORICAL DOCUMENT

TITLE I

SECTION 1

This Act may be cited as the "United States Information and Educational Exchange Act of 1948."

OBJECTIVES

SEC. 2. The Congress hereby declares that the objectives of this Act are to enable the Government of the United States to promote a better understanding of the United States in other countries, and to increase mutual understanding between the people of the United States and the people of other countries. Among the means to be used in achieving these objectives are–

(1) an information service to disseminate abroad information about the United States, its people, and policies promulgated by the Congress, the President, the Secretary of State and other responsible officials of Government having to do with matters affecting foreign affairs;

(2) an educational exchange service to cooperate with other nations in-

(a) the interchange of persons, knowledge, and skills; (b) the rendering of technical and other services; (c) the interchange of developments in the field of education, the arts, and sciences.

SEC. 3. In carrying out the objectives of this Act, information concerning the participation of the United States in the United Nations, its organizations and functions, shall be emphasized.

TITLE II-INTERCHANGE OF PERSONS, KNOWLEDGE AND SKILLS

PERSONS

SEC. 201 The Secretary is authorized to provide for interchanges on a reciprocal basis between the United States and other countries of students, trainees, teachers, guest instructors, professors, and leaders in fields of specialized knowledge or skill and shall wherever possible provide these interchanges by using the services of existing reputable agencies which are successfully engaged in such activity. The Secretary may provide for orientation courses and other appropriate services for such persons from other countries upon their arrival in the United States, and for such persons going to other countries from the United States. When any country fails or refuses to cooperate in such program on a basis of reciprocity the Secretary shall terminate or limit such program, with respect to such country, to the extent he deems to be advisable in the interests of the United States. The persons specified in this section shall be admitted as nonimmigrant visitors for business under clause 2 of section 3 of the Immigration Act of 1924, as amended, for such time and under such conditions as may be prescribed by regulations promulgated by the Secretary of State and the Attorney General. A person admitted under this section who fails to maintain the status under which he was admitted or who fails to depart from the United States at the expiration of the time for which he was admitted, or who engages in activities of a political nature detrimental to the interests of the United States, or in activities not consistent with the security of the United States, shall, upon the warrant of the Attorney General, be taken into custody and promptly deported pursuant to section 14 of the Immigration Act of 1924…

Deportation proceedings under this section shall be summary and the findings of the Attorney General as to matters of fact shall be conclusive…

BOOKS AND MATERIALS

SEC. 202.The Secretary is authorized to provide for interchanges between the United States and other countries of books and periodicals, including government publications, for the translation of such writings, and for the preparation, distribution, and interchange of other educational materials…

INSTITUTIONS

SEC. 203. The Secretary is authorized to provide for assistance to schools, libraries, and community centers abroad, founded or sponsored by citizens of the United States, and serving as demonstration centers for methods and practices employed in the United States. In assisting any such schools, however, the Secretary shall exercise no control over their educational policies and shall in no case furnish assistance of any character which is not in keeping with the free democratic principles and the established foreign policy of the United States...

TITLE V-DISSEMINATING INFORMATION ABOUT THE UNITED STATES ABROAD

GENERAL AUTHORIZATION

SEC. 501. The Secretary is authorized, when he finds it appropriate, to provide for the preparation, and dissemination abroad, of information about the United States, its people, and its policies, through press, publications, radio, motion pictures, and other information media, and through information centers and instructors abroad. Any such press release or radio script, on request, shall be available in the English language at the Department of State, at all reasonable times following its release as information abroad, for examination by representatives of United States press associations, newspapers, magazines, radio systems, and stations, and, on request, shall be made available to Members of Congress...

POLICIES GOVERNING INFORMATION ACTIVITIES

SEC. 502. In authorizing international information activities under this Act, it is the sense of the Congress (1) that the Secretary shall reduce such Government information activities whenever corresponding private information dissemination is found to be adequate; (2) that nothing in this Act shall be construed to give the Department a monopoly in the production or sponsorship on the air of short-wave broadcasting programs, or a monopoly in any other medium of information...

TITLE X-MISCELLANEOUS

LOYALTY CHECK ON PERSONNEL

SEC. 1001. No citizen or resident of the United States, whether or not now in the employ of the Government, may be employed or assigned to duties by the Government under this Act until such individual has been investigated by the Federal Bureau of Investigation and a report thereon has been made to the Secretary of State. Provided, however, That any present employee of the Government, pending the report as to such employee by the Federal Bureau of Investigation, may be employed or assigned to duties under this Act for the period of six months from the date of its enactment. This section shall not apply in the case of any officer appointed by the President by and with the advice and consent of the Senate...

Approved January 27, 1948.

GLOSSARY

construe(d): to interpret someone's words or acts in a particular way, sometimes incorrectly or for self-serving purposes

disseminate: to spread information widely and to as many people as possible

loyalty check: a background check common in the Cold War era to determine if the subject had prior connections or sympathy to the Soviet Union or to communist ideology

promulgate(d): the act of creating law or policy

Document Analysis

The excerpt begins with the standard statement of the formal name of the law and moves into Section 2, which outlines the objectives of the U.S. Information and Educational Exchange Act. As discussed above, the State Department's goal was to gain authorization to engage in officially sanctioned "positive" propaganda efforts to bolster support for American policies and actions in parts of the world thought to be vulnerable to Soviet influence and to serve as a counterbalance to Soviet propaganda. Within the text of the law, this very practical and realist goal is rhetorically softened into a desire to promote a "better understanding"—not of American policy and the ways that policy might be implemented—but a "better understanding" of the United States itself. This is a subtle distinction, but plays into a common assumption held by many Americans throughout the Cold War that if nations around the world simply understood America, they would seek to emulate it and shun rivals like the Soviet Union or the People's Republic of China. Another distinction drawn in Section 2 is that between promoting an understanding of the United States and the goal of increasing "mutual understanding between the *people* of the United States and the *people* of other countries" [emphasis added]. These two closely related, but distinct goals, are reflected in the law through the "means to be used" by the State Department. The first means is an "information service" which will present information directly from the government of the United States that will focus on "matters affecting foreign affairs." This will fulfill the goal of building support for American policies abroad. The second is an "educational exchange service," which will provide American experts in a variety of fields ranging from technology to artistic endeavors. This portion of the law aims to involve the citizens of nations directly.

Section 3, the last section excerpted in Title I, establishes that one of the goals of the State Department is to emphasize the leading role the United States plays in the United Nations. While the legislation does not expand on the reasons for this, identifying American goals with the broader goals of the United Nations would give the impression of American policy as being less monolithic than it really was.

Title II addresses the personnel exchange program between the United States and other countries. The law specifies international exchanges of both students and teachers in "fields of specialized knowledge or skill." It also mandates that existing organizations be used to manage such programs, although the State Department is to provide any specialized "orientation courses and other appropriate services" for people who arrive in the United States from other nations and provides guidance for how to classify exchange visitors under immigration law. Significantly, the language in this section about deportation of foreign exchange personnel place the determination solely in the hand of the Justice Department—the State Department has no role here. This addresses concerns from the Justice Department—particularly the Federal Bureau of Investigation (FBI)—about the danger of foreign nationals being at large in the United States.

Sections 202 and 203 establish the ability of the State Department to provide assistance and support in a number of ways including translation and dissemination of printed materials, including government publications.

Title V of the Smith-Mundt Act addresses the goal of "disseminating information about the United States abroad." Title V authorizes the use of every form of media, from print to film, popular at the time, but with language that is open enough ("other information media") that emerging technologies such as television were included. Section 502 requires the State Department to use private materials wherever appropriate rather than using public resources to create similar materials. Section 502, in many ways, prevents the State Department from monopolizing or dominating the field.

Title X, like Title II, addresses concerns held by the Justice Department as well as members of Congress about the political suitability of those involved in conducting "public diplomacy" on behalf of the United States. The implementation of a "loyalty check"—which would, in the 1950s, be required of nearly all federal employees—would, it was hoped, uncover those who were potentially politically subversive.

Essential Themes

The Smith-Mundt Act and the initiatives taken under its authority raise questions about the compatibility of a "state media" with a free press, the access Americans had to what was being broadcast under the authority of the American government, and the role of propaganda during the Cold War. The Smith-Mundt Act, with its long road from when the State Department saw a need to engage in public diplomacy to its eventual signing into law, had to cope with the burgeoning anti-Communism of the Cold War as well as concerns from the federal law enforcement community.

As the State Department established radio and television networks, such as Voice of America and *Radio y Televisíon Martí*, broadcast programming to Latin America, Asia, and the Middle East, and promoted countless cultural exchanges. The mission and role would change as the Cold War waned, but the Smith-Mundt Act provides a valuable snapshot of an era where the American government itself wielded the power of the press to promote its interests and policies around the world.

—Aaron Gulyas

Bibliography and Additional Reading

Cull, Nicholas J. *The Cold War and the United States Information Agency*. New York: Cambridge University Press, 2008.

Nelson, Michael. *War of the Black Heavens: The Battles of Western Broadcasting in the Cold War*. Syracuse, NY: Syracuse University Press, 1997.

Trent, Deborah L, ed. *Nontraditional US Public Diplomacy: Past, Present, and Future*. Washington, DC: The Public Diplomacy Council, 2016.

■ Universal Declaration of Human Rights

Date: 1948
Authors: Eleanor Roosevelt; John Humphrey; René Cassin
Genre: Charter; law

Summary Overview

The United Nations was formed in the aftermath of the Second World War. It was the successor to the League of Nations, which had been founded at the end of the First World War. Like the League, the United Nations hoped to be a place where the international community could come together to talk out international concerns before global war broke out. After two horrible wars that spread throughout the world, world leaders were concerned about what would happen during a third world war—especially after the American nuclear attacks on Hiroshima and Nagasaki in Japan.

Among its first acts was the drafting and passage of the Universal Declaration of Human Rights (UDHR). The document had been drafted by the Commission on Human Rights, chaired by Eleanor Roosevelt. The document has also been used as the basis for the International Bill of Human Rights, followed by the Covenant on Civil and Political Rights and the International Covenant on Economic, Social, and Cultural Rights. All these different declarations were designed to guarantee individual citizens certain universal rights.

The UDHR is a comprehensive statement about what the national community considers the immutable rights of every person in the world. It includes articles addressing religious freedom, torture, the right to leave one's country and return there, and many others. The Preamble introduces the document's goal and purpose, while Article 19 focuses on the freedom of the opinions and expression and to both receive and impart information and ideas through any media.

Defining Moment

Although some countries had enshrined freedom of expression in their founding documents, many countries offered no protection for the press or spoken word, and others actively persecuted those who spoke against the government. At the time that the United Nations was formed, in the aftermath of the Second World War, the censorship and oppression of the Nazi regime was impossible to ignore. While the Jewish people were by far the most affected by the Holocaust and the concentration and death camps, Hitler also focused attention on others deemed "undesirable." These individuals included political opponents, artists who spoke out against his work, and resistance fighters. The Ministry of Enlightenment and Propaganda aimed to make all work that did not support Nazis invisible, thereby making the Nazi beliefs pervasive and impossible to disregard.

The Nazis were far from the only government that attempted to control its people by prohibiting opposition viewpoints, but in 1948, when the Universal Declaration of Human Rights (UDHR) was unanimously adopted by the General Assembly of the United Nations, the more than six million who died in the concentration camps could not have been far from the writers' minds.

Author Biography

The UDHR does not have a specific author. The document was authored by the Commission on Human Rights that was chaired by Eleanor Roosevelt, widow of President Franklin D. Roosevelt. The committee was made up of eighteen members who worked together to draft the document. While the declaration was absolutely a work by committee and was later modified and adapted based on resolutions introduced by member states, certain individuals are generally acknowledged as having played pivotal roles as writers of the UDHR.

For example, René Cassin, a legal expert from France, wrote the first draft of the declaration. The blueprint of the document was prepared by John Humphrey of Canada, Director of the UN's Human Rights Division, Charles Malik of Lebanon, the Committee Rapporteur, and Peng Chung Chang of China, the committee's cochair. Eleanor Roosevelt, however, was generally considered the driving force behind the document.

The UDHR was considered and discussed by all members of the United Nations at that point in time. The declaration was universally passed, although eight nations did ultimately choose to abstain from voting.

The Universal Declaration of Human Rights, December 10, 1948. (United Nations Department of Public Information)

Eleanor Roosevelt holding poster of the Universal Declaration of Human Rights (in English), Lake Success, New York. November 1949. (FDR Presidential Library & Museum 64-165)

Engraving of the Four Freedoms at the Franklin Delano Roosevelt Memorial in Washington, D.C.

HISTORICAL DOCUMENT

Preamble

Whereas recognition of the inherent dignity and of the equal and inalienable rights of all members of the human family is the foundation of freedom, justice and peace in the world,

Whereas disregard and contempt for human rights have resulted in barbarous acts which have outraged the conscience of mankind, and the advent of a world in which human beings shall enjoy freedom of speech and belief and freedom from fear and want has been proclaimed as the highest aspiration of the common people,

Whereas it is essential, if man is not to be compelled to have recourse, as a last resort, to rebellion against tyranny and oppression, that human rights should be protected by the rule of law,

Whereas it is essential to promote the development of friendly relations between nations,

Whereas the peoples of the United Nations have in the Charter reaffirmed their faith in fundamental human rights, in the dignity and worth of the human person and in the equal rights of men and women and have determined to promote social progress and better standards of life in larger freedom,

Whereas Member States have pledged themselves to achieve, in co-operation with the United Nations, the promotion of universal respect for and observance of human rights and fundamental freedoms, Whereas a common understanding of these rights and freedoms is of the greatest importance for the full realization of this pledge,

Now, therefore the General Assembly proclaims this universal declaration of human rights as a common standard of achievement for all peoples and all nations, to the end that every individual and every organ of society, keeping this Declaration constantly in mind, shall strive by teaching and education to promote respect for these rights and freedoms and by progressive measures, national and international, to secure their universal and effective recognition and observance, both among the peoples of Member States themselves and among the peoples of territories under their jurisdiction.

Article 19.

Everyone has the right to freedom of opinion and expression; this right includes freedom to hold opinions without interference and to seek, receive and impart information and ideas through any media and regardless of frontiers.

GLOSSARY

aspiration: a hope or ambition for achieving something

barbarous: savagely cruel, exceedingly brutal

inalienable: unable to be either taken away from or given away by the possessor

tyranny: cruel and oppressive government or rule

Document Analysis

As we can appreciate from the point of view of today, the UDHR was not the UN's final word on the rights of world citizens. The declaration changed as more nations joined the UN, as the founders saw how their words were being used on the world stage, and how they could be better refined and clarified. One important detail of the UDHR is that it is written in plain language that is easy to understand; just compare the writing to any modern bill written by a state or national legislature, and the difference is obvious. The declaration has also been translated into many different languages so that it is accessible to everyone.

The preamble serves as an introduction to the complete document. It lays out the basic reasons why the UDHR is needed and what the drafters' goals were in writing it. The articles are then the more specific statements that the committee is making about various human rights. When looking at a document like this, reviewing the preamble is often as important as looking at the relevant articles. One learns a good deal about what the writers view as important, why they are concerned about the issues addressed, and what motivates them to act.

The preamble introduces the declaration and summarizes its core values. First, international peace and security are not just a matter of diplomacy. They are a function of human rights. Then, dignity is "inherent," a vital part of being human. All people have the right to respect and share certain rights that cannot be taken away. Finally, these rights are shared equally: All people have the same rights, and no one has more of one right than anyone else.

In the preamble's reference to "barbarous acts," the authors clearly had in mind World War II, but they do not mention the war, for they wanted the document to focus on the future. The second paragraph alludes to the "four freedoms" that were articulated by President Franklin Roosevelt in a 1941 speech. Although Roosevelt was speaking as an American, the delegates agreed that these are the "highest aspiration of the common people": freedom from fear and want (or poverty) and freedom of speech and belief. This list includes social, economic, political, and cultural rights. In a sense, the UDHR is an expansion of the four freedoms.

Article 19 is broader in scope, speaking of the right to "freedom of opinion and expression." Even more importantly, however, it goes beyond the right to hold your own views and offers the right to share your opinion in whatever way is available to you.

When countries want to control their citizens, one of the first things they tend to do is to restrict the expression of ideas in all forms. Human beings are essentially social creatures who want to share information. In the early years of the German oppression of the Jews, there were only rumors of what was happening, and no proof of any kind. In the age of social media, it seems much more likely that additional messages might have been able to escape the ghettos and other dangerous precursors to the concentration camps.

Essential Themes

The primary essential theme in the UDHR is the idea that freedom is universal; there is no person who does not have the rights described in the declaration. This is important, as many countries use categories such as race, ethnicity, gender, or religion to declare that certain people have fewer rights than others. This is precisely what happened during the Holocaust, when the rights of Jewish people were slowly stripped away until they were considered less than human.

Some commentators debate, however, whether the UDHR protects the rights of women. Later declarations worked to make this clearer, but at the time of the writing, many of the signatory nations did not offer women full rights. This included the United States: White women still had many limitations on their financial rights, and women who were not white had even more limitations in society. In other countries, the rights of all women were deeply restricted.

Not all countries who participate in the United Nations follow the rules of the UDHR or the other provisions that followed. In some ways, freedom of expression may be the most important right for the international community to promote and protect. After all, without the ability to learn of atrocities being perpetrated in one's own or other countries, we may not know of them until it is too late to do anything to address them.

—Kay Tilden Frost

Bibliography and Additional Reading

"About the UN," United Nations. https://www.un.org/en/sections/about-un/overview/index.html.

"The History of the Document," United Nations. https://www.un.org/en/sections/universal-declaration/history-document/index.html.

"Nazi Propaganda and Censorship," *Holocaust Encyclopedia*, United States Holocaust Memorial Museum. https://encyclopedia.ushmm.org/content/en/article/nazi-propaganda-and-censorship.

Roberts, Christopher N.J. *The Contentious History of the International Bill of Human Rights.* New York: Cambridge University Press, 2015.

■ William Faulkner's Nobel Prize Acceptance Speech

Date: December 10, 1950
Author: William Faulkner
Genre: Speech

Summary Overview

The selection of William Faulkner as the 1949 recipient of the Nobel Prize in Literature was a surprise for some in the United States. Although his work had received critical acclaim, it was not widely read, largely because of the experimental nature of his prose. Faulkner decided to use his acceptance speech at the Nobel ceremonies to speak about the writer's role during a time when tensions between East and West threatened the world with nuclear war. Faulkner urged young writers to focus on what he called the "eternal verities" of human nature rather than becoming distracted by passing events, no matter how dire. The speech garnered worldwide acclaim and made Faulkner an international spokesperson for the role of literature in the modern world.

Defining Moment

Though Faulkner's work was well regarded among intellectuals and academics at the time of his Nobel Prize win, he had produced no best-seller, and many readers found his experimental style difficult. Furthermore, unlike flamboyant literary personalities such as Ernest Hemingway, Faulkner was rather reclusive, choosing to let his work speak for him. He had earlier expressed some reluctance to accept the Nobel Prize if offered because he was skeptical about the work of previous American recipients, notably Sinclair Lewis and Pearl S. Buck.

Europeans were less surprised than Americans at Faulkner's selection. His novels and stories had been translated into several languages, and he had a strong, if limited, following on the Continent—especially in Sweden, the home of the committee charged with selecting the annual Nobel Prize recipients. In choosing Faulkner, the committee cited him for "his powerful and artistically unique contribution to the modern American novel."

Although Faulkner was named the Nobel winner for 1949, he did not actually receive the prize until 1950. In 1949, the Nobel committee was unable to select a clear winner, although contemporary newspaper reports indicated that Italian writer Benedetto Croce and British historian and statesman Winston Churchill were among the finalists. Faulkner's late selection meant he had to share the stage with the 1950 recipient, British philosopher Bertrand Russell. Faulkner was reluctant to travel

William Faulkner, photographed by Carl Van Vechten in 1954.

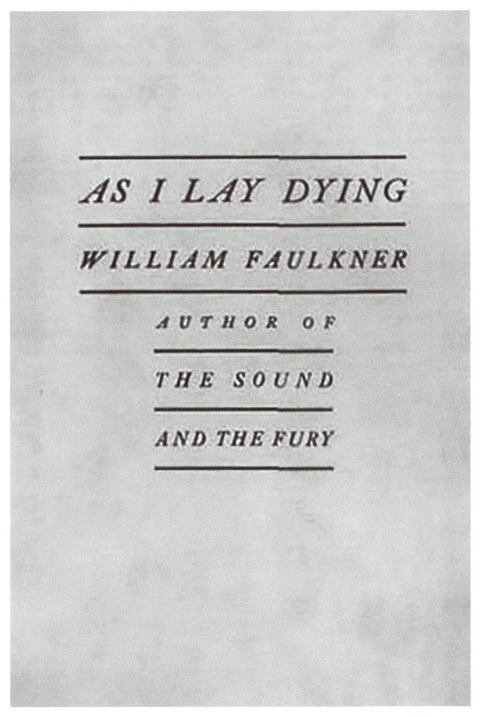

First edition cover of As I Lay Dying *(published in 1931, preceded by* The Sound and the Fury *in 1929 and followed by* The Sanctuary *in 1931).*

to Stockholm, but family and friends convinced him to make the trip. He prepared a rather lengthy acceptance speech but later cut it to a mere 553 words.

Mindful of the world situation, Faulkner decided to use the international platform to address young writers on the role and duty of the artist in a world where the future of civilization itself seemed at stake. The years following the end of World War II in 1945 had seen euphoria at the defeat of the German and Japanese war machines turn to apprehension and dread. The Soviet Union, a reluctant ally of the United States, Great Britain, and France during the war, almost immediately began a move to consolidate its hold on countries in Eastern Europe and thwart efforts of the other Allied powers to rebuild Europe along democratic lines. In 1946, Churchill declared that an Iron Curtain had fallen across Europe, beginning a near-fifty-year period of tension between the United States and the Soviet Union known as the Cold War, which would make citizens around the world fear a third global conflict. Since both sides possessed nuclear arsenals, the possibility existed that cities and even nations could be annihilated. What the role of literature could or should be in a world facing such looming catastrophe became the subject of Faulkner's brief address.

Author Biography

William Cuthbert Falkner was born on September 25, 1897, in New Albany, Mississippi. (He added the "u" to his surname in 1918). Just before his fifth birthday, his family moved to Oxford, Mississippi, where, except for brief periods, he would live and work for the rest of his life. Between 1926 and 1948, he published a dozen novels and several short-story collections that earned him critical acclaim but little financial reward; he supported himself by writing movie scripts and commercially successful short stories for periodicals such as the *Saturday Evening Post*. Renewed attention to his work after World War II led to international recognition and, in 1949, the awarding of the Nobel Prize in Literature. After receiving the award, Faulkner became a public figure, lecturing in the United States and abroad. He published five more novels before his death in 1962.

The brief acceptance speech Faulkner composed for the Nobel ceremony was immediately hailed as a major statement on the role of literature in modern life. It was reprinted in news publications worldwide and later anthologized as one of the best speeches of the century.

HISTORICAL DOCUMENT

Ladies and gentlemen,

I feel that this award was not made to me as a man, but to my work—a life's work in the agony and sweat of the human spirit, not for glory and least of all for profit, but to create out of the materials of the human spirit something which did not exist before. So this award is only mine in trust. It will not be difficult to find a dedication for the money part of it commensurate with the purpose and significance of its origin. But I would like to do the same with the acclaim too, by using this moment as a pinnacle from which I might be listened to by the young men and women already dedicated to the same anguish and travail, among whom is already that one who will some day stand here where I am standing.

Our tragedy today is a general and universal physical fear so long sustained by now that we can even bear it. There are no longer problems of the spirit. There is only the question: When will I be blown up? Because of this, the young man or woman writing today has forgotten the problems of the human heart in conflict with itself which alone can make good writing because only that is worth writing about, worth the agony and the sweat.

He must learn them again. He must teach himself that the basest of all things is to be afraid; and, teaching himself that, forget it forever, leaving no room in his workshop for anything but the old verities and truths of the heart, the old universal truths lacking which any story is ephemeral and doomed—love and honor and pity and pride and compassion and sacrifice. Until he does so, he labors under a curse. He writes not of love but of lust, of defeats in which nobody loses anything of value, of victories without hope and, worst of all, without pity or compassion. His griefs grieve on no universal bones, leaving no scars. He writes not of the heart but of the glands.

Until he relearns these things, he will write as though he stood among and watched the end of man. I decline to accept the end of man. It is easy enough to say that man is immortal simply because he will endure: that when the last dingdong of doom has clanged and faded from the last worthless rock hanging tideless in the last red and dying evening, that even then there will still be one more sound: that of his puny inexhaustible voice, still talking.

I refuse to accept this. I believe that man will not merely endure: he will prevail. He is immortal, not because he alone among creatures has an inexhaustible voice, but because he has a soul, a spirit capable of compassion and sacrifice and endurance. The poet's, the writer's, duty is to write about these things. It is his privilege to help man endure by lifting his heart, by reminding him of the courage and honor and hope and pride and compassion and pity and sacrifice which have been the glory of his past. The poet's voice need not merely be the record of man, it can be one of the props, the pillars to help him endure and prevail.

Faulkner supported himself by writing movie scripts and commercially successful short stories for periodicals such as the Saturday Evening Post. (George Gibbs)

Document Analysis

Like Abraham Lincoln's Gettysburg Address, Faulkner's Nobel Prize acceptance speech captures the imagination through its clarity of focus on a contemporary crisis and its optimistic assessment of humankind's ability to triumph over even the most extreme adversity. Unlike most Nobel laureates, Faulkner chose not to talk about his own accomplishments directly. Instead, as Mark LaVoie has observed, he took the opportunity afforded him by this international platform to speak on a matter of vital interest to people worldwide: the current condition of fear, approaching collective paralysis, generated by the threat of nuclear holocaust, and the role of literature in this time of international crisis. Aiming his remarks directly at young writers and indirectly at humankind as a whole, Faulkner argues that writers have a crucial role to play in helping their fellow citizens confront and prevail over the current challenge to civilization.

Faulkner first lays out what he believes is the problem with modern literature: its focus on fear. Faulkner wants writers to change this focus, asking not, "When will I be blown up?" but rather what it means to live as a human being, even in such a climate of fear. He urges his audience to put aside fear and embrace those qualities that have made life both bearable and noble for centuries: the "old verities" of "love and honor and pity and pride and compassion and sacrifice." These human qualities, dramatized in literature that deals with "the human heart in conflict with itself," are the basis of good literature, allowing it to be more than simply a report on the human condition. Those who write "of the heart," rather than "of the glands," can help humankind endure by "lifting [its] heart" and helping people "endure and prevail."

The speech draws heavily on literary tradition for its effect. David Rife points out that Faulkner embeds allusions to Henryk Sienkiewicz, Joseph Conrad, Nathaniel Hawthorne, Dylan Thomas, Élie Faure, Friedrich Hebbel, A. E. Housman, Rex Stout, and Plato; others have suggested that the lone man contemplating the end of civilization is a reference to the figure that appears in H. G. Wells' *The Time Machine* (1895). Faulkner's immediate audience would have appreciated the international lineup of writers he marshals to make his case for the value of literature.

Subsequent readers can appreciate his appeal to tradition as a means of bolstering his argument that literature can do more than report on the human condition; it can also serve as a guide for humankind in troubled times.

Essential Themes

In calling for a return to the "old verities and truths of the heart" and emphasizing the role of literature as a guide to life, Faulkner strikes out against modernism, the literary movement that came to prominence after World War I. Ironically, Faulkner was a modernist in several respects, most notably in his use of experimental techniques, such as stream of consciousness. Where Faulkner differed from his contemporaries was in his belief in concepts such as honor, courage, pity, pride, and glory, which many modernists rejected as hollow terms that led to the carnage of worldwide conflagration; for example, Ernest Hemingway's modernist hero Frederic Henry in *A Farewell to Arms* (1929) dismisses "abstract words such as glory, honor, courage" as "obscene," opting to focus instead on the physical aspects of his world. Faulkner believes this kind of reportage does a disservice to the craft of writing, which should help humankind endure in troubled times. Rather than rejecting the past and its values, he embraces both and argues that the only hope for humankind is to look to tradition for lessons in how to live well in the face of trouble, even if that trouble is the threat that civilization itself might be annihilated.

Faulkner's receipt of the Nobel Prize and the speech he delivered upon accepting it raised his status as a spokesperson for literature. For the last decade of his life, he traveled widely to speak to audiences about the function and value of literature in the modern world. His optimism served as a counterweight to many writers' pessimistic worldview. During the 1950s, his work drew widespread interest from academics and became staples in college classes, helping fuel interest in the genres of southern regionalism and historical fiction while introducing thousands of students to the experimental techniques employed by writers after World War I.

—*Laurence W. Mazzeno*

Bibliography and Additional Reading

Carothers, James B. "'In Conflict with Itself': The Nobel Prize Address in Faulknerian Contexts." In *Faulkner and Formalism: Returns of the Text*, edited by Annette Trefzer and Ann J. Abadie, 20–40. Jackson: University Press of Mississippi, 2012.

LaVoie, Mark. "William Faulkner's 'Speech Accepting the Nobel Prize in Literature': A Language for Ameliorating Atomic Anxiety." *Rhetoric & Public Affairs* 17.2 (2014): 199–226.

Rife, David. "Rex Stout and William Faulkner's Nobel Prize Speech." *Journal of Modern Literature* 10.1 (1983): 151–52.

Schwartz, Lawrence H. *Creating Faulkner's Reputation: The Politics of Modern Literary Criticism*. Knoxville: University of Tennessee Press, 1988.